UNIVERSITY OF NORTH CAROLINA
STUDIES IN THE ROMANCE LANGUAGES AND LITERATURES
Number 72

RENAISSANCE AND OTHER STUDIES IN HONOR OF
WILLIAM LEON WILEY

WILLIAM LEON WILEY

RENAISSANCE AND OTHER STUDIES
IN HONOR OF
WILLIAM LEON WILEY

EDITED BY
GEORGE BERNARD DANIEL, JR.

CHAPEL HILL
THE UNIVERSITY OF NORTH CAROLINA PRESS

DEPÓSITO LEGAL: V. 887 - 1968

ARTES GRÁFICAS SOLER, S. A. - JÁVEA, 30 - VALENCIA (8) - 1968

TABLE OF CONTENTS

Page

BIOGRAPHY
George B. Daniel — 11

TENDRES AND *GÉNÉREUX* IN THE LATER PLAYS OF CORNEILLE
Claude K. Abraham — 15

AN INTERESTING USE OF GENEALOGY IN HISTORICAL ROMANCE
James R. Beeler — 31

RONSARD'S TREATMENT OF IGNORANT POETS AND THE COMMON PEOPLE
Samuel M. Carrington — 41

ROTROU'S *VENCESLAS:* TRAGÉDIE OR TRAGI-COMÉDIE?
James H. Davis, Jr. — 55

A FEW COMPARISONS AND CONTRASTS IN THE WORDCRAFT OF RABELAIS AND JAMES JOYCE
Alfred G. Engstrom — 65

THE IMPACT OF FRÈRE JEAN ON PANURGE IN RABELAIS' *TIERS LIVRE*
Donald M. Frame — 83

CANDIDE'S QUARTERINGS
R. L. Frautschi — 93

AFFINITY AND ANTITHESIS IN THE VOCABULARY OF *PHÈDRE*
Stirling Haig — 107

LES COMMENTAIRES DE CHARLES PÉGUY SUR *POLYEUCTE*
Jacques Hardré — 115

	Page

BONAVENTURE DES PÉRIERS ABROAD
    J. Woodrow Hassell, Jr.   123

MONTAIGNE'S SPAS
    Urban T. Holmes   133

DRAMATIC TECHNIQUE IN *LES PRÉCIEUSES RIDICULES*
    Quentin M. Hope   141

THE GEOPHYSICS OF RABELAIS' FROZEN WORDS
    Abraham C. Keller   151

AN ASPECT OF OBSCENITY IN RABELAIS
    Raymond C. La Charité   167

CHAR'S SURREALIST EXPERIENCE: AN APPRAISAL OF *ARTINE*
    Virginia A. La Charité   191

THE SCUDÉRYS REVISITED: GEORGES DE SCUDÉRY
    Jerome W. Schweitzer   203

CREATIVE IMITATION, ORIGINALITY AND LITERARY TRADITION IN RONSARD
    Isidore Silver   215

PASCAL AND FRANÇOIS MAURIAC
    Maxwell A. Smith   229

THE CULT OF TASTE IN BOUHOURS' *PENSÉES INGÉNIEUSES DES ANCIENS ET DES MODERNES* (1689)
    Frederick W. Vogler   241

MONTAIGNE'S CONCLUSION TO BOOK II OF HIS *ESSAIS*
    Philip A. Wadsworth   249

MONTAIGNE'S READINGS FOR *DES CANNIBALES*
    Bernard Weinberg   261

A BIBLIOGRAPHY OF THE WRITINGS OF WILLIAM LEON WILEY
    George B. Daniel   263

EDITOR'S FOREWORD

I should like to acknowledge with grateful appreciation the wise counsel of my colleague, Urban T. Holmes, in bringing this volume to fruition. His constant interest and encouragement have made a pleasant endeavor even more pleasant.

WILLIAM LEON WILEY

George B. Daniel

The only child of William A. Wiley and Irma Stearns, Wiley, William Leon Wiley was born in Tate, Georgia, on March 14, 1903. His father had a long and productive career in the public schools of Georgia and was, for several years, principal of the Chickamauga High School. In addition to his interest in school administration, the father was a great admirer of classical Greek and Roman civilization and literature. The most lasting influence of the father upon the son was perhaps an enthusiasm for the classics transmitted to the son who has for over fifty years been first and foremost a student of classical literature. It is natural that he was drawn to teaching as a profession and to Classicism.

Another influence upon "Lee," as he is called by those who know him, was his mother. Her antecedents were long prominent in the Methodist Church. Her patrician dignity was distinctive everywhere she went.

Lee had his early education in the Georgia public schools. Upon graduating from Chickamauga High School, he entered the University of Chattanooga in 1917, and received the bachelor's degree in 1921.

He was not only an excellent student; he was a very fine athlete. Tennis is his favorite sport. Most of us know that his "wicked ball" can still cause embarrassment to the brashly young who think youth is superior to experience.

As testimony of her esteem for him, the University of Chattanooga awarded Lee a Distinguished Service Citation in 1955 and the Litt. D. in 1961.

After his father's death in 1921, Lee succeeded him as principal of the Chickamauga High School. He conntinued in this capacity until 1923 when he left to pursue his studies at Harvard. The Department of Romance Languages there was especially distinguished. Lee studied under such renowned professors as Ford, Wright, Grandgent, and Morize.

He received his master's degree in 1925 when he left Harvard to come to Chapel Hill as an instructor in French. His association with the late William M. Dey, Head of the Department of Romance Languages, was quite warm.

On June 18, 1927, William Leon Wiley and Dorothy Preston Ford were married in Clifton Forge, Virginia. "Dot," a charming and gracious lady had met her husband while working in the university library. They have one son, William Lee, who has continued the scholarly bent of the family. He received his doctorate from the university of North Carolina and is now a research chemist with the DuPont Corporation of Wilmington, Delaware.

Lee returned to Harvard in 1928-30; he was an instructor in French and Spanish there. He was named Sheldon traveling fellow to France and Spain for the scholastic year 1930-31. This was the beginning of his annual visits to Europe, usually to Paris.

In the fall of 1931, he returned with his family to Chapel Hill. There then ensued for him a long and distinguished career, not only as teacher and scholar but also as active citizen. He advanced from instructor to Kenan professor of French, being named to that position in 1955.

Between 1931 and the Second World War, Lee and Dot spent much time in renovating their ante-bellum home on Cameron Avenue, which is one of the best in Chapel Hill. At the outbreak of the war, Lee joined the Navy. From 1942-45 he served as air operations officer and then in Europe as an officer for the OSS. He rose from lieutenant to lieutenant commander in the USNR.

It is needless to list his achievements in the department, in the university community, and in the outside world. He has served as acting chairman of the department on various occasions, and has been a member of many university committees including the Athletic Council, the Board of Governors of the Press, and the Chancellor's Advisory Committee. He has been an assistant editor of *Studies in Philology* for many years, and has served on the Romance Department Series and on *Romance Notes*. He was a visiting professor of French at Brown University in 1965-66. He was, this past summer, a senior fellow in the Medieval-Renaissance Institute held on the Chapel Hill campus.

Giving one's accomplishments does not always reveal the man. This is surely the case with Lee Wiley. There is something in his urbane, civilized manner which sets a tone of dignity at any meeting or gathering.

Lee's active interest in professional organizations is evident from his affiliation since the beginning with the American Renaissance Society. He belongs also to the Modern Language Association, the South Atlantic Modern Language Association, and the Southeastern Renaissance Conference. He has read numerous papers before meetings of these groups, and has served as officer in various sections.

In recognition of his achievements, his outstanding qualities as a scholar and person, the University honored him in 1966 with the Thomas Jefferson Award: "Being that member of the academic community who through personal influence and performance of duty in teaching, writing and scholarship has best exemplified the ideals and objectives of Thomas Jefferson."

Another recognition came to him and the University in the spring of 1967. He was named to the chairmanship of their post-doctoral Fellowships of the Southern Region by the National Endowment for the Humanities.

One of Lee's associates of long standing expressed very aptly what he thought to be the essential nature of the man. "He must always be doing something," the friend said. As we go to press, he is busily engaged in doing research for another book and probably has a dozen or more projects in mind.

The chief beneficiary of Lee Wiley's presence has been the Department of Romance Languages, which has been well served by men like him. It has been a privilege to be associated with William Leon Wiley. Many of us have sat in his classes in the Renaissance, in the history of the drama, literary criticism, and phonetics. All of us have benefited from the presence of this truly Renaissance gentleman. It is with pleasure that we his colleagues, students, and associates throughout the country dedicate this volume to him on his sixty-fifth birthday.

TENDRES AND *GÉNÉREUX* IN THE LATER PLAYS OF CORNEILLE

CLAUDE K. ABRAHAM
University of Florida

The later plays of Corneille, with the exception of *Suréna,* are habitually dismissed by scholars and teachers alike with a disdainful comment or two. Invariably, these plays are compared to the masterpieces of the "middle period" and rejected as inferior. While we do not intend this study to be an attempt at rehabilitation, we would like to suggest that such a comparison, while fruitful to some extent, presents some grave dangers. Parallels and contrasts are fine tools for examining broad questions dealing with the very nature of the arts, but they all too often lead to obfuscation when the works compared are interpreted to suit the method or twisted to suit the preconceived notion. Centering our investigation around certain of the later heroines of Corneille, we would like to see if they reveal a clue to the better understanding of the mature author.

In the 1660 *Examen d'Horace,* Corneille, commenting on the death of Camille, states unequivocally that there *is* a difference between men and women and that certain feelings, such as "la frayeur, si naturelle au sexe,"[1] are to be expected from women. Sabine, in the first scene of the play, suggests no less a distinction:

Si l'on fait moins qu'un homme, on fait plus qu'une femme.
Commander à ses pleurs en cette extrémité,
C'est montrer, pour le sexe, assez de fermeté.   (vv. 12-14)

---

[1] *Œuvres complètes* (Paris: Seuil, 1963), p. 248.

Yet, how many female characters in the tragedies of Corneille forget just that? Péguy deplored the fact that Racine's male characters "sont femmes. ... Ils sont tous dévirilisés." [2] By the same token, it can be said that too many of Corneille's heroines are "déféminisées."

Some of Corneille's women never cease to be just that: eternally feminine, they move in a world not quite that of their male counterparts, one whose values may harmonize with those of the men, but never be the same. But such is not always the case, and Médée, in Corneille's first tragedy, has values far more masculine than the "fantoches d'opérette" [3] that surround her. While Créuse's feminine whims nearly elicit laughter — witness the speech in which her desire for Médée's *robe* is equated with her love for Jason (vv. 588-92) — Médée's entrance sets an entirely different tone. Jason, by rejecting her, is guilty of an *injure* (v. 206). If his faithlessness can be forgiven, his audacity cannot:

> S'il a manqué d'amour, manque-t-il de mémoire?
> Me peut-il bien quitter après tant de bienfaits?
> M'ose-t-il bien quitter après tant de forfaits?
> Sachant ce que je puis, ayant vu ce que j'ose,
> Croit-il que m'offenser ce soit si peu de chose?
>
> (vv. 230-34)

And so, while Créuse dies happy in the arms of her husband (vv. 1497-98, 1505), Médée, by killing her children, can only succeed in "noyer dans leur sang les restes de nos flammes" (v. 1542), an act that does little more than complete the previously contemplated divorce between Médée and the entire human race.

At the beginning of *Le Cid,* we are told of a relationship between a man and a woman, a relationship which exists primarily because they are worthy of each other. Rodrigue, as Jean Starobinski suggests, is *ébloui* by his father's famous question. To prove that he does indeed have courage, he will become *éblouissant* and, in the process, destroy the delicate balance that existed in the above-mentioned relationship. It is now *Chimène's* turn to be *éblouie,* and, not wanting to be outdone, she decides that "ma générosité doit

---

[2] *Œuvres en prose, 1909-1914* (Paris: Gallimard, 1961), p. 777.

[3] Albert Thibaudet, "Un tricentenaire," *Nouvelle Revue Française* (1 Sept., 1935), p. 407.

répondre à la tienne" (v. 930), a sentiment echoed by Rodrigue (v. 946). This has nothing to do with honor: she is told repeatedly that her honor has been satisfied by her first attempts, yet she will continue to strive to equal Rodrigue. Limited physically as a woman, he refuses to allow her conduct to be guided by these limitations, and even the king's final order fails to put an end to her quest. Corneille himself is quite explicit on this matter: "Je sais bien que le silence passe d'ordinaire pour une marque de consentement; mais quand les rois parlent, c'en est une de contradiction."[4] This sentiment is echoed by Pulchérie some twelve years later when she says that

> Les silences de cour ont de la politique.
> Sitôt que nous parlons, qui consent applaudit,
> Et c'est en se taisant que l'on nous contredit.
> (vv. 1578-80)

The Infante, on the other hand, is involved in a truly feminine struggle. She is aware of the existence of a love triangle; Chimène is not. Whenever the two meet (II, 3 or IV, 2), the contrast is obvious: it is through the Infante's femininity that Chimène's intransigence is made manifest. She, as "témoin d'une gloire," to use Horace's words, witnesses "first the depth and sureness of Chimène's love for Rodrigue, and then the seriousness of her intent to be his equal in heroism."[5] The Infante's quest for peace and tranquility — each one of her appearances is punctuated by mention of *repos* (vv. 107, 508, etc.) — serves "as a frame of reference and as a focus for the most important thing in the play — the heroic love affair of Rodrigue and Chimène."[6]

This does not mean that some of Corneille's heroines are less aware of their duty than others. All are conscious of their obligations to their rank, all have a concept of what is due their *maison*. None, as in Racine, would dishonor themselves for love. Dircé, in *Œdipe,* puts it as well as any in her opening monologue of Act III:

---

[4] *Œuvres complètes*, p. 219.
[5] A. Donald Sellstrom, "The Role of Corneille's Infante," *French Review* (Nov., 1965), p. 240.
[6] *Ibid.*

> Impitoyable soif de gloire,
> ....
> Ne crains pas qu'une ardeur si belle
> Ose te disputer un cœur
> Qui de ton illustre rigueur
> Est l'esclave le plus fidèle.
> Ce regard tremblant et confus,
> Qu'attire un bien qu'il n'attend plus,
> N'empêche pas qu'il ne se dompte.
> Il est vrai qu'il murmure, et se dompte à regret;
> Mais s'il m'en faut rougir de honte,
> Je n'en rougirai qu'en secret.   (vv. 779-98)

Dircé cannot understand how "aux soins de sa gloire on préfère l'amour" (v. 880). It is never otherwise in Corneille, and so the basic problem is never one of choice between love and duty. Péguy, viewing Corneille's drama as one of salvation,[7] claims that, "au fond, il n'y a pas une femme de Corneille dont on puisse dire: *C'est une malheureuse.*"[8] But this too is irrelevant: how can any woman be happy as a woman in a world of Horaces? The issue is neither what she will chose nor whether or not this choice will bring her happiness. The choice itself is intrinsically evil:

> Quiconque peut choisir consent à l'un des deux,
> Et le consentement est seul lâche et honteux.
>   (*Théodore*, vv. 773-74)

Rather, the issue lies in the heroine's attitude vis-à-vis the choice, her justification for this attitude, and her reconciliation with the result. Thus some heroines, like the Infante, find peace of mind, while others must either die or live out a life of frustration wearing the eternal mask of what André Rousseaux has called "le mensonge héroïque."[9]

The Infante sees the danger to her *gloire* and readily finds a cure:

> Quand je vis que mon cœur ne se pouvait défendre,
> Moi-même je donnai ce que je n'osais prendre.   (vv. 101-2)

---

[7] *Op. cit.*, p. 772.
[8] *Ibid.*, p. 787.
[9] *Le monde classique* (Paris: Albin-Michel, 1941), pp. 37-68.

Having done this, she awaits the wedding that will give her the much wanted *repos*. Queens and princesses will face the same problem in later plays with such regularity as to constitute a Cornelian commonplace, one that could readily be called *l'amant donné*. In its varied presentations, however, this commonplace shows no intrinsic value. Rather, through its nuances, it reveals the changes in Corneille's attitude vis-à-vis his heroines.

Basically, one may distinguish two types of heroines. While it is not always easy — or wise — to classify them, the classification can be made. On the one hand, there is the purely feminine woman, one who readily admits her powers and weaknesses as a woman; on the other, the woman endowed with a masculine mystique, demanding to be judged as an equal by the men around her and living by their standards. It is easy to see Pauline as a perfect example of the former. From the start, she is the dutiful wife striving to understand her husband; she finds happiness in becoming one with her husband while regaining her long-lost father (vv. 1784-85). Rodélinde herself makes her classification easy: "Je ne m'abaisse point aux faiblesses des femmes" (v. 871). On the other hand, a classification of Camille or Sabine along these lines would be extremely difficult and could only hinder any investigation of their ambivalence.[10]

In *La mort de Pompée*, Corneille reintroduces the juxtaposition first used in *Le Cid*, that of a feminine heroine with a truly masculine one. Again, as in *Le Cid*, the feminine role is minor, and Cornélie's *raison d'être*, from the theatrical point of view, seems to be to make manifest Cléopatre's total defeminization. Cornélie, in love with one man, mourns his death and nurtures a hatred for his foes that is her new reason in life: "Je veux vivre avec elle, avec elle expirer" (v. 1724). Cléopatre, on the contrary, "semble n'avoir point d'amour qu'en tant qu'il peut servir à sa grandeur," as Corneille puts it in his *Examen*.[11] Pompée and César are equally loved by

---

[10] Two fine studies have been made of this ambivalence: L. E. Harvey, "Corneille's *Horace*. A study in tragic and artistic ambivalence," *Studies in Seventeenth-Century French Literature Presented to Morris Bishop* (Cornell Univ. Press, 1962), and R. A. Mazzara, "More on unity of character and action in 'Horace'," FR (May, 1963), 588-94.

[11] *Œuvres*, p. 316.

her simply because "Ou l'une ou l'autre main me rendra ma couronne" (v. 334).

This juxtaposition of opposites, absent in *Théodore*, reappears in *Rodogune*. Rodogune, although ready to follow the dictates of her duty (vv. 373-80, 930-38), has fallen in love because of "ce je ne sais quoi" (v. 362). Like the Infante, she is torn between love and duty, and like her, readily makes the just decision. She seems feminine compared to Cléopatre, but still lacks the tenderness already hinted at in the creation of Théodore, and so obvious in the later plays. Cléopatre is entirely *déféminisée*. Her main motive is a lust for power (v. 423) so strong as to make her cheat her sons out of their legitimate legacy. Her husband's infidelity concerns her only insofar as it threatens this thirst:

> J'aurais vu Nicanor épouser Rodogune,
> Si content de lui plaire et de me dédaigner,
> Il eût vécu chez elle en me laissant régner. (vv. 464-66)

This difference between the two women is nowhere made more manifest than in the motives behind the proposition presented to the two brothers: Cléopatre merely wants to rid herself of any rival; Rodogune wishes to forestall disaster. As Corneille has suggested in his *Examen*, Rodogune knows that neither brother will accept the challenge and thus force her to choose.[12] This gesture, blemishing her *gloire* while preventing strife between the brothers, can be considered as the beginning of a transformation in Corneille's concept of the perfect tragic heroine. From the first tragedy to the last, the Cornelian hero is alone. But while in the earlier works, this solitude is forced on the hero, with Rodogune we see the first hint of a trend that will be readily recognized a few plays later. In his presentation of *Don Sanche*, André Stegmann remarks that "la pièce marque une évolution dans sa conception même de la tragédie: il est pour le héros d'autres périls plus graves que la mort, capables de susciter l'admiration et la pitié, qui demeurent la fin de la tragédie: c'est la solitude intérieure, l'incompréhension et l'injustice du monde dans lequel il vit."[13] It is precisely this

---

[12] *Ibid.*, p. 418.
[13] *Ibid.*, p. 495.

inner solitude that becomes manifest at Rodogune's above-mentioned sacrifice.

Solitude is also the main theme in *Nicomède*, where two worlds face each other, doomed to eternal misunderstanding. Arsinoë, like the Cléopatre of *Rodogune*, wants to rule men and through men. For this, she, a mediocre soul, must rely on other mediocre beings and cannot hope to win in a world ruled by a Nicomède she judges by her own standards. Understanding between the two is impossible: Nicomède sees others as human beings; Arsinoë, intent on "éblouir le Roi, Rome et la cour" (v. 346), moves by "artifice" (v. 296) and treachery, and sees others as things to use (vv. 337-38). This search for gloire can only be a "dessein avorté" (v. 1661). Arsinoë's son will rule, but he will hold the crown from Nicomède, and so, from Arsinoë's point of view, the plot has worked "pour moi contre moi-même" (v. 1836).

Laodice is also concerned for her *gloire:* "Je suis Reine" (v. 57), and a queen

> ... ne prendra jamais un cœur assez abjet
> Pour se laisser réduire à l'hymen d'un sujet.
> (vv. 65-66)

Unlike the Infante, however, Laodice can hope that her lover will one day rule and, putting her trust in his capabilities — "Faites que l'on vous craigne et je ne craindrai rien" (v. 98) — she finds the path to *gloire* by admitting her love, while the Infante finds hers in painful silence.

Pertharite was a complete failure, and this reception may be blamed in part on the bad presentation of the female duo. Eduige, as a woman, demands complete servitude of her lover, not to serve her ambition, but her love (vv. 475-98). This entirely unselfish devotion that she demands is preposterous in view of her own wavering, not only between the men, but between love and "la haine d'un frère" (v. 324). If Eduige is a poor standard-bearer for the feminine mystique, Rodelinde is a caricature of the masculine counterpart. Rodelinde, like Chimène, is torn between hatred and esteem for the usurper Grimoald. As the king's widow, she admits that Grimoald "règne avec amour" (v. 174), but forces herself to hate him "par devoir" (vv. 182-83). When he offers to rule for her son, her inner struggle intensifies, for now she must "porter cette haine aussi loin que l'estime" (v. 704). Seeking her *gloire* in this hatred, she is frustrated by the reappearance of her husband. Having warned the audience that "je ne m'abaisse point aux faiblesses des femmes" (v. 871), she proves it, in her reunion with Pertharite, by scorning feminine emotions (vv. 1411-14). When Pertharite suggests that

> Vous avez assez fait pour moi, pour votre honneur.
> Il est temps de tourner du côté du bonheur,   (vv. 1421-22)

she attempts to assume a role that is not hers and fails, being forced at the end of the play to submit her *gloire* to that of the men around her.

In *Sertorius,* this confrontation is presented again, but with a slight twist. Both women claim to scorn love, but their protestations are quite dissimilar. Aristie, the rejected wife of Pompée, exaggerates to such an extent that she fails to convince, and lines such as

> Laissons, Seigneur, laissons pour les petites âmes
> Ce commerce rampant de soupirs et de flammes
>   (v. 285-86)

are in sharp contrast to Viriate's frank statement:

> Ce ne sont pas les sens que mon amour consulte,
> Il hait des passions l'impétueux tumulte,
> Et son feu, que j'attache aux soins de ma grandeur,
> Dédaigne tout mélange avec leur folle ardeur.   (vv. 401-4)

While Viriate's dedication to her *gloire* is manifest in every speech, Aristie's mask is seldom effective. Still in love with Pompée, she readily admits her feelings to him:

> Mon feu qui n'est éteint que parce qu'il doit l'être
> Cherche en dépit de moi le vôtre pour renaître.
>   (vv. 1005-6)

If she plans to give herself to Sertorius, it is precisely because of that love:

> Oui, Seigneur, il est vrai que j'ai le cœur sensible;
> Suivant qu'on m'aime ou hait, j'aime ou hais à mon tour,
> Et ma gloire soutient ma haine et mon amour. (vv. 994-96)

Having lost one title when Pompée rejected her, she must have another even though such a quest "coûtera bien des têtes" (v. 1126). But, while this decision is the result of a jilted love, that of Viriate is not:

> Je sais vous obéir,
> Mais je ne sais que c'est d'aimer ni de haïr,
> Et la part que tantôt vous aviez dans mon âme
> Fut un don de ma gloire, et non pas de ma flamme.
> (vv. 1283-86)

Viriate, in fact, does not know love, and readily admits it: "L'amour n'est pas ce qui me presse" (v. 1390). Aristie, seeking only revenge (v. 1547), abandons this quest and forces her heart to forget past miseries (v. 1888) when happiness beckons, while Viriate can only accept "la paix ... offerte" (v. 1889).

Corneille presents the same problem in the next play, *Sophonisbe*. While, as the author states, Sophonisbe has "un peu d'amour, mais elle règne sur lui," sacrificing it to her hatred of Rome,[14] Eryxe, truly feminine, wants to be loved freely — "Mais que sert une main par le devoir forcée" (v. 480) — and submits her *gloire* to the greater good:

> J'aime donc Massinisse, et je prétends qu'il m'aime:
> Je l'adore, et je veux qu'il m'adore de même,
> Et pour moi son hymen serait un long ennui,
> S'il n'était tout à moi, comme moi toute à lui.
> (vv. 499-502)[15]

If this trend of setting off two women to show the two possible attitudes can barely be detected in *Rodogune*, it is omnipresent in *Attila*. Honorie loves Valamir but refuses a king "qu'on force d'obéir" (v. 420), because "ainsi que mon amour, ma gloire a ses

---

[14] *Ibid.*, p. 643.
[15] In a bantering mood, *Agésilas* reverses the problem in that it shows two women equally feminine, equally in love with the same man, one loved in return, the other sought for reasons of state.

appas" (v. 443). Promised in marriage to Attila, she fears his choice: if he accepts her, she must relinquish Valamir; if he rejects her, her *gloire* will suffer. The only possible solution is to forestall Attila's decision by leaving with Valamir (vv. 475-76), but this is only possible if Valamir acts as a king: "Je veux un roi: regardez si vous l'êtes" (v. 490). Ildione, also promised to Attila, is Honorie's unwilling rival. She not only knows her duty, but realizes that her *gloire* can only be satisfied if she marries Attila, even if only to kill him. Yet, in spite of this knowledge, she fervently hopes that Attila will reject her:

> ... puisse être Honorie
> La plus considérée, ou moi la moins chérie!
> (vv. 625-26)

Furthermore, she admits her love far more readily than Honorie, her unselfish love ready for any sacrifice for her lover's happiness:

> Je vous aime: Ce mot me coûte à prononcer,
> Mais puisqu'il vous plaît tant, je veux bien m'y forcer.
> (vv. 671-72)

Ildione repeatedly tries to assume a male posture, but every attempt fails, her last one (IV, 7) ending in complete surrender:

> Et qu'aisément le sexe oppose à sa fierté
> Sa douceur naturelle et sa timidité! (vv. 1447-48)

Honorie has repeatedly sought the help of others (Valamir or Attila) to achieve a *gloire* which, being based on masculine values, she cannot attain on her own. Ildione, on the other hand, sees her happiness on a completely different plane. As a result, the death of Attila affects the two women quite differently: now that Attila is no longer there to hinder her happiness, Ildione will live happily ever after; Honorie, however, doomed to remain on her treadmill, the impotent victim of her own *gloire,* can only assure her lover that his problems are just beginning, and that "nos destins changés n'ont point changé mon cœur" (v. 1788).

In *Tite et Bérénice,* as in so many plays before — and as in the few that follow — this confrontation of two women will be coupled with another Cornelian commonplace: the juxtaposition of selfish and unselfish characters. In fact, the world of *Tite et Bérénice* can be analyzed according to several lines, all manifestations of the same trend — that of an older, gentler Corneille, further and further removed from the Horatian "grandeur romaine." Domitie is selfish, Bérénice is not; Domitie loves power, Bérénice does not; as a result, Domitie must constantly ask for proof of a man's love while Bérénice *knows* that this love exists.

Though Domitie loves Domitian, she loves power more (vv. 217-24). She feels that to love less than an emperor is to "aimer contre mes intérêts" (v. 230). Domitian readily realizes that she "ne regarde et n'aime que soi-même" (v. 276). This is no rare occurrence, as Albin suggests, and Domitian admits that he, like any other lover, "ne voit, il n'entend, il ne croit que sa flamme" (v. 340). For Domitie, this is readily understandable: victim of her "intérêts," of her *gloire,* she must, like Honorie, rely on others to achieve her goals. This is why she must ask for proof of Domitian's love: if he cannot sacrifice his love to her desires — "Si vous m'aimez, Seigneur, il faut sauver ma gloire" (v. 1187) — if she cannot be empress, "je suis à qui me venge" (v. 1204). Such a prostitution is not surprising. In fact, it is a Cornelian commonplace in itself — witness Chimène, Emilie, etc. — precisely because all these masculine heroines, with their search for *gloire,* require the help of others better suited for such a struggle.

Bérénice lives in an entirely different world, so far removed from that of Domitie that the two women will not even understand each other. Even though Domitie once loved (v. 1510), she neither understands nor believes in Bérénice's purer love (vv. 1528-46). Bérénice not only loves without regard for politics, she is impatient with whoever considers them,

> Vos chimères d'Etat, vos indignes scrupules,
> Ne pourront-ils jamais passer pour ridicules,
> (vv. 927-28)

and, secure in her love, she demands only one thing of Tite: that he love her. Although Rome adopts her, she refuses to endanger her lover or her love. Thus her lines "On nous aime, faisons qu'on nous aime à jamais" (v. 1702), and "Jamais un tendre amour n'expose ce qu'il aime" (v. 1712), show to what extent she is ready to give Tite a lesson in "amour généreux." Tite had become "malgré l'amour, ... maître du dehors" (v. 950); Bérénice attains this condition because of her love. Content with Tite's love (v. 1714), she is mistress of herself and of the situation, and thus in a position to give to Domitie the rank that the Roman could not attain by herself.

Suréna, Corneille's last effort, sees the ultimate refinement of this problem: both Palmis and Eurydice are feminine, both are faced with the same problem, and in their opposing views to the solution, Corneille defines the mystique of the eternal feminine.

Eurydice, a more *tendre* Infante, loves a man whose worth is such that he is above "un Roi qui n'est que Roi" (v. 64), but if Suréna, like Rodrigue, "sait rétablir les Rois" (v. 60), and if his hand is better than a diadem (v. 233), he is, nonetheless, not a king and therefore unworthy of a love that Eurydice reveals to everyone she meets — *confidente,* Palmis, Suréna:

> Je veux...
> Toujours aimer, toujours souffrir, toujours mourir,
> (vv. 267-68)

a line that Suréna will echo in closing the most touching love duet in Corneille (v. 348). Eurydice is one of the most open and frank of all Cornelian heroines. To Pacorus, to whom she has been promised, she gives her hand if not her heart: "Et mon cœur avec vous n'a point fait de traité" (v. 504). Though she promises to do her best to move her heart for him, she confesses that "je ne sais si le temps l'y pourra disposer" (v. 507). This frankness has distinct disadvantages: when Pacorus makes her admit her love for another, she refuses to marry him unless he can make her love him and forget the love of Suréna (vv. 549-64).

As a matter of fact, all the lovers of *Suréna* are remarkably frank. Palmis scolds Pacorus for forsaking her and promises to forgive him if he can truly say that duty forced him to do it. When he openly admits that he did it for love, she reacts only by saying that it really makes no difference: "Je ne puis vous haïr" (v. 674).

Both women realize that the presence of the beloved is a painful necessity, though the reasons are not quite the same. Eurydice sees in her torment a further proof of her love. Palmis wants to be near "cet ingrat qui me tue" (v. 1001) because

> Je verrai l'infidèle inquiet, alarmé
> D'un rival inconnu ...
> ....
> .... devenir ma victime,
> (vv. 1007-10)

in other words, to force him to "avoir regret à moi" (v. 1020). Yet, it is Palmis, seemingly here most selfish and tenacious, who, at the crucial moment, most readily reveals her tenderness. With Suréna's life in danger, Eurydice feigns a lack of concern that brings a quick reproach from Palmis:

> Cette male vigueur de constance heroïque
> N'est point une vertu dont le sexe se pique.
> (vv. 1097-98)

Eurydice explains:

> Mon intrépidité n'est qu'un effort de gloire,
> Que, tout fier qu'il paraît, mon cœur n'en veut pas croire.
> Il est tendre... (vv. 1117-19)

Tender, but selfish, Eurydice refuses to surrender him, even though her refusal may cost his life:

> Donner ce qu'on adore à ce qu'on veut haïr,
> Quel amour jusque-là put jamais se trahir?
> (vv. 1703-4)

Palmis cannot mention all the Cornelian heroines who were able to sacrifice themselves to this extent, but her reproach certainly indicates that she herself could have been of that number. Eurydice's love, in Palmis' eyes, was not only "inutile" (v. 1725) but, since it existed only to cause Suréna's death (v. 1728), far from perfect.

As we have suggested earlier, the contrast in two such women is merely one manifestation of a far more general trend. Nowhere is the change from the heroic to the tender more obvious than in *Œdipe* (1659). Created seven years after Rodelinde, Dircé is her logical heir. Like her predecessor, she is only too aware of her *vertu*. Wanting to equal Thésée in every way (vv. 690-700, 704), she, like Chimène, goes beyond the demands of her *gloire*. Seeing in each effort to save her from her fanatical desire to sacrifice herself "un piège adroit qu'on tend à sa vertu" (v. 988), she is basically guilty of what Œdipe calls an "excès de générosité" (v. 956). Yet, as the play goes on, love becomes stronger and stronger. Already in Act II, Dircé announces a change:

> Ma vertu la plus forte à votre aspect chancelle:
> Tout mon cœur applaudit à sa flamme rebelle,
> Et l'honneur, qui charmait ses plus noirs déplaisirs [16]
> N'est plus que le tyran de mes plus chers désirs.
> (vv. 719-22)

By Act IV, she has gone even further when she admits that

> l'amour pour les sens est un si doux poison,
> Qu'on ne peut pas toujours écouter la raison.
> (vv. 1255-56)

Needless to say, her *générosité* is rewarded, but it is her love that triumphs in the end.

While it is difficult to consider *La Toison d'or* a tragedy, Médée is here presented as a very logical — though at times romanesque — link between the earlier and later heroines. Scorned by Jason, she wishes to hate him, but her love won't allow it (vv. 765-67). Jason, it is explained, scorned her to do his duty. But she does not want "un cœur noble et vraiment généreux" (v. 802), but "seulement amoureux" (v. 803). To be sure, the characters of this mythological fairy tale are difficult to adapt to really tragic situations, and one cannot expect to find unrefined in the later plays the extreme outpourings of Médée. After all, how far from Rodrigue's "l'infamie est pareille..." (v. 1063) is Jason's "Des paroles enfin ne sont que des paroles!" (v. 1681). Yet, the trend is there, as it will be in Corneille's last "comédie héroïque," *Pulchérie*.

Pulchérie loves Léon with a love that has "la vertu pour âme, et la raison pour guide" (v. 10), and while love may speak only to the heart, "l'hyménée a de plus leur gloire à soutenir" (v. 80). The choice must once more be made, and "L'amour gémit en vain sous ce devoir sévère" (v. 85). Thus, like the Infante, Pulchérie will have

---

[16] Note the past tense.

to give up the lover she cannot have herself lest she forget her duty to herself and to her *gloire:* "Je le crains, je me crains, s'il n'engage sa foi" (v. 867). Her decision is as obvious as the Infante's, but she is far less decisive. Her love is too strong to be easily denied. Even when prodded to rush her decision, she hesitates, indecisive and reluctant: "Laisse-moi consulter mieux mon âme" (v. 878). As late as Act IV, the issue remains in doubt: "Je ne t'en ai point fait un don irrévocable" (v. 1174). The decision must be made, however, and when Pulchérie decides, it is in favor of her *gloire.* In this respect, she is alone in the play. Only Aspar, an ambitious "esprit flottant" (v. 1756) who would do anything for power, is equally selfish. Martian, like Bérénice, loves selflessly, because, as he claims,

> L'amour hors d'intérêt s'attache à ce qu'il aime,
> Et n'osant rien pour soi, le sert contre soi-même.
> (vv. 425-26)

The advice he gives to his daughter Justine is in the same vein: "Le véritable amour n'est point intéressé" (v. 719), and he suggests that the two work against their own interests, and for those of the ones they love. Irène, too, loves unselfishly: "Je vous aime/ Plus que moi" (vv. 1373-74), she tells Aspar when his Machiavellian schemes endanger his life. "L'amour tendre est timide, et craint pour son objet" (v. 1375), and her fears are such that she is willing to sacrifice herself, and her *gloire,* for him: "Dédaignez, quittez-moi, mais ne vous perdez pas" (v. 1384). This type of "grandeur d'âme" is beyond Pulchérie.

It must be admitted that all of Corneille's heroines are aware of their obligation to themselves and to their reputation. Most of them find the path to fulfillment in the assumption of a masculine mystique which can only frustrate them and make true happiness impossible. However, a few — and their number grows as Corneille grows older — seek a different path to fulfillment. If the early heroines all too often violate nature to attain their *gloire,* later ones frequently sacrifice their *gloire* for the sake of their true nature. If, in *Rodogune,* Cléopatre reminds us of Lady Macbeth's "unsex me," Ildione, in *Attila,* violates her *gloire* for the sake of her "douceur naturelle" (v. 1448). Also, in later plays, those heroines seeking their fulfillment in the glorious manner find their path more and more difficult, not because of outside barriers, but because of a growing awareness of their true nature and because of hearts that will not be stilled. Time and time again, it is in the assumption of their true nature that these heroines attain a level far above that reached by the slaves of the *grandeur romaine* so readily associated with Corneille's earlier plays.

AN INTERESTING USE OF GENEALOGY IN HISTORICAL ROMANCE

James Rush Beeler
College of William and Mary

By the year 1690, when Madame d'Aulnoy published *Histoire d'Hypolite, comte de Duglas,* the novel had established itself in France as an important literary form. Scorned by critics and men of learning, denounced by the pious, and hampered by official censorship, the relatively new *genre* had nevertheless achieved unprecedented popularity and could no longer be ignored. Although the novel had its apologists in the seventeenth century — notably Pierre-Daniel Huet, the learned Bishop of Avranches — the measure of its popularity is best taken by reference to bibliographies and histories of printing in the seventeenth century. The *Bibliothèque des romans* (Amsterdam, 1734) of Lenglet du Fresnoy is an annotated catalogue some four hundred pages in length composed largely of novels that were published in France during the seventeenth century. The Ralph Copplestone Williams *Bibliography of the Seventeenth Century Novel in France* (New York, 1931) has over twelve hundred listings. Both of these works list only first editions. While a comprehensive study of reprints and subsequent editions of seventeenth-century French novels has never been made, it is possible by consulting the catalogue of the Bibliothèque Nationale (where the list of seventeenth-century editions and reprints of individual novels sometimes runs to more than a page) to obtain some notion of the popularity then enjoyed by the *genre*. This popularity is further attested by the wealth accumulated by booksellers and publishers of novels in the seventeenth century and by the emergence at the end of the century of the novelist as a professional man-of-letters. Since for him writing was a trade and means of livelihood, he studied popular taste and, perforce, was guided by it. In 1690, when she was forty years old, Madame d'Aulnoy embarked upon such a career and, pursuing it vigorously for the next thirteen years, won acclaim and considerable fortune.

Seventeenth-century readers required an historical framework for the novel. Whether the need for reliance upon history is to be explained by (1) the view, held at least until 1670,[1] that the novel was an epic in prose, similar to the poem both in arrangement and in subject matter, or (2) the verisimilitude lent to fiction by historical fact, seventeenth-century novelists were at pains to satisfy the readers' desire. In doing so, they outlined the principal forms which the historical novel was to take:

1) The setting is loosely historical. The characters and plot are of the author's invention. Example: The *Astrée* of Honore d'Urfé.

2) The setting is historical and well defined. Imaginary characters mingle with historical personages and participate in well-known historical events. Example: *Ariane* by Desmarets de Saint-Sorlin.

3) The characters are famous historical personages. History is supplemented in the plot by a series of extravagant adventures invented by the author. Example: *Cassandre* by la Calprenède.

4) The *roman à clef*. Contemporary society is represented under borrowed historical names in a falsely historical setting. Example: *Le Grand Cyrus* by Mademoiselle de Scudéry.

5) The *histoire secrète*. An invented sentimental plot purports to explain famous events of political history. Example: *Histoire secrète d'Henri IV, roi de Castille* by Mademoiselle de la Force.

6) The apocryphal memoir. A series of imaginary adventures is offered as an authentic memoir. Example: *Mémoires d'Artagnan* by Courtilz de Sandras.

Madame d'Aulnoy wrote four novels: *Histoire d'Hypolite, comte de Duglas* (1690); *Histoire de Jean de Bourbon, prince de Carency* (1692); *Mémoires de la cour d'Angleterre* (1695); and *Le*

---

[1] The date of Huet's *Traité de l'origine des romans*. It is chiefly his insistence that the novel conform to the rules of the epic poem which makes Huet's treatise seem *passé*.

Comte de Warwick (1703). Following the general trend, she gave an historical setting to each of her novels; in the management of plot and characters she utilized history in such a variety of ways as to include some feature of each of the typical forms of the historical novel that are listed above. In this paper I propose to examine the second novel, *Jean de Bourbon,* with special reference to Madame d'Aulnoy's use of genealogy to flatter a patroness.

Whereas in her first novel Hypolite and the other major characters are creatures of the author's own invention and acquire a luster of truth through association with prominent historical personages and famous events, Jean de Bourbon is known, albeit obscurely, to history; and Madame d'Aulnoy's fictitious narrative amplifies or enlarges upon the meager data of his recorded biography. The historical Jean de Bourbon, d. *ca.* 1458, was, as Madame d'Aulnoy says, a "proche parent du roi de France," and it is largely on account of his illustrious ancestry that his name has survived.[2] She accurately identifies him as the youngest son of Jean de Bourbon, Comte de la Marche, d. 1393. His grandfather, Jacques de Bourbon, d. 1361, was also Comte de la Marche, and his great-grandfather, Louis de Bourbon, d. 1341, was both Duc de Bourbon and Comte de la Marche. His great-great-grandfather was Robert de France (1256-1317), sixth son of King Louis IX (Saint Louis), who by his marriage in 1272 to Béatrice de Bourgogne, Dame de Bourbon et de Charolais and heiress in the fourteenth generation of the Counts of Bourbon, acquired the vast estates of the Bourbons and founded the dynasty which was to produce the royal house of France as well as the various branches of the august house of Bourbon.

Jean de Bourbon, second of the name, was Seigneur of Carency in Artois, of Buquoi, of l'Écluse, and of Duisant. He was never called *Prince de Carency,* nor was his *seigneurie,* or manor, of Carency, which had been a part of his grandmother's dowry, ever erected into a principality. Hence Madame d'Aulnoy, in calling her hero *Prince de Carency,* styled him erroneously. Whether she did

---

[2] For what information exists on the life of Jean de Bourbon, the reader must turn to genealogical records; his role in history is not significant. The chief sources consulted by me are La Chesnaye-Desbois, *Dictionnaire de la noblesse...,* 2d ed. (Paris, 1770-86), and Henri Vrignault, *Généalogie de la maison de Bourbon* (Paris, 1957).

so by accident or by design is difficult to ascertain. As several of her biographers have pointed out, Madame d'Aulnoy had herself used the title of countess when apparently she was only privileged to be called baroness, and it might be concluded that she would not have been overscrupulous in the use of titles in her novels. It should be mentioned, however, that Charles de Bourbon, who inherited the title at the beginning of the sixteenth century, did style himself *Prince de Carency*; and this practice was continued by his descendants until the end of the century. Carency subsequently passed by marriage into the estates of the Rochechouart-Mortemart family, and the latter did not take up the title.

Little is known of the life of Jean de Bourbon, Seigneur de Carency, etc., except that he was Chamberlain to Charles VI of France; that he went with his two elder brothers, Jacques de Bourbon, Comte de la Marche, and Louis de Bourbon, Comte de Vendôme, into England to make war against King Henry IV, usurper of the crown of Richard II; that he conducted the Queen of Cyprus to Basle in 1411; and that he died before the year 1458. He married, first, Catherine d'Artois, second daughter of Philippe d'Artois, Comte d'Eu (it is with this marriage that Madame d'Aulnoy concludes her novel). Then, in 1420, he married Jeanne Vendômois, who had been his mistress for some years during the lifetime of her husband, Gervais Ronsart. By his second wife he had eight children, three born prior to the marriage.

In selecting a hero so obscure, the author made herself less vulnerable to attack by Boileau and other critics than did Mademoiselle de Scudéry and the novelists who audaciously chose their heroes from among the most famous men of history. It could scarcely have been a matter of concern to any critic that she had deformed the character of Jean de Bourbon by turning him into a typical *héros de roman*, "plus fou que tous les Céladons et tous les Sylvandres ... qui ne sait du matin au soir que lamenter, gémir et filer le parfait amour." [3] I myself do not believe that caution prompted her to choose Jean de Bourbon. In her two English novels, *Mémoires de la cour d'Angleterre* and *Le Comte de Warwick*, she did not

---

[3] Thus Boileau describes Mademoiselle de Scudéry's Artamène in his "Discours sur le Dialogue des héros de roman," in *Œuvres complètes de Boileau Despréaux*, ed. Daunou (Paris, 1825), III, 44.

hesitate to alter or arrange historical facts as she delineated the amours of Charles II, the Dukes of Monmouth and Buckingham, and Warwick the Kingmaker.

In the dedicatory epistle of *Le Comte de Warwick*, Madame d'Aulnoy says that in order to tell the story which she had begun in a lively way and which she had not been permitted to finish in the same spirit because the events were too recent and too well known, she was obliged to seek in the past a court and names suitable to the ones of which she really wished to speak. One wonders if perhaps in her earlier novel she chose Jean de Bourbon because the events of his life corresponded to a narrative she desired to relate. Comparison does not confirm this, but it does point the way to an interesting alternate explanation of why she chose Jean de Bourbon. As has been indicated above, he was the youngest son of Jean de Bourbon, Comte de la Marche, d. 1393, who married in 1364 Catherine de Vendôme, heiress of the Counts of Vendôme. As Jean was the third of their seven children, it is possible that he was born prior to 1380, the year which Madame d'Aulnoy indicates. The Comte de la Marche played a rather prominent role in military affairs during the reigns of Charles V and Charles VI. In 1366 he took part in the Spanish expedition led by Du Guesclin. He was at the battle of Rosebecke in 1382, at the siege of Taillebourg in 1384, and participated in the Gueldres campaign in 1388. The diplomatic mission in Spain that led, in the novel, to the engagement of Jean de Bourbon and Léonide de Velasco is not recorded, however. Léonide, her family, and her friends likewise appear to be imaginary.

The crusade of Nicopolis provides a suitable setting for the first exploits of Jean de Bourbon. Here, according to Madame d'Aulnoy, he proved his courage and strength in battle and, in the aftermath of the disaster, found the occasion for his first amorous adventure. In 1394 Sigismund, King of Hungary, sent letters to Venice, and in 1395 to the kings of France and England, the emperor and other reigning princes, asking for volunteers in a great campaign against the Ottoman Turks then threatening the whole eastern Danube region. Dread of the Turks combined with a temporary cessation of the Hundred Years War and consequent restlessness of the unoccupied and undisciplined chivalry to produce an enthusiastic response to Sigismund's request. In the spring of 1396 there gathered at Buda nobles and their attendants from all parts of Germany, France, England, and The Netherlands, making up in all perhaps 100,000 men. From France alone came about a thousand knights and nobles of the highest rank, accompanied by several thousand attendants, mercenaries, and women. They were under the command of John of Nevers, son of the Duke of Burgundy and grandson of King John of France.

The story of the assemblage of the hosts loses nothing in its telling by Froissart (whom Madame d'Aulnoy probably follows), and the other chroniclers who have described this, perhaps the last of the tournaments on a grand scale which in the Middle Ages took the place of scientifically waged warfare. Having proceeded by various routes into northern Bulgaria, pillaging the countryside along their march, the crusaders gathered under the walls of Nicopolis on the right bank of the Danube, the most recent conquest of the Ottomans. They besieged it for two weeks, but did not assault the city, uncertain whether they should go farther to seek the Turkish sultan or await his coming.

Bayezid (Bajazet) did not leave them long in uncertainty. Abandoning the siege of Constantinople in which he was engaged, he moved quickly to face the crusaders in the plain before Nicopolis. Refusing to submit to any formulated plan of attack or defense, the French knights with many of those of England and Germany and their followers, recklessly keen for glory, galloped against the Turks and to their own destruction. They broke, it is true, the first line of the enemy, made up of irregular troops, and massacred their opponents and prisoners indiscriminantly on the ground that they were unbelievers. But they were, after the first onslaught, now facing the veteran and disciplined army of the Turkish sultan. There could be only one result: numbers of the proudest nobles of France were killed, and the rest were forced to surrender to the overwhelming numbers of fresh and well-handled troops of Bayezid or take flight as best they could. In anger and retaliation for the massacre of prisoners by the French knights, the sultan ordered a general execution of all prisoners taken by his troops. By the interposition of a French knight who could speak Turkish, and in expectation of a rich ransom, Bayezid was induced to spare the Count of Nevers, Marshal Boucicault, and some twenty others. (That Bayezid was moved to pity by the youth and noble bearing of Jean de Bourbon is an invention of Madame d'Aulnoy's.) But they were all forced to stand beside the sultan and watch the execution of their friends and companions. The massacre went on through a whole day and the number put to death has been estimated at 10,000. When the sun set those who had not been put to death were turned over to the soldiers to be sold as slaves. The few nobles reserved for ransom were taken to Brusa, where they were allowed a certain amount of liberty while the ransom of 20,000 pieces of gold was being obtained. Eventually, within a year, through the mediation of certain Genoese and Venetian bankers who negotiated with the Ottomans, the ransom was paid and those of the prisoners who were still living returned to their homes. Among them were the Count of Nevers, John, surnamed The Fearless because of his recklessness at Nicopolis, and Jacques de Bourbon, who in 1393 had succeeded his father as Comte de La Marche. Froissart and the other chroniclers make no mention of the ransoming of Jean de Bourbon, younger brother of the Count, or of his having participated in the crusade. [4]

No novelist could be blamed for having chosen to write of the crusade of Nicopolis; its pageantry and heroics are the very stuff of romance. Why, however, did Madame d'Aulnoy not choose to tell of the exploits of a known survivor of the battle? The deeds of Boucicault, whom she mentions incidentally in the novel, and especially the story of his almost miraculous escape from the general

---

[4] When referring to Jacques de Bourbon, Comte de la Marche, Froissart sometimes wrote *Jean de Bourbon,* calling him by the same name as his father's and his brother's (see *Œuvres de Froissart,* ed. Kervyn de Lettenhove, XXII [Bruxelles, 1875], 157). It might be supposed that this confusion of names led Madame d'Aulnoy to believe that Jean de Bourbon, Seigneur de Carency, participated in the crusade of Nicopolis, were it not perfectly clear in the chronicles that *Jean de Bourbon* and *Comte de la Marche* are used to refer to the same person. In her romance Madame d'Aulnoy says that both the Comte de la Marche and his younger brother followed John of Nevers to Nicopolis.

The list of chronicles and histories of the reigns of Charles VI and Charles VII given by Charles Sorel in his *Bibliothèque françoise* (Paris, 1664), 292-295, has been used as a guide to historical works concerning the period of Jean de Bourbon that would have been available in printed editions at the time Madame d'Aulnoy wrote. In addition, the chronicles quoted either in part or in full in Kervyn's monumental edition of Froissart have also been consulted. All point to the conclusion that Jean de Bourbon was not at Nicopolis.

slaughter of prisoners, might well have suited a novelist's purpose. [5] If she preferred a hero of higher rank, she might have chosen John of Nevers, leader of the crusade, or even Jacques, Comte de la Marche. The Comte de la Marche undoubtedly took part in the crusade and battle of Nicopolis. He was also captured by the Turks and held prisoner until a large ransom was paid for his release. The remainder of his life was adventurous, although not always heroic. Upon his return to France in 1397, this elder brother of Jean de Bourbon was made Grand Chamberlain and ordered to lead a maritime expedition against England. After having apparently squandered the greater part of the money allocated for the expedition, he at length, for form's sake, put to sea. When a storm forced him to return to port, the project was abandoned. This incident was commemorated by an epigram which jeering students chanted as he passed through Orléans: *Mare videt et fugit*. He fought in the civil wars on the side of the Burgundians from 1409 until 1411, when he was captured by the Armagnacs. Freed after a year's imprisonment, and now a widower, he went to Italy where in 1415 he married Giovanna II, Queen of Naples. Following an episode in which he caused one of the Queen's lovers to be assassinated, a group of Neopolitans captured him and imprisoned him in the Castello dell' Uovo. He managed to escape, returned to France, and took up arms for Charles VII. In 1424 he was made governor of Languedoc, but after a short time he relinquished that office in exchange for a pension of 12,000 *livres*. Finally, in 1435, he withdrew to the monas-

---

[5] "A icelle piteuse procession feut mené le maréschal de France Boucicaut tout nud, fors de ses petits draps. Mais Dieu qui voulut garder son servant pour le bien qu'il debvoit faire le temps à venir, tant en vengeant sur Sarrasins la mort de celle glorieuse compaignée, comme des autres grans biens qui par son bon sens et à cause de luy debvoient advenir, feit que le comte de Nevers sur le poinct que on vouloit férir sur luy, le va regarder moult piteusement, et le maréschal luy. Adonc prist merveilleusement à douloir le coeur au dict comte de la mort de si vaillant homme, et luy souvint du grand bien, de la prouesse, loyauté, et vaillance qui estoit en luy. Si l'advisa Dieu tout soubdainement de joindre lex deux doigts ensemble de ses deux mains en regardant Bajazet, et feit signe qu'il luy estoit comme son propre frère, et qu'il le répitast: lequel signe Bajazet entendit tantost, et le feit laisser." *Le Livre des faicts du bon Messire Jean de Maingre, dit Boucicaut*, in *Collection des mémoires relatifs a l'histoire de France*, ed. Claude Bernard Petitot (Paris, 1820-26), VI, 466-467.

tery of Cordelier monks at Bensançon, remaining there until his death on September 24, 1438. Thus he had, according to the humorous remark of Jules Quicherat, "goûté de la captivité dans toutes ses formes." [6]

The Comte de la Marche left no offspring. His brother, Jean de Bourbon, had eight children and a long line of descendants stretching down to Madame d'Aulnoy's day. An investigation of these descendants is of interest because it reveals a possible motive for the author's choice of Jean de Bourbon as the hero of her novel. Jean de Bourbon was succeeded as Seigneur de Carency by his son Jacques de Bourbon, who was in turn succeeded by his son Charles de Bourbon (who nevertheless called himself Prince de Carency). The male line having failed in the third generation, the estates now passed to Isabeau, daughter and heiress of Charles de Bourbon. She was married to François d'Escars, Seigneur de Vauguyon; and their son and heir Jean d'Escars was called Prince de Carency as well as Comte de Vauguyon. He was succeeded by his daughter Diane d'Escars, Princesse de Carency, Comtesse de Vauguyon, etc., who was married to Charles, Comte de Maures. She was the last to use the title Carency; her daughter and heiress Louise was simply styled Comtesse de Maures. The Comtesse de Maures was twice married, first to Odet de Matignon, Comte de Thorigny, and then to Gaspard de Rochechouart, Marquis de Mortemart, etc., by whom she had two sons. The elder was Gabriel de Rochechouart, Duc de Mortemart, Pair de France, etc., father of Françoise-Athénaïs de Rochechouart, Demoiselle de Tonnay-Charente — the future Madame de Montespan. Her daughter by Louis XIV, Louise-Françoise de Bourbon, legitimated de France and called Mademoiselle de Nantes, was married in 1685 to Louis III, Duc de Bourbon-Condé. Thus, Madame d'Aulnoy's patroness, the Duchesse de Bourbon, was a direct descendant, in the tenth generation, of Jean de Bourbon, Seigneur de Carency (see table). Through her royal father she was also a collateral descendant. Louis de Bourbon, Comte de Vendôme, from whom the house of France was descended, was a brother of Jean de Bourbon. He was also the ancestor of the family of Bourbon-Condé, to which her husband belonged.

---

[6] Cited by Antoine Thomas in his biographical sketch of Jacques de Bourbon: *La Grande Encyclopédie*, VII, 720.

The name of the Duchesse de Bourbon has been associated with the novel *Histoire de Jean de Bourbon, prince de Carency* since the date of its publication. In his letter to the reader, which serves as a preface to the first edition, Barbin, the publisher, said: "Madame D['Aulnoy] eut à peine fini l'histoire du Comte de Duglas, qu'elle commença celle du Prince de Carency; ensuite elle la laissa, pour écrire à la prière de ses amis, les Mémoires et le Voyage d'Espagne. Madame la Duchesse [the Duchesse de Bourbon] et Madame la Princesse de Conty ayant vu le commencement de l'Histoire de ce Prince, que je vous donne, en jugèrent si avantageusement qu'elles souhaitèrent de la voir achevée et Madame D['Aulnoy] la continua; mais ayant entrepris des ouvrages plus sérieux, elle ne sut s'attacher à finir celui-ci et peut-être qu'il n'aurait jamais vu le jour, sans qu'une personne de qualité qui en avait une copie, me l'a donnée pour l'imprimer." The identity of the "personne de qualité" who gave a copy of the novel to Barbin is not known; it is logical to think that it may have been the Duchesse de Bourbon, anxious to insure the publication of a work in which Madame d'Aulnoy evidently had lost interest.

The Princesse de Conti (daughter of Louis XIV and Mlle de la Vallière, and half-sister to the Duchesse de Bourbon) had received the dedication of Madame d'Aulnoy's first published works, *Histoire d'Hypolite, comte de Duglas* and *Mémoires de la cour d'Espagne*. For each, the author had composed a flattering dedicatory epistle and into the text of the latter work had inserted an account of the Princess's wedding at Versailles in 1680. An anonymous letter, published in the *Mercure Galant*, praised Madame d'Aulnoy for choosing this means of flattering a patroness:

> "Elle ne pouvait lui faire un compliment plus spirituel, qu'en lui faisant voir, comme dans un miroir, l'éclat surprenant de sa beauté, les deux plus beaux jours de sa vie, la veille et le jour de ses noces."

In the case of *Histoire de Jean de Bourbon, prince de Carency*, a knowledge of fourteenth-century genealogy enabled Madame d'Aulnoy to pay a less obvious, but equally witty, compliment to her other royal patroness.

---

[7] March, 1692, p. 131.

RONSARD'S TREATMENT OF IGNORANT POETS AND THE COMMON PEOPLE

SAMUEL M. CARRINGTON
Rice University

In formulating for French letters of his day a new poetic doctrine, Pierre de Ronsard incorporated into this doctrine an exaggerated disregard and aristocratic disdain for what he termed the *moderne ignorant* and the *vulgaire*. Into the first of these two classifications he placed the cultural obstructionists in the Catholic and Protestant Churches of the period; those poets who tended to preserve certain medieval traditions in their poetry, especially the remnants of Marot's group led by Mellin de Saint-Gelais; and finally toward the end of his life the insipid writers at the court of Henri III. Into the second classification were placed the common people with the admirers of the above groups of poets. For Ronsard these two classes of people constituted the main forces opposed to the perfection of France's literature and language as outlined in the Pléiade's reforms. In order to counteract this retrogressive attitude toward art and literature, the poet portrayed himself and his colleagues as part of the legions of enlightenment battling the forces of ignorance.

In his criticisms of the people placed into the first classification, Ronsard adopts as his point of departure the differences between the poetic doctrine followed by him and his colleagues and that adhered to by the so-called ignorant poet. As may be seen in the arts of rhetoric of the fifteenth and sixteenth centuries and in Thomas Sebillet's *Art poétique françoys* (1548), French poetry before the publication in 1549 of Du Bellay's *Deffence et illustration de la langue françoyse* did not possess a truly intellectual and philosophical base upon which it could justify its existence. The poetic treatises of such poets as Molinet were primarily concerned with the mechanical aspects involved in the writing of verses; Sebillet, while skirting the philosophical aspects of poetic doctrine, was never able to give a clear, comprehensive treatment of the subject and thus contented himself in large measure with cataloguing and describing the poetic forms used by Marot's group and with trying to relate these forms to those used by the poets of antiquity.[1] With the arrival of Dorat, Ronsard, and Du Bellay onto the literary scene, the concept of poetic doctrine changed drastically and was elevated above the idea of technique and form; from this point on, the poet needed divine inspiration in writing verse, and he became the intermediary between the gods and mankind. Thus, from the beginning of his literary career, Ronsard was faced with the dual task of questioning and attacking the entire structure of poetic values adhered to by the court poets under the leadership of Saint-Gelais while attempting to institute and popularize the poetic ideas of his own group; in later years, with the success of the Pléiade's reforms and with the disappearance of the older generation of poets, he would turn his attention to the opposition coming from certain Protestant writers and from the court poets led by Desportes.[2]

When he discusses the versification of his opponents, Ronsard adopts in his argumentation the device of comparison. Serving as a criterion of cultural and literary excellence is the erudite who embraces the innovations of the Pléiade; into this elite group are placed the new generation of poets, such as Du Bellay and Jacques Bouju, and the admirers and supporters of its poetic goals; to describe these people Ronsard uses almost exclusively the terms *docte* and *doctement*. When these words qualify the learned poet and his works, they indicate not only his erudition and knowledge

---

[1] See for example Bk. II, chap. vi of the *Art poétique françoys*, édition critique avec une introduction et des notes publiée par Félix Gaiffe, 2e tirage; Société des Textes Français Modernes (Paris, 1932).

[2] For detailed studies on Ronsard's relationships with his literary opponents at court, see Paul Laumonier's *Ronsard poète lyrique*, 2e édition (Paris, 1923), pp. 70-119 and Marcel Raymond's *L'Influence de Ronsard sur la poésie française (1550-1585)*, nouvelle édition; Travaux d'Humanisme et Renaissance, LXXIII, 2 vols. (Genève, 1965), I, 9-71 and II, 70-77.

but also his skill and ability to transfer this erudition into the rigid structure of a poem:

> Il faut que ta [Du Bellay's] docte main face
> Un euvre dinne de son bruit. ³

In describing the admirers of the erudite poet, the terms indicate the possession of the knowledge necessary to appreciate the results of the poet's frenzy and to obtain from it a certain intellectual and aesthetic satisfaction:

> J'ai sous l'esselle un carquois
> Gros de fleches nompareilles,
> Qui ne font bruire leurs vois
> Que pour les doctes oreilles ...   (I, 73)

Opposing these intellectuals are all writers of inane and superficial verses. For Ronsard an attack on this group of people represents an effort on the part of the erudite to eradicate the vestiges of medieval ignorance found in the literature of the first half of the sixteenth century and, later, to censure the shallow verses of the court poets of Henri III. Throughout his poetry, Ronsard is obsessed with the idea of the ignorance of his opponents, which may be defined as an insufficiency of knowledge and an inadequacy of experience resulting from a lack of intellectual curiosity; to combat these deficiencies, the learned poet must present

> Un vers qui soit industrieus,
> Foudroiant la vieille ignorance
> De nos peres peu curieus.   (I, 237)

In many of the references to ignorance, the word is personified as a monster which acts as an obstructionist to any emancipation of thought and art and which must be overcome. Several scenes of

---

³ Pierre de Ronsard, *Œuvres complètes*, édition critique avec introduction et commentaire par Paul Laumonier; Société des Textes Français Modernes, 17 vols. (Paris, 1914-), II, 43. All citations are taken from this edition except for those preceded by the letters LL., which are from the Laumonier edition of the text of 1584 (Paris: Lemerre, 1914-1919).

battle emerge from the poet's verses: the Muse of Jacques Bouju is depicted as having chased away "la sourde ignorance" (I, 124), while Jean Dorat is credited with having broken this monster into pieces with his erudition (I, 127). In an ode addressed to Marguerite de France in 1550, Ronsard relates how the French cultural climate in the first half of the sixteenth century was devoid of intellectual enlightenment and presents Marguerite as a modern day Pallas who has righteously struck down

> Le vilain monstre Ignorance
> Qui souloit toute la France
> Desous son ventre couver.   (I, 75)

Finally, at the end of his life, Ronsard decries in the "Caprice à Simon Nicolas" the ignorance which has again gained favor and has supplanted him at court. Obviously embittered by the treatment which he has received at the hands of the group of poets led by Desportes, the old man mourns the days when the Pléiade poets had reigned supreme over French poetry, and he wonders whether all of his work has come to naught and is to be displaced by Ignorance in a new guise:

> Que m'a serui de me trauailler tant
> D'vn bras vainqueur l'Ignorance dontant,
> Si par aueu elle se rend plus forte,
> Si les plus grands ores lui font escorte,
> Passionnez d'vn langage fardé,
> Que les neuf Sœurs n'ont jamais regardé,
> D'vn vers trainant, d'vne prose rithmée,
> De qui leur ame est si tres affamée,
> Que si Virgile esclairoit à leurs yeux,
> Il leur seroit je m'asseure ennuyeux?   (LL., VI, 63)

Weighted down by their lack of erudition and incapable consequently to compose lofty verses, the ignorant poets adopt a narrow approach to poetry and believe that their primary function is to please and to amuse without paying too much attention to content. Thus there can be no reconciliation between this style of poetry and that of the Pléiade. The first comprehensive treatment which Ronsard gives to the differences in poetic doctrine existing between the divine poet and his human counterpart is contained in the "Au Lecteur" to *Les Quatre premiers livres des Odes* (1550);

in this preface, he sees himself and his colleagues following a new route in poetry which is separated by a wide, intellectual gap from the verses of his marotique contemporaries:

> ... tu ne me diras imitateur de leurs écris, car l'imitation des nostres m'est tant odieuse (d'autant que la langue est encores en son enfance) que pour cette raison je me suis éloingné d'eus, prenant stile apart, sens apart, euvre apart, ne desirant avoir rien de commun avecq' une si monstrueuse erreur .... Et pour parler rondement, ces petis lecteurs Poëtastres, qui ont les yeus si agus à noter les frivoles fautes d'autrui, ... montrent evidemment leur peu de jugement, de s'attacher à ce qui n'est rien, laissant couler les beaus mots sans les louer, ou admirer. Pour telle vermine de gens ignorantement envieuse ce petit labeur n'est publié ....
> (I, 45-48)

At the end of the preface, Ronsard underscores the mercenary tendancies of the *poëtastres* who write verses only for the honors bestowed upon them by their patrons and whose poetry will never survive the critical scrutiny of posterity.

As may be seen in the preceding passage, the principal criticism which Ronsard levels at the past generations of poets is that they have sacrificed intellectual content, poetic inspiration, and phonetic harmony to poetic form and technique. Probably having uppermost in mind the verbal gymnastics of the Grands Rhétoriqueurs and their imitators, Ronsard shows a clear scorn for technique as well as for any poetic form which superimposes itself upon a poem's content; this attitude is elaborated upon in much of his early poetry. In a poem addressed to Du Bellay in the *Quatre premiers livres des Odes*, he ridicules those poets who must rely on poetic rules in their futile attempts to write poetry equal to his own; it is as painful for them to write verse as it is for a woman to give birth to a child:

> Mais ces rimeurs qui ont apris
> Avec travail, peines, & ruses,
> Tousjours ils enfantent des vers
> Tortus, & courans de travers
> Parmi la carriere des Muses:
> Eus égualés à nos chants beaus
> Ils sont semblables aus corbeaus

>   Lesquels desous l'ombre quaquetent
>   Contre deus aigles, [Ronsard and Du Bellay] ...
>   (I, 111)

Thus, what comes naturally through divine inspiration to the erudite poet can only be acquired imperfectly through poetic rules and painful labor by the ignorant rhymer.

In the well-known ode to Michel de l'Hospital, published in the *Cinquiesme livre des Odes* (1552), Ronsard sums up his initial ideas concerning the question of the learned poet's inspiration and the technique of the versifier. Applying the Pindaric doctrine of the *beau désordre,* he reclaims complete freedom from form and rules for the *docte* poet who in his frenzy does not need these tools and who will accomplish his task "Sans art, sans sueur, ne sans peine" (III, 144). Believing that without inspiration there is no poetry, Ronsard condemns categorically the necessity for technique which has enslaved French versification and which he terms "Cét art penible, & miserable" (III, 143); without the aid of divine fury, the rhymer can only produce verses devoid of grace and grandeur, for

>   ... les vers viennent de Dieu,
>   Non de l'humaine puissance.
>   (III, 145)

Toward the middle part of his life, Ronsard begins to admit that there is a need for rules to govern the composition of poetry, and from the *Abbregé de l'Art poëtique françois* (1565) comes the idea that the arrangement of a work depends on "la belle invention, laquelle consiste en une elegante et parfaicte collocation & ordre des choses inventées, ... se gouvernant par artifice, estude & labeur ..." (XIV, 14). However, a distinction has already been made in the *Response aux injures* (1563) between the poet's artifices and the rhymer's technique:

>   En l'art de Poësie, un art il ne faut pas
>   Tel qu'ont les Predicans, qui suivent pas à pas
>   Leur sermon sceu par cueur, ou tel qu'il faut en prose,
>   Où toujours l'Orateur suit le fil d'une chose.
>   Les Poëtes gaillards ont artifice à part,

> Ils ont un art caché qui ne semble pas art
> Aux versificateurs, d'autant qu'il se promeine
> D'une libre contrainte, où la Muse le meine. (XI, 160)

Such artifices are beyond the capabilities of the *poètes ignorants* who

> ... ne sont seulement que de mots inventeurs,
> Froids, grossiers, & lourdaux, comme n'ayant saisie
> L'ame d'une gentille & docte frenaisie ... (XI, 161)

Ronsard's final treatment of ignorant poets comes in the *Preface sur la Franciade,* published in 1587, where the *versificateurs* are likened to charlatans; in their compositions they "se contentent de faire des vers sans ornement, sans grace et sans art ..." (XVI, 336).

Complementing Ronsard's criticisms of ignorant court poets are his denunciations of the general public which he deems incapable of accepting or understanding the Pléiade's approach to literature. Referred to as the *vulgaire, populaire, multitude,* and *peuple,* the members of this group are portrayed as living in an environment permeated with intellectual, moral, and artistic sterility. In many of the passages describing these individuals, Ronsard often chooses terms which denote hardness and weight and which impart to these people inanimate qualities; the "dur populaire" was, according to him, born from rocks and possesses

> ... l'esprit gros & plombé,
> Tousjours vers la terre courbé,
> Jamais au beau ne dresse l'aile ... [4] (III, 165)

In the "Complainte contre Fortune," published in the *Second livre des Meslanges* (1559), a more complete description of the ignorant public is given:

> Le lourd peuple ignorant, grosse masse de chair,
> Qui a le sentiment d'un arbre ou d'un rocher,
> Traine à bas sa pensée, & de peu se contente,
> D'autant que son esprit hautes choses n'atente.
> Il a le cueur glacé, & jamais ne comprend
> Le plaisir qu'on reçoit d'aparoistre bien grand. (X, 36)

---

[4] See also II, 161.

Only the "gaillard esprit" is capable of loftier thoughts. A passage in the *Remonstrance au peuple de France* (1563) imparts more specifically these inanimate qualities to the multitude; Ronsard accuses the Protestants of having deceived with their theological arguments the young merchant, the boastful gentleman, the debauched student, and

>... le vulgaire innocent,
>Grosse masse de plomb qui ne voit ny ne sent ...
>(XI, 76)

In these verses it is also interesting to note the new dimension given to the multitude's character; not only does the poet deprive it of its senses, but he also pictures it as having the type of naïveté which permits it to be easily led astray.

Unable to feel and to see, the masses are also incapable of being virtuous (IX, 64); therefore, the divine poet's pronouncements will make no impression on them. Like the ignorant poets, the multitude is motivated by greed and materialism; by its moral standards, a man's essence is determined by the amount of money he possesses and not by the type of life he leads or by the manner in which he puts his possessions to work. In the opinion of the *vulgaire,* gold

>... faict l'ignorant sage, & par luy le lourdaut
>Est tenu pour accort, & s'éleve plus haut
>En l'honneur, qu'un sçavant, ou qu'un vertueux, pource
>Que la simple Vertu n'a jamais bonne bourse.
>Combien voit-on de gens qui seroient estimez
>Sotz, nyez, & badins, s'ilz n'estoient bien armez
>De madame Richesse, escu de leur sotize,
>Qui faict que le vulgaire ainsi que Dieux les prise?
>(VIII, 187)

Standing in contrast to this materialistic attitude are the poet and philosopher who need money solely for the simple necessities of life; an excess amount of wealth is to them quite superfluous and

>... ne sert qu'à nous faire
>Ou proye des larrons, ou fable du vulgaire.[5]
>(XII, 92)

---

[5] See VIII, 180.

So worldly are the members of the *vulgaire* that, if the poet receives gifts from admirers whom he has celebrated in his poetry, they accuse him of being a materialist:

> Pourquoy vay-je comptant, moy François, les bienfaicts
> Qu'à ces Grecs estrangers, liberal, tu as faicts,
> Et je ne compte pas cette faveur honneste,
> Que je receu du Roy n'aguere à ta requeste?
> Si je la celebrois, le vulgaire menteur,
> Babillard, & causeur, m'appelleroit flateur,
> Et diroit que tousjours ma Muse est favorable
> Vers ceux, qui m'ont receu d'un visage aymable ... [6]
> (X, 47-48)

As is indicated in the preceding citation, the poet is often misunderstood by the people, who scorn everything which is foreign to their way of life and who do not readily accept change. Lacking the knowledge to appreciate the results of the poet's frenzy, they ridicule the universal truths found in his verses and deem him mad:

> Tu seras du vulgaire appellé frenetique,
> Insencé, furieux, farouche, fantastique,
> Maussade, mal plaisant, car le peuple medit
> De celuy qui de mœurs aux siennes contredit.
> (XII, 49)

As a result of their lack of knowledge, the people unwittingly become the ally of ignorance, in which state it takes very little to please them: a great lord dressed in the regalia of his rank causes "esbahir les yeux du populaire" (VIII, 11), while the mediocre versifier can amuse them with his banal rhymes:

> ... ce n'est moy qui sers
> De bateleur au peuple, & de farce au vulgaire ...
> (XI, 175)

Ronsard's distaste for the ignorant masses extends even into the realm of love. Unfeeling and possessing the non-human characteristics attributed to rocks and trees, they do not understand the

---

[6] See VII, 247-48.

intricacies of human love which is reserved by the poet for "les bons espris" (V, 120). The type of woman whom the erudite poet should love is of equal importance, and in "A son Luc," published in the *Continuation des amours* (1555), Ronsard discusses the differences between the erudite lady of the city and her ignorant counterpart in the village and the reasons why one should prefer the former to the latter. In a light-hearted curse, the poet damns "mon haineux" to love the village girl "Qui soit badine, sote, & qui ne sache rien" (VII, 138), for the greatest misfortune which can befall one in love is to give his attentions to "une femme indocte, & mal-habille." Due to her lack of education, the ignorant woman will be unable to reciprocate the lover's feelings, and in her vanity she will not understand the underlying meanings of his words:

> Vous l'aurez beau prescher, & dire qu'elle est belle,
> Sans s'esmouvoir de rien, vous entendra pres d'elle
> Parler un jour entier, & ne respondra mot. [7]   (VII, 139)

Standing in contrast to the ignorant village girl in the poem is the "femme de ville" who in her beauty and manners represents the ideal type of lady whom the poet's friends may love. Being born into a distinguished family where she may acquire the necessary intellectual attainments which will be pleasing to a discriminating suitor, the lady will be naturally sensitive to the pleasures which one receives from love. In another poem, Ronsard emphasizes the importance of the lady's intelligence which, combined with her physical charms, is sufficient to please any man:

> Car est-il home que n'enchante
> La voix d'une dame savante,
> Et fust-il Sythe en cruauté:
> Il n'est point de plus grand magie
> Que la docte voix d'une amie,
> Quand elle est jointe à la beauté.   (VI, 249)

---

[7] In the versions of the poem published between 1560 and 1572, Ronsard uses the stone motif, employed earlier to describe the populace. The phrase "Froide comme un rocher" replaces "Sans s'esmouvoir de rien."

To resolve to his own satisfaction the conflict between his group of erudites and the members of the *vulgaire*, Ronsard chooses to ignore the latter and to make no attempt to placate it:

> Mais que ferai-je à ce vulgaire
> A qui jamais je n'ai seu plaire,
> Ni ne plais, ni plaire ne veus?
> Porterai-je la bouche close
> Sans plus animer quelque chose
> Qui puisse etonner nos neveus? [8]
> (III, 106, ll. 157-62 var.)

As with the ignorant rhymers, the divine poet must separate himself from the masses, lest he be contaminated by them:

> Car voulentiers l'esprit d'un personnage rare
> Ne veut s'acompaigner de la tourbe barbare.
> (IX, 64)

> Pour la vertu j'ay quitté le vulgaire,
> Villes, chasteaux, bourgades & marchez ...
> (XIV, 142)

The poet's usual refuge will be in the forests where he can contemplate the beauties of nature and communicate with his Muse and God, who will remain mute to man if he is not virtuous and alone:

> Car Dieu ne communique aux hommes ses mysteres
> S'ils ne sont vertueux, devots & solitaires,
> Eslongnés des tyrans, & des peuples qui ont
> La malice en la main, & l'impudence au front,
> Brulés d'ambition, & tourmentés d'envie,
> Qui leur sert de bourreau tout le temps de leur vie.
> (XII, 47)

In his treatment of ignorant poets and the common people, Ronsard makes no attempt to understand them; this attitude, fired by the poet's pride; and influenced by certain writers of classical antiquity, may have resulted in part from the type of fear which an intellectual feels when he is confronted by a social and intel-

---

[8] Cf. VII, 115-116.

lectual level inferior to his own. However, in his poetry, Ronsard tempers his fear, which is always implied, and his disdainful attitude toward his opponents by using general, somewhat vague terms to describe them. Although by implication he leaves little doubt to which groups of people he is criticizing, Ronsard seldom attacks individual members of these groups [9]; instead, he relies primarily on such general terms as *moderne ignorant, rimeur, vulgaire,* and *peuple* to describe each group as whole. The principal reason behind this use of generalities is that, while denying any desire to please his opponents, the poet wants to be read by them and to receive for his works their approval. In discussing poetic doctrine, Ronsard might condemn the approach to versification employed by unspecified but easily identifiable schools of poetry, but he does not alienate outright in his denunciations the individual members of these schools who might eventually elect to join his own poetic movement. It should be noted that this tactic achieved some measure of success, when many of the court poets under Saint-Gelais eventually sought a reconciliation with Ronsard's group and began to imitate its poetry as well as that of the poets of antiquity. [10]

Coupled with the hope of winning over many of his literary opponents to his new approach to poetry is Ronsard's desire to be recognized by his countrymen as a truly national poet. It is not surprising then that the poet seeks and obtains for his poetry

> ... ensemble & des grands Rois
> Faveurs & biens & du peuple la voix ...   (XV, 16)

Elsewhere, he relates how the people of Bourgueil are familiar with his poems to Marie (XII, 256-77) and how the general public has favorably received his compositions (XII, 15).

From Ronsard's treatment of his literary adversaries and the common people, there emerges a dilemma whose resolution is paradoxal. The Pléiade's style of poetry must replace that of the preceding generations, and to accomplish this task, the poet must

---

[9] One of the rare exceptions to this statement is found in the *Cinquiesme livre des Odes,* where Ronsard speaks of having been "Mellinisé" (III, 106, l. 144). However, subsequent editions of the poem replace this verse with one which makes no reference to Saint-Gelais.

[10] See Raymond, *op. cit.,* I, 52-71.

vociferously denounce all who do not accept or understand this new approach to poetry. However, in his denunciations, he must not alienate too much these people, for it will be from many of them that he will eventually receive the national praise and recognition which he seeks for his poetry. Thus, Ronsard resolves the problem by the use of vague, general terms to describe his opponents and the general public and to attack their approach to poetry without compromising his own position concerning poetic doctrine.[11]

---

[11] I wish to thank Professor Isidore Silver who so kindly furnished me with some of the references used in this paper.

ROTROU'S *VENCESLAS: TRAGÉDIE* OR *TRAGI-COMÉDIE?*

JAMES HERBERT DAVIS, JR.
University of Georgia

When in 1648 Jean de Rotrou published his *Venceslas,* which had been performed a year earlier, it appeared as a *tragi-comédie.* The next seven editions —those of 1655, 1698, 1705, 1708, 1716, 1718, and 1737— likewise classified the play as a *tragi-comédie.*[1] In the seventeenth and early eighteenth centuries, therefore, the appellation *tragi-comédie* presented no real problems with regard to the genre and form of Rotrou's play. Here, indeed, was a type of drama, adapted from Francisco de Roja's *No hay ser padre siendo rey,* which presented in classic form aristocratic characters involved in a happy dénouement, and which ended with a possible marriage.[2] These traits were apparently sufficient for Rotrou's generation —and the generation following— to justify the play as characteristic of a genre well established by 1628, and, by the time of the performance of *Venceslas,* at the height of its popularity. But, in the case of Rotrou, as Lancaster remarks, the distinction between *tragédie* and *tragi-comédie* is tenuous and "its assignment to either

---

[1] The 1705 and 1708 editions are not listed in the *Catalogue Général des Livres Imprimés de la Bibliothèque Nationale* (Paris: Imprimerie Nationale, 1938) CLIV, 814. See: Rotrou, *Venceslas, tragi-comédie, édition critique par W. Leiner* (West-Ost-Verlag Saarbrücken Gmbh: 1956), pp. XLIII-XLIV.

[2] Henry Carrington Lancaster, *The French Tragi-Comedy. Its Origin and Development from 1552 to 1628* (Baltimore: J. H. Furst Co., 1907), pp. xxii-xxiv.

genre can be defended." [3] This study purports, therefore, to show the principal attitudes and concepts, relative to genre, which developed in the course of years, regarding what might possibly be Rotrou's strongest dramatic creation.

I

The dubious credit for changing the genre title of *Venceslas* belongs to Jean-François Marmontel, protégé of Voltaire, literary spokesman for the *encyclopédistes*, and author of the *Contes moraux*. In his *Mémoires*, today perhaps the best known of his works, Marmontel tells how he came to prepare his edition of *Venceslas:*

> Madame de Pompadour ayant désiré que le *Venceslas* de Rotrou fût purgé des grossièretés de mœurs et de langage qui déparaient cette tragédie, j'avais bien voulu, pour lui complaire, me charger de ce travail ingrat... [4]

In wishing to rejuvenate an old text, which could now be brought within the grasp of a new public, Marmontel meant no sacrilege. Corneille, himself, for the new edition of his works in 1660 had proceeded with a revision of style. [5] Later, in 1734, Jean-Baptiste Rousseau published a *retouchement* of Corneille's *Le Cid*, in which the role of the Infanta was suppressed. [6] Respect for old texts was no law; and so it was that the new *Venceslas*, this time (and for the very first time) bearing the name "tragédie," appeared in 1759.

Marmontel's principal motives, as can be observed by the above passage, in tampering with the creation of a respected dramatist, were those of modernization. In the *Mercure* (June, 1759), he explains that he has tried to conserve the fine lines of the original

---

[3] Henry Carrington Lancaster, *French Dramatic Literature in the Seventeenth Century* (9 vols.; Baltimore: The Johns Hopkins Press, 1932), II, pt. 2, 530; 546.

[4] Jean-François Marmontel, *Œuvres complètes* (18 vols.; Paris: Verdière, 1818-1819), I, 369.

[5] S. Lenel, *Un Homme de lettres au XVIIIe siècle. Marmontel* (Paris: Hachette, 1902), p. 169.

[6] Jean-Baptiste Rousseau, *Pièces dramatiques choisies et restituées* (Amsterdam: F. Changuion, 1734).

and even to restore the flavor of Rotrou's language in the new lines which were mixed into the original. At the same time he has "précipité le dialogue," and has tried to give the *discours* a more noble and proper tone.[7] Marmontel, however, goes a step further. Finding Ladislas too violent, too impetuous, for a prince who will be crowned at the conclusion of the tragedy, he has preferred to give a certain depth of kindness and rectitude to his character.[8] What is perhaps most important from the standpoint of genre, Marmontel creates a new dénouement in which Cassandre, despairing because the murderer of her bridegroom has become king, commits suicide. Thus, in the eyes of Marmontel, she triumphs over false justice and morality.

Against the attacks of his detractors, chiefly the editor of the *Année Littéraire*, Elie Fréron, Marmontel defends his change in the dénouement. He declares that through the punishment of Ladislas, Cassandre's death gives a certain morality to the play.[9] Later (in the *Mercure* of July, 1759), he maintains that Cassandre's death is consistent with her character, her passion, and her position in the drama. She can by no means enter the marriage bed covered with the blood of her lover, nor can she accept as master this monster, whose very actions have reinforced her concept of love, honor, and virtue. Marmontel concludes:

> En vérité, dans de telles circonstances, je ne vois pas qu'elle ait à délibérer et dans son désespoir, il ne lui reste d'autre ressource que son désespoir; car, enfin Cassandre n'est pas comme nos dames d'aujourd'hui qui se consolent assez volontiers de la perte d'un amant dans les bras même de son rival.[10]

Although Marmontel's reaction, with regard to dénouement, is more a question of morality than of art, his *dénouement funeste* justifies his idea that *Venceslas* should be considered a *tragédie*.

---

[7] Leiner, p. lvii.
[8] Lenel, p. 172.
[9] Léonce Person, *Histoire du Venceslas de Rotrou* (Paris: Léopold Cerf, 1882), p. 73.
[10] Ibid., p. 78.

Here, as he says, is a subject which is "terrible, touchant, et moral." [11] Furthermore, Marmontel sees in Venceslas's son the key to the tragic action of the play:

> Que Ladislas soit fougueux, violent, emporté dans les accès de sa passion, c'est en cela qu'il est tragique; mais c'est pour lui qu'on doit trembler et s'attendrir; c'est lui qui doit arracher des larmes; c'est à lui qu'on doit s'attacher... Il faut donc que son caractère soit celui d'un prince naturellement bon, mais égaré, rendu furieux et coupable par des passions qu'il n'a pu dompter. Tout ce qui annonce la dureté, la méchanceté d'un cœur naturellement féroce, est donc une tache dans ce caractère... [12]

The *Venceslas retouché* of Marmontel evoked not only the hostility of Fréron, but also the animosity of the actor Lekain, who refused to acknowledge in performance Marmontel's changes. In collaboration with Colardeau, whom Marmontel had encouraged in his literary débuts, [13] the tragedian prepared a third version of the play, finally printed in 1774. Although the Colardeau-Lekain text contains numerous changes, it is much closer to the original Rotrou than is Marmontel's. [14] The new version, however, will not admit Marmontel's idea of Cassandre's suicide, nor will it accept Rotrou's concept that the murderer Ladislas can marry the wife of his victim. [15] Instead, Cassandre simply does not appear at all in the last scene of the play, a change which necessitates the removal of eighteen lines of the 1648 *tragi-comédie*. [16] Despite the Colardeau-Lekain effort to rehabilitate the original *Venceslas*, six out of the thirteen published versions of the play during the remainder of the eighteenth century follow Marmontel's corrections. [17]

---

[11] Rotrou, *Saint Genest and Venceslas*, ed. Thomas Frederick Crane (Boston: Ginn and Co., 1907), p. 116. This edition is henceforth referred to as Crane.

[12] Ibid., p. 117.

[13] Lenel, p. 176.

[14] Leiner, p. xxx.

[15] Ibid, p. xliii.

[16] *Venceslas. Tragédie en cinq actes par M. Rotrou* (Paris: chez la Veuve Duchesne, 1774), pp. 94-96.

[17] The 1767, 1773, 1775, and 1784 editions follow the original; the 1774 and 1785 editions are the Colardeau-Lekain version. Leiner does not comment on the 1780 edition. See Leiner, pp. xliv-vi.

II

Although there are presumably no editions of *Venceslas* in the nineteenth century which follow Marmontel's text, his idea that the play should be called a tragedy appears, in some manner, to have affected the general concept of the play's genre. An 1813 edition, for example, cites in the "observation de l'éditeur" that *Venceslas* is here being given the name of "tragédie," a denomination under which it has previously been printed. The editor does remark, however, that "Rotrou ne l'a jamais qualifié que de tragi-comédie, comme le prouve l'édition faite en 1648." [18]

Even in 1820, when Viollet-le-Duc published what might be considered the first modern edition of *Venceslas* (his edition is certainly the first edition of the complete works of Rotrou), he presents a title page which bears the following designation: "*Venceslas. Tragédie. 1647.*" [19] In his "Notice historique et littéraire sur *Venceslas*," Viollet-le-Duc refers to the play as a tragedy which alone has placed Rotrou "au niveau des plus grands tragiques dont notre théâtre s'honore" (V, 175). There is no comment about its having been considered a *tragi-comédie*, but there is an allusion to Marmontel's efforts to reconstruct the play (V, 176).

The second half of the nineteenth century is a period of revival of interest in Rotrou. Two editions of his *Théâtre choisi* appear, as well as other items, such as a study of his work by Jules Jarry, [20] Léonce Person's *Histoire de Venceslas*, and a somewhat limited discourse by Saint-René Taillandier. [21]

In his chapter on Rotrou's *tragi-comédie*, Jarry does not include a discussion of *Venceslas*. Obviously, from the start, he wishes to relegate this play to a more lofty genre. For him it is, indeed, a creation worthy of being ranked with *Saint Genest* and *Cosroès*,

---

[18] *Théâtre des auteurs du second ordre* (Paris: A. Belin, 1813), XXVIII, 7.

[19] Jean Rotrou, *Œuvres*, ed. Viollet-le-Duc (5 vols.; Paris; Chez Th. Desoer, 1820), V, 173. Volume and page numbers in this paragraph refer to this specific edition.

[20] *Essai sur les œuvres dramatiques de Jean Rotrou* (Paris: A. Durand, 1868). Citations in parentheses in the section on Jarry refer to this volume.

[21] *Rotrou et ses œuvres* (Paris: Ch. Lahure, 1865). Citations in parentheses in the paragraph on Taillandier refer to this volume.

"grandes tragédies," as he calls them (p. 277). In another section of his essay, Jarry refers to *Venceslas* as a "tragédie passionnée," and in still another as a "tragédie sanglante" (pp. 198; 211). He finds, moreover, that Ladislas, as a sublime, durable creation, has served as something of a model for all "ces héros éminemment dramatiques qui intéressent par la passion, les transports, les fluctuations de l'amour" (p. 81). His passion and his vehemence, his vitality and his exuberance cause one to compare him to Othello. Ladislas is truly the "amoureux tragique" (p. 94). The character of Venceslas also possesses tragic proportions, for "on se l'imagine volontiers avec la taille surhumaine et la gravité superbe d'un antique demi-Dieu" (p. 228).

Saint-René Taillandier refers to *Venceslas* neither as a *tragédie* nor as a *tragi-comédie*. Most often it is called a "drame" — "drame moral," "ce beau drame," "le drame sanglant," "ce terrible drame" (pp. 33; 40; 35). It is a play, the subject of which even Aeschylus and Shakespeare did not imagine. Rotrou, our critic concedes, is of course no Aeschylus; but had the Greek playwright been enlightened by Christianity, he would have shown Orestes bowing to the laws of nature and humanity —as Ladislas does— instead of obeying fate and executing the decree of the oracle. In this case, Rotrou is elevated to a more lofty position than is Aeschylus; the French poet has captured true tragic spirit and interest (p. 41).

The Jouaust edition of Rotrou, which appeared in 1882, reestablishes, and for the first time in almost a century and a half, the original genre title of *Venceslas*, with the play now bearing the designation "tragi-comédie." [22] In the general introduction to this two-volume edition, Louis de Ronchaud comments very briefly on Marmontel's *retouchement* of *Venceslas* but includes no remarks concerning the evolution of the play's genre; he does little more than praise the fine characterization of Ladislas and the king, evaluate Cassandre as a "Chimène dégénerée," and hail *Venceslas* as Rotrou's masterpiece. [23]

---

[22] Jean de Rotrou, *Théâtre choisi, avec une étude par Louis de Ronchaud* (2 vols.; Paris: Librairie des Bibliophiles, 1882), II, 93.

[23] Ibid., I, xlvi-vii.

Félix Hémon, in the introduction to his 1883 edition of Rotrou's *Théâtre choisi*, [24] finds that the distinctive feature of Rotrou's theater is the perpetual confusion of genres (p. 41). *Venceslas*, as far as he is concerned, bears the deceptive title of *tragi-comédie*, although admittedly "ce drame se sépare malaisément de certains autres, qui l'ont précédé ou l'ont suivi" (pp. 395; 456). One may recognize in Ladislas the jealous prince of another of Rotrou's *tragi-comédies*, *Laure persécutée*, but here in *Venceslas*, the playwright has at least portrayed jealous passion with all its frightening effects. Here also the poet touches the most lofty questions that can preoccupy us — "l'amour, la politique et la famille" (p. 63).

Hémon, therefore, prefers to classify *Venceslas* as a *tragédie* (he designates it as such both on the title page and in the table of contents) and to discuss it accordingly in a section of his commentary dealing with Rotrou's "trois grandes tragédies." The other two tragedies are, of course, *Saint Genest* and *Cosroès*, which together with the play in question compose "cette trinité dramatique" (p. 63). The true tragic interest of the play, as others have been prone to note, is centered about Ladislas, who possesses savage grandeur and brutal love; this Ladislas, who as an assassin, transforms himself into a hero; this "sombre prince du Nord," who becomes worthy of a crown instead of the woman he loves (p. 68). He is a character to be placed in tragedy, not tragi-comedy. Venceslas, also, the father and king, who triumphs over personal emotion to accept the decree of his people with dignity, is a true tragic figure, worthy of being placed in a scene from Corneille (p. 68; 70-72). In Hémon's opinion, Rotrou perhaps never really cultivated *tragi-comédie* for the sake of *tragi-comédie*; it was as if he had an awareness of the falseness of a genre in which he was ill at ease (p. 47).

---

[24] Jean de Rotrou, *Théâtre chosi, nouvelle édition avec une introduction et des notes par M. Félix Hémon* (Paris: Laplace, Sanchez et Cie, 1883). The volume and page numbers in parentheses in the section on Hémon refer to the Garnier edition of 1925, which is a reprint of the 1883 edition.

III

Even in our present century, scholars devoting attention to Rotrou as an important predecessor to Corneille and as a successful cultivator of *tragi-comédie,* are not in complete accord with regard to the designation of the genre of *Venceslas.* The region inhabited by this 1647 *tragi-comédie* is, indeed, surrounded by rarefied and unstable boundaries; however, based on certain modern concepts, the following statements are presented as at least a partial view of the question and as a matter of conclusion:

1. All of Rotrou's *tragi-comédies, Venceslas* included, "follow very closely the seventeenth-century understanding of the genre: noble characters, tragic plot, happy dénouement," although these characteristics are not always found together. [25] Rotrou was essentially a *romanesque* poet, and as such, the form of *tragi-comédie* was the one best adapted to his genius. [26]

2. Obviously certain *tragi-comédies* differ from the typical members of the genre. Rotrou's *Bélissaire* (1644), for example, ends with the death of the hero; whereas *Venceslas* contains a reconciliation scene, a scene of pardon similar to the one found in *Cinna.* [27] *Venceslas,* like many classical tragedies, emphasizes to some degree moral problems at the expense of events. [28] At any rate, *tragi-comédie* is, indeed, a "genre mixte," for together with its usual *dénouement heureux,* one can expect to find a combination of tone and characters. [29]

3. *Venceslas* is definitely closer to tragedy than Rotrou's *Laure persécutée* (1638) and might be considered "a tragedy with a happy ending," a tragedy in which a self-sacrificing father and a violent son contribute to a situation

---

[25] Crane, p. 55.

[26] Ibid., p. 135.

[27] Antoine Adam, *Histoire de la littérature française au XVIIe siècle* (5 vols.; Paris: Domat, 1954), II, 318.

[28] Lancaster, *History of French Dramatic Literature in the Seventeenth Century,* II, pt. 2, 252.

[29] René Bray, *La Formation de la doctrine classique en France* (Paris: Librairie Nizet, 1951), pp. 329-30.

which is genuinely tragic.[30] Fernand Brunetière considers *Venceslas* a *tragédie*, since for him *dénouement heureux* and marriage at the conclusion of the drama do not necessarily constitute a true concept of *tragi-comédie*. One would be closer to a definition by saying that it differs from *tragédie* "par la qualité des personnes, n'y ayant de *Tragédie* que de palais ou de cour..."[31]

4. Raymond Lebègue proposes that Rotrou, under the influence of the Spanish *comedia*, be considered a baroque dramatist. As such, his *Venceslas* is something of a baroque *tragédie*, a play in which there is a mingling of the genres, a certain display of horror and violence; an evidence of concrete, descriptive, *précieux* style, which characterizes the baroque; and grandeur of character, seen principally in Ladislas.[32]

---

[30] Marvin T. Herrick, *Tragicomedy. Its Origin and Development in Italy, France, and England* (Urbana: The University of Illinois Press, 1955) (Illinois Studies in Language and Literature, vol. 39), p. 207.
[31] Fernand Brunetière, "L'Evolution d'un Genre," *Revue des Deux Mondes*, VI (Nov., 1901), p. 143.
[32] Raymond Lebègue, "Rotrou Dramaturge Baroque," *Revue d'Histoire Littéraire de la France*, L (Dec., 1950), pp. 379-81.

A FEW COMPARISONS AND CONTRASTS IN THE WORD-CRAFT OF RABELAIS AND JAMES JOYCE

ALFRED G. ENGSTROM
University of North Carolina

> "*Que diable de langaige est cecy?
> Par Dieu, tu es quelque hérétique.*"
> Pantagruel.

Rabelais and Joyce appear in our time as two gigantic representatives of the comic spirit in the western world. They employ some of the same literary techniques in their writings, and show in general certain similarities in style and outlook that have frequently attracted brief critical attention; but I know of no major study that has been devoted to the relationships between them.[1]

It is not clear how well Joyce knew Rabelais. In a lecture delivered in Trieste in 1907, he cites the author of *Gulliver's Travels* as sharing with Rabelais "the place of the best satire in world literature,"[2] and in *Ulysses* he has Molly Bloom in her famous soliloquy refer with distaste to the account of a child born out of the mother's ear in a book she has read by "Master Francois somebody supposed to be a priest";[3] but, in 1927, Joyce himself wrote that he never read Rabelais, "though nobody will believe

---

[1] The most detailed examination I have seen is Duncan Mallam's excellent article on "Joyce and Rabelais" in *The University of Kansas City Review*, XXIII (Dec., 1956: Winter Number), 99-110.

[2] *The Critical Writings of James Joyce*, ed. by Ellsworth Mason and Richard Ellmann (New York: The Viking Press, 1959), p. 170. The text is translated from Joyce's holograph manuscript in Italian.

[3] James Joyce, *Ulysses* (New York: Random House, 1934), p. 736.

this" — adding, however, that he will read him soon and that he has read "a few chapters of a book called *La langue de Rabelais*." [4]

It is hard to believe that Joyce could have read much of Rabelais without reading to the end; and many of the similarities in the two authors hardly appear to result from pure chance. Yet one cannot be sure. Duncan Mallam cites Joyce's and Rabelais' use of many of the same forms of discourse — "most conspicuously letters, speeches, catechisms, anecdotes, beast fables, riddles, poems (or pieces of doggerel), and a dramatic montage of drinkers' remarks." [5] He cites also the multilingual play of both writers, with Joyce using a score or more of languages [6] and Rabelais nearly a dozen, [7] and shows their common employment of digressions ("deliberately calculated"), onomatopoeic words and comic polysyllables, puns, slips of the tongue, stuttering, humorous enumerations ("by the hundreds"), genealogical sequences, etc. — and, in general, their "prodigal abundance." [8]

All this is impressive evidence of similarities in Rabelais and Joyce; but Mallam does not urge the necessity of influence, concluding merely that "Joyce may have conceived all his comic linguistic modes by himself, but he need not have done so. He

---

[4] Letter of May 31, 1927 to Harriet Shaw Weaver, in *The Letters of James Joyce*, ed. by Stuart Gilbert (New York: The Viking Press, 1957), p. 255. *La langue de Rabelais* is L. Sainéan's famous study that appeared in two volumes in 1922-1923.

[5] Duncan Mallam, *op. cit.*, p. 105.

[6] According to Joseph Campbell and Henry Morton Robinson (*A Skeleton Key to "Finnegans Wake"* [New York: Harcourt, Brace and Co., 1944], p. 358), Joyce had a fluent speaking knowledge of English, French, German and Italian, and a scholarly familiarity with Latin, Greek, Sanskrit, Gaelic and Russian. He had learned Norwegian in his youth to study Ibsen and had in his baggage scraps of Finnish, Arabic, Malay, Persian and Hindustani. "Obscure dialects, argots and the slang of many nations clung to his ear like limpets" — and "he outrivals Sinclair Lewis in his ability to burlesque the American Babbitt."

[7] In Chapter IX of *Pantagruel* when the hero meets Panurge.

[8] "Joyce and Rabelais," pp. 105 ff. Mallam cites here "140 anatomical similitudes" in Rabelais, "24 miracles, 14 acts of demagoguery" in Joyce; 60 generations of genealogical sequence for Pantagruel, 32 for Bloom; 210 epithets for *fool* applied to Triboulet by Pantagruel and Panurge (*Le Tiers Livre*, Chap. XXXVIII), Earwicker's list of 120 abusive names he has been called; a long list in a satiric catalogue of books in the library of Sainct Victor (*Pantagruel*, Chap. VII), 2 1/2 pages of subjects studied by the children in *Finnegans Wake*, etc.

could have found ample inspiration, precedent, and example in Rabelais, whom he need not have read in entirety for the purpose." [9]

Our present examination of selected materials from Rabelais and Joyce is not seriously concerned with matters of influence. It is intended rather to suggest, by a few representative examples of Rabelaisian and Joycean word-craft, certain comparisons and contrasts in the attitude shown towards language and in its use by two comic geniuses whose powers of expression have helped to change our vision of the world.

I

A reader discovers very quickly the peculiar vitality of Rabelais' language. Words in *Gargantua* and *Pantagruel* are like living things; and Pantagruel himself cites the *Rhetoric* of Aristotle on Homer's words being "voltigeantes, volantes, moventes, et par conséquent animées." [*Le Quart Livre,* Chap. LV, p. 713.] [10] This is at the famous point in Pantagruel's adventures when he and his comrades, on the shore of "la mer glaciale," hear words and other sounds, frozen during a battle the preceding winter, become audible as they thaw out with the coming of warm days. Pantagruel, trying to account for the sounds, cites the singing head of Orpheus, and Antiphanes' reference in Plutarch to frozen and thawing words; and he discovers and picks up some of the sounds that have not yet begun to melt.

> Lors nous jecta sus le tillac plenes mains de parolles gelées et sembloient dragée, perlée de diverses couleurs. Nous y veismes des motz de gueule, des motz de sinople, des motz de azur, des motz de sable, des motz doréz. Lesquelz, estre quelque peu eschaufféz entre nos mains, fondoient comme neiges, et les oyons réalement, mais ne les entendions, car c'estoit languaige barbare. [*Le Quart Livre,* Chap. LVI, p. 714.]

---

[9] Ibid., p. 109.
[10] All quotations from Rabelais will be from the *Œuvres complètes de Rabelais,* texte établi et annoté par Jacques Boulanger, revu et complété par Lucien Scheler (Bibliothèque de la Pléiade; Paris: Gallimard, 1955).

The frozen words have colors of heraldry: red, green, azure, sable, and gold.

A passage from Joyce's *A Portrait of the Artist as a Young Man* affords here an interesting comparison and contrast with the passage from Rabelais:

> [Stephen] drew forth a phrase from his treasure and spoke it softly to himself:
> —A day of dappled seaborne clouds. —
> The phrase and the day and the scene harmonised in a chord. Words. Was it their colours? He allowed them to glow and fade, hue after hue: sunrise gold, the russet and green of apple orchards, azure of waves, the grey-fringed fleece of clouds. No, it was not their colours: it was the poise and balance of the period itself. Did he then love the rhythmic rise and fall of words better than their associations of legend and colour? Or was it that, being as weak of sight as he was shy of mind, he drew less pleasure from the reflection of the glowing sensible world through the prism of a language manycoloured and richly storied than from the contemplation of an inner world of individual emotions mirrored perfectly in a lucid supple periodic prose. [11]

Here one sees clearly some of the notable differences between Rabelais and Joyce — the changes in European sensibility that had come with Romanticism and Symbolism, as well as essential differences of individual temperament in artistic consciousness. But there are equally interesting comparisons of a different nature to be drawn from the episode of the *parolles gelées*.

At Panurge's request, Pantagruel throws three or four handfuls of frozen words on deck ... some "bien picquantes," others "sanglantes," some "horrificques et aultres assez mal plaisantes à veoir." As the motley collection melts, strange sounds arise:

> ...hin, hin, hin, hin, his, ticque, torche, lorgne, brededin, brededac, frr, frrr, frrr, bou, bou, bou, bou, bou, bou, bou, bou, traccc, trac, trr, trr, trr, trrr, trrrrrr, on, on, on, on, ouououon, goth, magoth et ne sçay quelz aultres motz

---

[11] James Joyce, *A Portrait of the Artist as Young Man* (New York: The Modern Library, 1928), pp. 193-194.

barbares; et disoyt que c'estoient vocables du hourt et hannissement des chevaulx à l'heure qu'on chocque. [*Le Quart Livre,* Chap. LVI, p. 715.]

The narrator wants to preserve some of the red words in oil; but Pantagruel says this is folly, since *motz de gueule* are never lacking to good and joyous Pantagruelistes.

Joyce's tangible words are as remarkable as the *parolles gelées* of Rabelais. Rather early in *Finnegans Wake* we come upon reference to the low hero's "cantraps of fermented words, abracadabra calubra culorum." [12] But the most interesting parallel to Rabelais' passage here occurs deep in the book when we are offered the amazing spectacle of chewed foods being metamorphosed before our eyes into the forms of changing words:

> ...I want to get outside monasticism. Mass and meat mar no man's journey. Eat a missal lest. Nuts for the nerves, a flitch for the flue and for to rejoice the chambers of the heart the spirits of the spice isles, curry and cinnamon chutney and cloves. All the vitalmines is beginning to sozzle in chewn and the hormonies to clingleclangle, fudgem, kates and eaps and naboc and erics and oinnos on kingclud and xoxxoxo and xooxox xxoxoxxoxxx til I'm fustfed like fungstif.... [13]

Here, amidst the somewhat hasty action of the vitamins as the food is being chewed, one can see what is happening to the former *steak* and *peas* and *bacon* and *rices* and *onions* and *duckling,* until the speaker is "stuffed like stuffing." The more completely chewed items at the last ("xoxxoxo and xooxox xxoxoxxoxxx") have been plausibly identified (with *x* for a consonant and *o* for a vowel) as "cabbage and boiled protestants [i.e., Irish potatoes]." [14] Amusingly, Joyce seems here to have kept something of the integrity of language in his metamorphoses, for *kates* and *eaps* and *naboc* and *erics* and *oinnos* and *kingclud* appear to carry some meaning still. [15]

---

[12] James Joyce, *Finnegans Wake* (New York: The Viking Press, 1945), p. 184.

[13] Ibid., p. 456.

[14] Joseph Campbell and Henry Morton Robinson, *A Skeleton Key to "Finnegans Wake,"* p. 280, footnote 16.

[15] *Kates* (for *cates*: food, dainties), *eaps* (heaps?), *erics* (blood fines for the crime of murdering an Irishman), *oinnos* (*oinos,* the Greek word

Both Rabelais and Joyce organize comic effects in dialogue through the use of excessively pedantic or foreign or ingeniously contrived artificial or composite language. In Rabelais this is particularly effective as high comedy in two well-known passages in *Pantagruel*. In the first, Rabelais' hero is walking with friends by the gate on the road to Paris when he meets a Limousin, "un escholier tout jolliet," coming along the way. After an exchange of greetings Pantagruel begins a conversation:

>"Mon amy, dont viens-tu à ceste heure?"
>L'escholier luy respondit:
>"De l'alme, inclyte et célèbre académie que l'on vocite Lutèce.
>—Qu'est-ce à dire? dist Pantagruel à un de ses gens.
>—C'est (respondit-il) de Paris.
>—Tu viens doncques de Paris? (dist-il). Et à quoy passez-vous le temps, vous aultres messieurs estudiens audict Paris?"
>Respondit l'escolier:
>"Nous transfretons la Sequane au dilucule et crépuscule; nous déambulons par les compites et quadrivies de l'urbe; nous despumons la verbocination latiale, et, comme verisimiles amorabonds, captons la bénévolence de l'omnijuge, omniforme et omnigène sexe féminin...."
>A quoi Pantagruel dist:
>"Que diable de langaige est cecy? Par Dieu, tu es quelque hérétique." [*Pantagruel*, Chap. VI, pp. 212-213.]

The second passage is one of the most famous of its kind in all literature (Chapter IX of *Pantagruel*, "Comment Pantagruel trouva Panurge, lequel il ayma toute sa vie"). Here, as Pantagruel is strolling outside Paris, he is attracted by the elegant bearing of a poorly dressed and apparently destitute stranger and offers him help. As in the earlier scene with the Limousin, Pantagruel's questions lead

---

for wine). Even *naboc* has, at least, a *nab* in it and a French *bock* as well; and *kingclud* suggests a *clod* (a lump of solid matter). Joyce writes otherwise in *Finnegans Wake* of "once current puns, quashed quotatoes, messes of mottage" [183] and of "Tenderest bully ever I ate with boiled protestants (allinoilia allinoilia!)" [456]; and he even cites "the legal eric for infelicitous conduict" [537], which is a rather gay way for an Irishman to refer to killing an Irishman.

him into a deluge of words as Panurge asks in thirteen different languages for food and drink.

> [Pantagruel:] "Mon amy... dictes-moy: Qui estes-vous? Dont venez-vous? Où allez-vous? Que quérez-vous? Et quel est vostre nom?" [P. 229.]

Panurge replies (in the Lyon edition of 1542, the last text seen and corrected by Rabelais) in turn in German, a made-up language, Italian, deformed Scotch, Basque, a second made-up language, Dutch, Spanish, Danish, Hebrew, Ancient Greek (transcribed according to the pronunciation of modern Greek), a third made-up language, and Latin (13 tongues in all). They are all Greek to Pantagruel:

> —Dea, mon amy, dist Pantagruel, ne sçavez-vous parler françoys?
> —Si faictz très bien, Seigneur, respondit le compaignon, Dieu mercy. C'est ma langue naturelle et maternelle, car je suis né et ay esté nourry jeune au jardin de France: c'est Touraine. [P. 234.]

Joyce's most remarkable use of an analogous technique occurs in the hilarious conversation between Mutt and Jute in *Finnegans Wake*:

> ...Scuse us, chorley guy! You tollerday donsk? N. You tolkatiff scowegian? Nn. You spigotty anglease? Nnn. You phonio saxo? Nnnn. Clear all so! 'Tis a Jute. Let us swop hats and excheck a few strong verbs weak oach eather yapyazzard abast the blooty creeks.
>
> Jute. —Yutah!
> Mutt.—Mukk's pleasurad.
> Jute. —Are you jeff?
> Mutt.—Somehards.
> Jute. —But you are not jeffmute?
> Mutt.—Noho. Only an utterer.
> Jute. —Whoa? Whoat is the mutter with you?
> Mutt.—I became a stun a stummer.
> Jute. —What a hauhauhauhaudibble thing, to be cause! How, Mutt?
> Mutt.—Aput the buttle, surd.
> Jute. —Whose poddle? Wherein?
> Mutt.—The Inns of Dungtarf where Used awe to be he.

> Jute.—You that side your voise are almost inedible to me. Become a bitskin more wiseable, as if I were you.... [*FW*, p. 16.]

The conversation ends with Mutt's inquiring, "Ore you astoneaged, jute you?" and Jute's reply: "Oye am thonthorstrok, thing mud."

In Rabelais, pedantic exuberance leads on one occasion to a stream of anatomical details that provide a highly amusing parody of mediaeval epic narrative. Here the description is of Frère Jean des Entommeures (in *Gargantua*) defending his beloved vineyard against its hapless invaders. Frère Jean seizes *le baston de la croix* and, using it as a weapon, kills 13,622 of the invading enemy, "sans les femmes et petitz enfans, cela s'entend toujours" [p. 109]:

> Es uns escarbouilloyt la cervelle, ès aultres rompoyt bras et jambes, ès aultres deslochoyt les spondyles du coul, ès aultres demoulloyt les reins, avalloyt le nez, poschoyt les yeux, fendoyt les mandibules, enfonçoyt les dens en la gueule, descroulloyt les omoplates, sphaceloyt les grèves, desgondoit les ischies, débezilloit les faucilles. [P. 107.]

Rabelais depends for some of his finest effects on the wonderfully vital rhythm of his prose, as in the description of Gargantua's great mare swishing her tail against insects and knocking down all the forest around Orléans: "...A tort, à travers, de çà, de là, par cy, par là, de long, de large, dessus, dessoubz, abatoit boys comme un fauscheur faict d'herbes...." [*Gargantua*, Chap. XVI, p. 75]. We find the same qualities in the following passage describing Gargantua's return to activity after the shock of his wife Badebec's death in giving birth to Pantagruel:

> "...Ha, Badebec, ma mignonne, m'amye... Ha, pauvre Pantagruel... Ha, faulce mort...
> Et, ce disant, pleuroit comme une vache; mais tout soubdain rioit comme un veau, quand Pantagruel luy venoit en mémoire.
> "Ho, mon petit filz (disoit-il)... Ho, ho, ho, ho! que je suis ayse! Beuvons, ho! laissons toute mélancholie! Apporte du meilleur, rince les verres, boute la nappe, chasse ces chiens, souffle ce feu, allume la chandelle, ferme ceste porte, taille ces souppes, envoye ces pauvres, baille leur ce qu'ils demandent! Tiens ma robbe, que je me mette en

pourpoint pour mieux festoyer les commères." [*Pantagruel,* Chap. III, pp. 203-204.]

Joyce accomplishes a somewhat similar effect in *Finnegans Wake*:

> ...Bolt the grinden. Cave and can em. Single wrecks for the weak, double axe for the mail, and quick queck quack for the radiose. Renove that bible. You will never have post in your pocket unless you have brasse on your plate. Beggards outdoor. Goat to the Endth, thou slowguard! Mind the Monks ad their Grasps. Scrape your souls. Commit no miracles. Postpone no bills. Respect the uniform.... Herenow chuck english and learn to pray plain. [P. 579.]

Rabelais on occasion shows himself to be a master of wit in rhythm — a rare skill, whose peerless French exemplars are Marot and La Fontaine. The following passage from the "Prologue de l'autheur...pour *Le Tiers Livre*" (pp. 344-345) describes the philosoper Diogenes on the hill and promontory called "le Cranie" at the siege of Corinth agitating the famous tub (in which he lived) so as not to seem idle while his fellow-citizens busy themselves preparing the city's defense. The rhythms and sounds of the 64 verbs describing the motions of the tub become increasingly funny as one reads, and the conclusion is a fine stroke of stylistic and comic art.

> Diogènes.... roulla le tonneau fictil qui pour maison luy estoit contre les injures du ciel, et en grande véhémence d'esprit desployant ses braz le tournoit, viroit, brouilloit, garbouilloit, hersoit, versoit, renversoit, nattoit, grattoit, flattoit, barattoit, bastoit, boutoit, butoit, tabustoit, cullebutoit, trepoit, trempoit, tapoit, timpoit, estouppoit, destouppoit, détraquoit, triquotoit, tripotoit, chapotoit, croulloit, élançoit, chamailloit, bransloit, esbranloit, levoit, lavoit, clavoit, entravoit, bracquoit, bricquoit, blocquoit, tracassoit, ramassoit, clabossoit, afestoit, affustoit, baffouoit, enclouoit, amadouoit, goildronnoit, mittonoit, tastonnoit, bimbelotoit, clabossoit, terrassoit, bistorioit, vreloppoit, chaluppoit, charmoit, armoit, gizarmoit, enharnachoit, empennachoit, caparassonnoit, le dévalloit de mont à val, et praecipitoit par le Cranie, puys de val en mont le rapportoit, comme Sysiphus faict sa pierre: tant que peu s'en faillit, qu'il ne le défonçast.

I know of nothing quite comparable in Joyce, though the sound of the "polylingual thunderclap... (bababadalgharaghtakamminarronnkonnbronntonnerronntuonnthunntrovarrhounawnskawntoohoohoordenenthurnuk! [*FW*, p. 31), which is the voice of God made audible through the noise of Finnegan's fall"[16] has, perhaps, some of its simpler elements in common with the sounds of the philosopher's tub in Rabelais.

Words for both Rabelais and Joyce have a life of their own, a kind of concrete reality that lends itself to purposes transcending the usual limits of word usage. Mallarmé has written in a famous passage on the creative power of the word from the viewpoint of the poet:

> Je dis: une fleur! et, hors de l'oubli où ma voix relègue aucun contour, en tant que quelque chose d'autre que les calices sus, musicalement se lève, idée même et suave, l'absente de tous bouquets.[17]

In the great comic poetry of Joyce and Rabelais we find analogous creation by the word — and this, too, is part of the ideal process by which the imaginative "maker" recreates the world for himself and for the rest of mankind.

When Gargantua carries off the great bells of Notre-Dame de Paris, the Sorbonne faculty selects the sophist Maistre Janotus de Bragmardo as its representative to plead for their return. After a long, nonsensical introduction, Maistre Janotus clears his throat ("Hen, hen, ehen, hasch!") and sets out to make his point as follows:

> "*Omnis clocha clochabilis, in clocherio clochando, clochans clochativo clochare facit clochabiliter clochantes. Parisius habet clochas. Ergo gluc...*" [*Gargantua*, Chap. XIX, p. 80.]

The late Leo Spitzer, in a fine essay on Rabelais, called the first statement here "a nonsensically axiomatic sentence which means

---

[16] Joseph Campbell and Henry Morton Robinson, *op. cit.*, pp. 15-16.
[17] Stéphane Mallarmé, *Œuvres complètes* (Bibliothèque de la Pléiade; Paris: Gallimard, 1945), p. 368.

simply: 'all bells ring.'" And he added a penetrating comment on the significance of Rabelais' word-play:

> Here the disappearance of meaning before mere sound is intended satirically as parody of contemporary scholasticism which was satisfied with meaningless, learned-sounding verbiage. But as always with Rabelais satire does not explain his creation: we sense Rabelais' positive delight in meaningless sound. And if Rabelais is able to envisage the possibility of language without meaning, it is precisely because he has witnessed the phenomenon of the medieval scholastic language become, out of self-exhaustion, devoid of meaning.[18]

Joyce's ebullient spirit reflects rhetoric of a somewhat different kind in a different way in the 34-page *tour de force* of the Aeolus episode in *Ulysses*, which takes place, quite appropriately, in a newspaper office.[19] Stuart Gilbert has listed examples of 94 different rhetorical forms employed here by Joyce in what Gilbert calls "a veritable thesaurus of rhetorical devices [which] ... might, indeed, be adopted as a text-book for students of the art of rhetoric."[20] Here, in the one episode of the book whose concerns are exclusively rhetorical, Joyce has assembled "nearly all the important, misleading enthymemes elenchated by Quintilian and his sucessors."[21]

Leo Spitzer contrasts the inscription on the gate of Dante's Hell with that on the gate of Rabelais' Thelema Abbey and finds in the latter "an acoustic equivalent" to the late Gothic gargoyles.[22] The first stanza of the 98-verse inscription is as follows:

> Cy n'entrez pas, hypocrites, bigotz,
> Vieux matagotz, marmiteux, borsoufléz,
> Torcoulx, badaux, plus que n'estoient les Gotz

---

[18] Leo Spitzer, "The Works of Rabelais," in *Literary Masterpieces of the Western World*, ed. by Francis H. Horn (Baltimore: The Johns Hopkins Press, 1953), p. 144.

[19] James Joyce, *Ulysses*, pp. 115-148.

[20] Stuart Gilbert, *James Joyce's Ulysses: A Study* (New York: Alfred A. Knopf, 1934), p. 172. The "Examples of Rhetorical Forms" occupy pp. 176-179.

[21] Ibid.

[22] Leo Spitzer, *op. cit.*, p. 143.

> Ny Ostrogotz, précurseurs des magotz
> Haires, cagotz, caffars empantouflez,
> Gueux mitouflez, frapars escorniflez,
> Beffléz, enfléz, fagoteurs de tabus;
> Tirez ailleurs pour vendre vos abus.
>
> [*Gargantua*, Chap. LIV, p. 173.]

Spitzer writes on these verses a remarkable appreciation of the hidden power in Rabelais' language:

> ...In this colossal onomatopoeic sequence of vilifications which I can never read aloud without a shudder of fear before the words become autonomous, the grotesque art of Rabelais is at its acme: usual French words are here assembled according to sound, rhyme and rhythm; they are transmogrified by the linguistic alchemy of Rabelais to give a sensuous impression of the being of the hypocrites (by the muffled sounds *fl*) — and at the same time of the whip with which Rabelais lashes out against them (the *go* syllables in *cagots, magots*) to create a climate of grotesque nowhereness on the brink between the comic and the dreadful, between the amusement provoked by automatic repetition of sounds and the fear inspired by the unknown shapes the sounds suggest.[23]

The power of Rabelais is that of a great master of prose, who could create humor endowed with his own prodigious vitality. Yet, as Spitzer has suggested, there is something rather frightening at times in Rabelais' monstrous verbal creations. They induct us into worlds we have not seen before and leave their lasting mark upon our cheese-shaped brains.

II

In *Finnegans Wake*, where the examples and the texture of Joyce's wordplay are most rich, ideas echo and re-echo and combine and disintegrate and meet again in intricate patterns of a subtlety unmatched in Rabelais. Joyce's techniques are so skillful and complex, and the resonance of his vocabulary is so significant that

---

[23] Ibid.

his practice can probably be best indicated only through examples in point from his writing; and even then, without elaboration, the surrounding texture in Joyce's network of meanings can only be imagined. No one before him has ever developed word-craft of this sort to such a degree of art. In the following pages we shall try briefly to suggest something of this element in Joyce's style through pertinent quotations from *Finnegans Wake* grouped around key ideas that recur in Joyce, in somewhat the same way that certain of them recur in Rabelais — only with Joyce in infinitely richer and more complex patterns of sound and reference.

Drinking is a structural element in the writings of Rabelais and in *Finnegans Wake*. *Gargantua* is dedicated to "beuvuers très illustres, et...véroléz très précieux"; and Rabelais' characters have names drawn from various references to drinking (Grandgousier, Gargantua, Gargamelle, Pantagruel, la Dive Bouteille, Bacbuc, etc.), which forms a sort of leitmotif for the whole narrative. In similar vein, the title of Joyce's work refers to the celebration in honor of the supposed death of Finnegan, a drunken hod-carrier who fell off a ladder. The following examples of Joyce's word-play in *Finnegans Wake* on the subject of drink will suggest various elements in his use of words and verbal patterns:

> ...one yeastyday (4) — he would caligulate ... the alltitude and malltitude until he seesaw by neatlight of the liquor (4) — alcoherently (40) — Noah Beery (64) [24] — the deserted *champ de bouteilles* (162) — to give them their beerings (321) — they had been malttreating themselves to their health's contempt (322) — Sir, kindest of bottleholders and very dear friend (366) — Once upon a drunk (453) — absintheminded (464) — with half a glance of Irish frisky (470) — beers o'ryely (498) [25] — For we're all jollygame fellhellows which nobottle can deny! (569).

---

[24] The name of the American movie-actor was apparently irresistible here for its dual reference to drink.

[25] Persse O'Reilly (from the French *perce-oreille*, "earwig") appears among the metamorphoses of Joyce's hero HCE (Here Comes Everybody, H. C. Earwicker, etc.). Joyce seems to have done a considerable amount of research on earwigs (see postcard, stamped Aug. 29, 1940, to Nino Frank [*Letters*, Vols. II, III, ed. by Richard Ellmann (New York: The Viking Press, 1966), III, 483]). It may be pertinent to note that Chap. VII of Rabelais' *Tiers Livre* is entitled "Comment Panurge avoit la pusse en l'aureille, et désista porter sa magnificque braguette."

On the subject of physical love, Joyce's vision is mixed, like that of Rabelais, who has a rather difficult time deciding whether Panurge should risk getting married.

> ...in her cozy-dozy bachelure's flat (61) — (she sall eurn bitter bed by thirt sweet of her face!) (291) — in the green of the wood where obelisk rises when odalisks fall (335) — heavinscent houroines (348) — malestream in shegulf (547).

Beyond all this passing play on words for Joyce there is the vast pattern of relations between HCE and ALP that move in the endless cycle of the fall and metamorphoses of man and woman. [26]

In *Finnegans Wake* one hears overtones from familiar songs that take on new meanings in their new forms: "...three jeers for the grape, vine and brew" (117) — "yea, he hath no mananas" (170). Familiar quotations sound far away and say something different from what they said before, often with a sharply ironic pertinence: "...my shemblable! My freer!" (489) — "where the bus stops there shop I" (540) — "Walhalloo, Walhalloo, Walhalloo, mourn in plein!" (541).

Unexpected word-coinage affords constant surprises as one reads:

> ...reminiscensitive (230) [27] — plenary sadisfaction (445) — sotisfiction (452) — tootoological (468) — Ruemember (488) — a doblinganger (490) — metandmorefussed (513) — torporature (597) — Humid nature (597).

One phrase of this sort has a special touch of virtuosity: "...nobirdy aviar soar anywing to eagle it!" (505).

Joyce writes of "slauchterday" (539) and "irkdays" and "folliedays" (553) and "jesterday" (570); and he provides a phrase on

---

[26] *Finnegans Wake* is, in a sense, the modern *Metamorphoses*; and the form-changes in the names of female ALP and male HCE are legion. Joyce was much attracted to Ovid; and he took the name Dedalus from the great artificer in the *Metamorphoses* and used a quotation from the passage on Daedalus there ("Et ignotas animum dimittit in artes," VIII. 188) as an epigraph for *A Portrait of the Artist as a Young Man*.

[27] Joyce may have been familiar with the writings of Jules Laforgue (who created such words as *violupté*, *Eternullité*, *sangsuelles*, and *crucifiger*); for he quotes in Italian Laforgue's phrase, "Ah! que la Vie est quotidienne..." (Letter of June 3, 1935 to George Joyce, *Letters*, III, 360).

the space of a week that affords a summation unique of its kind: "All moanday, tearsday, wailsday, thumpsday, frightday, shatterday till the fear of the Law" (301).

Word-play devoted to social commentary in *Finnegans Wake* often has barbs of sharp criticism aimed in many directions and at much of the contemporary scene:

> ...dumbestic husbandry (38) — yore Loudship (53) — our notional gullery (57) — muddlecrass pupils (152) — agricolous manufraudurers (173) — the crime ministers (242) — the unhappitents of the earth (258) — grand operoar style (442) — fecundclass family (444) — gossipocracy (476) — dullaphone (485) — chrome sweet home (494) — with fixed baronets (568) — jurisfiction (574) — a long jurymiad (575) — in a more or less settled state of equonomic ecolube equalobe equilab equilibbrium (599).

Like Rabelais, Joyce plays with religion and irreligion and at times approaches blasphemy;[28] but his uneasiness is apparent and lends a strange tone to his word-creation:

> ...Stay us wherefore in our search for tighteousness, O Sustainer ... in the night and at the fading of the stars! (5) — O foenix culprit! (23)[29] — Per omnibus secular seekalarum. Amain. (81) — a tumass equinous (93) — Let us pry (188) — But O felicitous culpability, sweet bad cess to you for an archetypt! (263) — his frighteousness (343) — die and be diademmed (353) — In the buginning is the woid, in the muddle is the sound-dance and thereinofter you're in the unbewised again (378) — smolking a spatial brunt of Hosana cigals (417) — Shunt us! shunt us! shunt us! If you want to be felixed come and be parked (454) — There's no plagues like rome (465) — Dies Eirae (481) — rocked of agues, cliffed for aye (505) — Pontifical mess (514) — Dollarmighty! (562) — Tickle, tickle. Lotus spray (598).[30]

---

[28] Rabelais' Franciscan and Benedictine background and Joyce's association with the Jesuits seem to have provided fuel for their fires.

[29] Joyce's distortion of St. Augustine's "O felix culpa" suggests again his preoccupation with only the dark side of original sin.

[30] There is analogous word-play in Rabelais. For example, when Frère Jean is accused of interrupting "le service divin" he puns on "le service du vin" (*Gargantua*, Chap. XXVII, p. 106) and later (ibid., Chap. XLI, pp. 143-144) declares "*brevis oratio penetrat celos, longa potatio evacuat cyphos* [les coupes] ... *venite apotemus.*"

The lyric element that is strong in Joyce and relatively absent in Rabelais recurs all through *Finnegans Wake* and provides unforgettable effects in the midst of what Joyce called "many counterpoint words" (482). A few examples will suggest the undercurrent of lyricism in Joyce's style:

> She tossed her sfumastelliacinous hair (157) — But the dormer moonshee smiled selene (192) — Still we know how Day the Dyer works, in dims and deeps and dusks and darks (226) — Quiet takes back her folded fields (244) — And I'd lie as quiet as a moss (626).

Time seems to have haunted Joyce, as it does so many writers of our century, and the time element is recurrent in his word-play in *Finnegans Wake* (often in combination with other motifs that recur in the book):

> ...thirsty p.m. (100) — at lighting up o'clock sharp (219) — Thyme, that chef of seasoners (236) — Dark ages clasp the daisy roots (272) — nuncandtunc and for simper (290) — from the night we are and feel and fade with to the yesterselves we tread to turnupon (473) — seeking spoor through the deep timefield (475) — it was eleven thirsty (517) — at six o'clock shark (558) — At half past quick in the morning (583) — Cocoree! ... Echo, choree chorecho! .... Echolo choree choroh choree chorico! (584-585).

The cyclic structure of *Finnegans Wake* that Joyce borrowed from the theories of Vico finds echo-points in the language of the book, beginning with the very first line:

> riverrun, past Eve and Adam's, from swerve of shore to bend of bay, brings us by a commodius vicus of recirculation back to Howth Castle and Environs (3) — they newknow knowwell their Vico's road (246) — Old Vico Roundpoint (260) — he spoorlessly disappaled and vansshed ...from circular circulatio. Ah, mean! (427) — The Vico road goes round and round to meet where terms begin (452) [31] — Our wholemole millwheeling vicociclometer (614).

---

[31] Even the structure of *Finnegans Wake* follows "the Vico road," beginning as it does in the middle of a sentence and ending the same way so that,

Notable also are Joyce's preoccupation with death and the overtones and undertones one hears on occasion when he writes of it:

> ...lastly when all is zed and done (123) — He points the deathbone and the quick are still. *Insomnia, somnia, somniorum. Awmawm.* (193) — even though ... the Tarara boom decay (247) — their dance McCaper in retrophoebia (415) — Remember, maid, thou dust art powder but Cinderella thou must return (440) — Howday you doom? (517) — doom adimdim adoom adimadim (552) — how it is triste to death, all his dark ivytod! (571) — It's Phoenix, dear. And the flame is, hear! (621).

Finally, there is what has been called Joyce's choice of "night logic, expressed in dream language, as his method of communication." [32] Leo Spitzer suggested, as we have seen earlier, something analogous to this in the grotesque word-coinage of Rabelais. But in Joyce the "night logic" is different from anything in Rabelais, and the "dream language" is like nothing we have experienced before in such detail. A hypnotic example is the last paragraph of the first part of *Finnegans Wake* (pp. 215-216) with its unforgettable passage on night waters flowing:

> Can't hear with the waters of. The chittering waters of. Flittering bats, fieldmice bawk talk. Ho! Are you not gone ahome? What Thom Malone? Can't hear with bawk of bats, all thim liffeying waters of. Ho, talk save us! My foos won't moos. I feel as old as yonder elm. A tale told of Shaun or Shem? All Livia's daughter-sons. Dark hawks hear us. Night! Night! My ho head halls. I feel as heavy as yonder stone. Tell me of John or Shaun? Who were Shem and Shaun the living sons or daughters of? Night now! Tell me, tell me, tell me, elm! Night night! Telmetale of stem or stone. Beside the rivering waters of, hitherandthithering waters of. Night!

---

like the Ouroboros, the serpent or dragon with its tail in its mouth ("the symbol of the endless cycle of metamorphoses," uniting good and bad [Kurt Seligman, *The Mirror of Magic* (New York: Pantheon Books, 1948), p. 106]), it ends in its beginning and so never ends.

[32] Joseph Campbell and Henry Morton Robinson, *op. cit.*, p. 361.

Rabelais' use of words helped turn the minds and sensibilities of western men to this world and this life. Joyce, coming at a precarious moment for man's beliefs, in his very discomfort before Church and God and Religion, tends in his word-craft to make men more conscious than most of his contemporaries of humanity's complexity and instability and spiritual longing. He belongs in part with the great Romantics and the Symbolist poets.

The Freudian world of guilt and anxiety was inherited by Joyce, along with the notion of Original Sin, and he was a transmitter of part of its message. In turning back to Rabelais, we breathe a freer air and find a healthier and more optimistic play of words. But the comic spirit pervades the imagination and the vision of life of both writers, and Joyce, with an essentially comic verve, can write (in *Finnegans Wake*) "when they were yung and easily freudened" (115),[33] and refer to someone as having "an eatupus complex and a drinkthedregs kink" (128-129), and comment on a "freudful mistake" (411). Still, Joyce was never, even on the surface, "a buffoon Homer," as Nodier and Hugo once called Rabelais.

One may see both Joyce and Rabelais as comic artists on a grand scale; but one is likely to have an afterthought about Joyce, as he would not about Rabelais, in agreeing with the author of *Gargantua* that "rire est le propre de l'homme." Even in high comedy, the word-craft of Rabelais and Joyce reveals their inner preoccupations. In Rabelais one may find especially pertinent the phrase "Fay ce que vouldras" — in Joyce, "O foenix culprit!"; in Rabelais, "Je boy pour la soif advenir" — in Joyce, "from the night we are and feel and fade with...seeking spoor through the deep timefield."

---

[33] When Jung wrote Joyce praising Molly Bloom's soliloquy in *Ulysses* as "a string of veritable psychological peaches" (*The Letters of James Joyce*, III, 253), Joyce commented in a letter to Georg Goyert of Oct. 22, 1932 that Jung "seems to have read *Ulysses* from first to last without one smile. The only thing to do in such a case is to change one's drink" (ibid., p. 262).

THE IMPACT OF FRERE JEAN ON PANURGE IN RABELAIS'S *TIERS LIVRE*

Donald M. Frame
Columbia University

When Rabelais, after twelve years of silence following *Gargantua*, publishes his *Tiers Livre* in 1546, several things strike the reader as new. The book is less outspoken than its predecessor, for apparently since the Affaire des Placards and the condemnation of the first two books Rabelais has become concerned not to court trouble. It is signed with his own name, no longer with that of "Maistre Alcofribas Nasier, abstracteur de Quinte Essence." Its unabashed display of erudition, together with the lack of giant stories and the change in the title from "Vie tres horrificque" and "horribles et espouvantables faicts et prouesses" to the much less sensational "faicts et dicts héroïques du bon Pantagruel," all suggest that Rabelais has a more learned, less popular public in view than before. By chapter 47 the subject of Books IV and V is announced, and the Prologue explicitly heralds the *Quart Livre* as well as the *Tiers*. One passage in the Prologue clearly suggests that Rabelais is uneasy about the reception of this new kind of book. After telling of the failure of Ptolemy I to delight and impress his people with his two-colored Bactrian camel, Rabelais comments:

> Cestuy exemple me faict entre espoir et craincte varier, doubtant que pour contentement propensé je rencontre ce que je abhorre, mon thésaur soit charbons, pour Vénus advieigne Barbet le chien, en lieu de les servir, je les fasche, en lieu de les esbaudir, je les offense, en lieu de leurs complaire, je desplaise et soit mon adventure telle que du coq de Euclion tant célébré par Plaute en sa *Mar-*

mite, et par Ausone en son *Gryphon* et ailleurs, lequel, pour en grattant avoir descouvert le thésaur, eut la couppe guorgée.[1]

It is hazardous but tempting to speculate about what else Rabelais had in mind. The giant hero was obviously to be Pantagruel, with Gargantua in the background if present at all. The center of attention was to be Panurge and his marital problems. This much seems clear.

For the first quarter of the *Tiers Livre* —nearly 13 chapters out of 52— Frère Jean (from then on spelled Jan) seems to have vanished from the scene without a trace. In the praise and rejection of debts, the inquiry why newlyweds are exempt from going to war, the business of the flea in Panurge's ear to get married, and Panurge's first consultations on the question with Pantagruel and the "sors virgilianes," there is no mention of Frère Jean or of any other characters except Pantagruel and Panurge. Finally, as Panurge is preparing to seek counsel in dreams and Pantagruel has told him how, according to Homer and Virgil, these come to men through the gates of ivory and horn, all of a sudden (p. 376) Frère Jean speaks up just as if he had been there all along: "Vous voulez inférer (dist Frère Jan) que les songes des coqüz cornuz, comme sera Panurge, Dieu aydant et sa femme, sont tousjours vrays et infallibles."

Has Rabelais planned this entrance all along and been simply playing possum? It is possible, but I doubt it. Consistency of this sort seems to have been no major concern of his; I suspect that he deliberately sacrificed it to spontaneity. Anyway, in the very next paragraph, which introduces chapter 14, he brings on (the next morning) the rest of the crew, Carpalim and Epistémon from *Pantagruel,* Ponocrates from *Gargantua,* and Eudémon from both (for Rabelais gives him one short speech in *Pantagruel,* chapter 9). Later (chapter 38) Gymnaste and Rhizotome will be named; now, after the list above, Rabelais adds "et aultres" to leave the field open.

This sudden influx of characters onstage is in striking parallel with chapter 9 of *Pantagruel.* Rabelais had started that book with

---

[1] Rabelais, *Œuvres complètes,* ed. Boulenger and Scheler, Paris: Gallimard (Pléiade), 1959 ed., pp. 326-27. All subsequent references to Rabelais are to this edition.

some fairly obvious giant materials —Pantagruel's genealogy and nativity, Gargantua's alternation between joy at this and grief over Badebec's death, Pantagruel's *enfances*— and followed these with three virtuoso episodes, the "écolier Limousin," the Librairie de St. Victor, and the letter from Gargantua to Pantagruel. At this point he seems to have needed something or someone to give him a sustained comic line, and it was not yet time for the war with Anarche; so (p. 207) "Pantagruel trouva Panurge, lequel il ayma toute sa vie." Then after the Baisecul-Humevesne trial, for nine chapters (14-22) including the debate with Thaumaste, Panurge moves to center stage and Pantagruel takes a back seat.

What makes the parallel closer yet is that in earlier chapters of *Pantagruel* (6-7) Rabelais had alluded to companions of the young giant king but not named any. Suddenly in chapter 9 (pp. 207-09, 211) we meet not only Panurge but also Epistémon, Eudémon (for the only time in the book), Carpalim, and Eusthenes.

By calling this an analogy I do not mean that Frère Jean promptly takes over in chapter 13 or 14 of the *Tiers Livre*; he does not. I mean that I think Rabelais, in this hazardous new type of book —almost without a story line— that he was undertaking, came to feel at about this point that he needed new characters, especially for comedy, and more variety in his dialogue. He had even had to make his philosopher king play the role of a jester in the "chanson de Ricochet" of chapter 9. Pantagruel, even with Panurge, simply could not sustain the comedy alone; hence the sudden arrival of Frère Jean, and in the next breath of Epistémon and the three others.

Incidentally, nowhere will these minor characters from *Gargantua* (Eudémon, Gymnaste, Ponocrates, Rhizotome) seem noticeably older than Carpalim and Epistémon from *Pantagruel*. Nor will Frère Jean or anyone else refer to an earlier fealty to Gargantua. It seems clear that Rabelais would have us forget that his characters in Books III-V (except Gargantua) represent two generations.

At all events, from the end of III: 13 to the end of the story in Book V, we now have a third important figure to keep Pantagruel and Panurge company: Frère Jean. As far as the story tells us, or rather fails to tell us, he has never before met the younger man and younger giant; after all, when *Pantagruel* was written, he had not been invented. The wise Pantagruel of the last three books is so like the mature Gargantua that Frère Jean had known in Book I as to make him now feel quite at home; more important, he and the two giants have completely different roles.

Not so with Frère Jean and Panurge. Their relationship is completely new, and, as characters, they are potential rivals. Each, in "his own" earlier book (so to speak), has been the number two —almost the number one— character, the leading human personage, coming on the scene about when Rabelais (it would seem) was tiring of giant humor and ready, or nearly ready, to transform his now educated, mature giant into a kind of philosopher king. Here in the *Tiers Livre*, for the first time, they must compete for the king's attention and, perhaps more important, for the reader's. Their presence together need have no effect on the character of Pantagruel (unless to free him from any comic tasks); but on one another's characters it seems it must.

Now as I see it, the lusty, dynamic, courageous monk —or anti-monk— Frère Jean had from the first been a more flesh-and-blood, three-dimensional character than Panurge, who in *Pantagruel* is more a type, a stock character in the old tradition of the student scamp. Rabelais uses Panurge more for special purposes of his own —to tell jokes and play tricks— and seems to give him less independent life than Frère Jean. I cannot help thinking of his name as meaning (to quote Liddell and Scott for πανουργος) not merely "knavish, roguish," but also (still quoting) "ready to do anything" —anything his creator has in mind. When he is courting the "dame de Paris" (II: 21, p. 264) he flees in haste "de peur des coups, lesquelz il craignoit naturellement," for Rabelais has no mind to make of him a courageous Don Juan figure; but in the war with the Dipsodes he is courageous as well as ingenious (II: 25-26, etc.) and even a source of moral support for the brave Pantagruel. There is consistency in his character, of course; but I find in it also certain inconsistencies which suggest that Rabelais uses him as he will, in much the same way as he makes the giants vast or man-size as he chooses.

In short, I think that because of their similar roles, earlier and now, Frère Jean and Panurge are bound to affect one another as characters in the *Tiers Livre*; above all they cannot be too much alike; and Frère Jean, the more solid of the two characters, is less subject to change than Panurge. We cannot of course test Frère Jean's stability in the *Tiers Livre* before and after chapter 13, since he is not there before; but Panurge's we can. After chapter 13 we find some new developments in him which may be accident, but I believe are not.

Of course much of Panurge's character is already set in the *Tiers Livre* before Frère Jean arrives on the scene. He is a master of specious eloquence; a victim of *philautie* — unless we take chapter 28 to show retroactively that his boastfulness is merely a cover for an inferiority complex; eager to marry mainly to avoid the hazards of adultery; showing no sign of readiness to marry a good woman or be a good husband; hopeful that he can marry as he likes, live as he likes, and still keep his wife satisfied and faithful; thus hopeful that he can outwit destiny and divine law; yet still not quite confident enough to be able to make up his mind. In short, in most respects his character is consistent throughout the *Tiers Livre*.

His concern with heresy, however, seems to grow after chapter 13. Non-existent in the *Pantagruel*, it peeps out, to be sure, as early as chapter 2 (p. 335) of the *Tiers Livre*, when Panurge says his indebtedness is an imitation of the "Université et Parlement de Paris," where he finds "la vraye source et vive idée de panthéologie, de toute justice aussi," and goes on to proclaim: "Hæreticque qui en doubte, et fermement ne le croyt." On the next page (same chapter) he claims to have manifested the virtue of strength by cutting down forests and thus ruining "retraictes d'hæreticques." Though this does point in that direction, I do not think it prepares us at all fully for the heresy-sniffing Panurge of the Raminagrobis episode (chapter 22)[2] or the remark in chapter 29 (p. 434) that most theologians are heretics.

One clear change in Panurge after III: 13 is that he becomes a coward. As we noted earlier, he had been inconsistent in this res-

---

[2] Especially p. 407 (Panurge speaking of Raminagrobis): "Il est, par la vertus Dieu, hæreticque. Je dis hæreticque formé, hæreticque clavelé, hæreticque bruslable comme une belle petite horologe. Son âme s'en va à trente mille charrettées de diables."

pect in *Pantagruel*, but brave more often than cowardly. In the early chapters of the *Tiers Livre* nothing clearly reveals him as one thing or the other. True, he comes to the subject of marriage (chapter 6) apropos of the exemption of newlywed men from going to war; but in view of that fact the surprising thing about that whole chapter is that he never acts like a coward. He raises the question quite matter-of-factly, and when Pantagruel has answered seriously, responds with brief stories about the "prescheurs de Varennes" and Frère Enguainnant, and theories about why newlyweds would be useless in war. If Rabelais had had any urge to show him up here as cowardly, the occasion was perfect; a blubbering, blustering Panurge like that of the tempest in the *Quart Livre* would have fitted the situation perfectly. On the contrary, as I see it, Panurge's attitude toward the hazards of war is one of equanimity.

However, once Frère Jean has made his appearance, we do not have to wait long to find comical cowardice in Panurge. The weird ritual of the Sibylle de Panzoust in chapter 17 gives him such a fright that he is ready to give up all plans of marriage (p. 389):

> "Par la vertus Dieu, je tremble! je croy que je suys charmé; elle ne parle poinct christian. Voyez comment elle me semble de quatre empans plus grande que n'estoit lorsqu'elle se capitonna de son davantau. Que signifie ce remument de badiguoinces? Que prétend ceste jectigation des espaulles? A quelle fin fredonne-elle des babines comme un cinge démembrant escrevisses? Les aureilles me cornent, il m'est advis que je oy Proserpine bruyante; les diables bien toust en place sortiront. O les laydes bestes! Fuyons! Serpe Dieu, je meurs de paour! Je n'ayme poinct les diables; ilz me faschent et sont mal plaisans. Fuyons! Adieu, madame, grand mercy de vos biens! Je ne me mariray poinct, non! Je y renonce dès à præsent comme allors."

Four chapters later Panurge, Frère Jean, and Epistémon consult the dying poet, the "bon vieillard" Raminagrobis; and when he has told them of the varicolored vermine who have been plaguing him, Panurge, "comme tout effrayé" (chapter 22, p. 405), pronounces him, as we have seen, a dangerous heretic. After some debate on this, Panurge starts the following chapter by urging that they all return to admonish Raminagrobis about his salvation; but suddenly he imagines the poet's room already full of devils waiting (pp. 408-09) "à qui humera l'âme raminagrobidicque, et qui premier, de broc en bouc, la portera à messer Lucifer." Immediately he is off on a long and delightful account of his fear and his reasons for not going back:

> "Houstez-vous de là! Je ne y voys pas; le diable me emport si je y voys. Qui sçait s'ilz useroient de *qui pro quo*, et, en lieu de Raminagrobis, grupperoient le paouvre Panurge quitte? Ilz y ont maintes foys failly, estant safrané et endebté. Houstéz-vous de là! Je ne y voys pas. Je meurs, par Dieu! de male raige de paour."

As one possible alternative Panurge proposes (p. 411) that Frère Jean go back to Raminagrobis instead with his "froc et domino de grobis," promising that "En cas que trente mille batelées de diables ne t'emportent ainsi qualifié, je payeray pinthe et fagot." But Frère Jean is not in the least daunted or even dismayed: "Je ne m'en souciroys (respondit frère Jan) pas tant, par adventure, que l'on diroyt, ayant mon bragmard on poing."

Thus already by chapter 23 Rabelais has established Panurge not only as a coward, but as a coward in striking, direct contrast with the courageous Frère Jean. Here already is the pattern of their behavior in the tempest and elsewhere in the *Quart Livre*.

The only other occasion in the *Tiers Livre* involving the idea of peril to Panurge is in chapter 47, when he first suggests the trip to consult the Dive Bouteille. He does so with no mention of danger, and when Pantagruel reminds him (p. 492) that their long peregrination would be "plene de azard, plene de dangiers évidents...," Panurge interrupts to dismiss this notion almost with contempt:

> "Quelz dangiers? (dist Panurge interrompant le propous). Les dangiers se refuyent de moy, quelque part que je soys, sept lieues à la ronde..."

However, this seems not to be courage but foolhardiness and braggadoccio; it sets Panurge up perfectly for such humiliating episodes in the *Quart Livre* as the tempest, the encounter with the whale, and the island of Ganabin.

The other new element in the last three quarters of the *Tiers Livre* is Panurge's age. In *Pantagruel* (chapter 16, p. 237) he had been represented as about thirty-five. No appreciable time seems to have elapsed, in the fiction, between the end of *Pantagruel* and the beginning of the *Tiers Livre*. Frère Jean's age is never given anywhere beyond the statement in *Gargantua* (chapter 27, page 83) that he is young; but he belongs to Gargantua's generation and thus, by any normal fictional chronology, has no place in the *Tiers Livre* unless that of an older man — though hardly an elder statesman.

Now it is true that already in chapter 6 of the *Tiers Livre* Panurge, speaking to Pantagruel of the law that exempted planters of new vines and builders of new lodgings, as well as newlywed men, from going to war, comments: "Des planteurs de vigne, je suis trop vieulx pour me soucier" (p. 349); and M. A. Screech in his edition calls this an early indication that Panurge is to be that stock comic character, the elderly lover. However, I do not see that this proves very much about Panurge's age. — It is also true that in chapter 31 (p. 443) Rondibilis pronounces Panurge fit for marriage: "bien proportionné en ses membres, bien tempéré en ses humeurs, bien complexionné en ses espritz," and, more important for our purpose, "en aage compétent, en temps oportun, en vouloir équitable de soy marier."

However, the striking comments on Panurge's age both come in the last three quarters of the *Tiers Livre*. In chapter 46 Pantagruel, who has never mentioned the subject before, in his comment on Triboulet's words is outspoken and —for him— surprisingly harsh (p. 489): "Il dict que vous estes fol? Et quel fol? Fol enragé, qui sus vos vieulx jours voulez en mariage vous lier et asservir." But Frère Jean —once again— has already come into the picture on the subject much earlier; it is he who makes the most of Panurge's advancing years. After giving him advice in chapter 27, he opens chapter 28 (pp. 428-29) as follows:

> "Je t'entends (dist frère Jan), mais le temps matte toutes choses: il n'est le marbre ne le porphyre qui n'ayt sa vieillesse et décadence. Si tu ne en es là pour ceste heure, peu d'années après subséquentes je te oiray confessant que les couilles pendent à plusieurs par faulte de gibessière. Desjà voy-je ton poil grisonner en teste. Ta barbe par les

> distinctions du gris, du blanc, du tanné et du noir, me semble une mappemonde. Reguarde icy: voylà Asie; icy sont Tigris et Euphrates. Voylà Afrique; icy est la montaigne de la Lune. Voidz-tu les paluz du Nil? Deçà est Europe. Voydz-tu Thélème? Ce touppet icy tout blanc sont les mons Hyperborées. Par ma soif, mon amy, quand les neiges sont ès montaignes, je diz la teste et le menton, il n'y a pas grand chaleur par les vallées de la braguette!"

Panurge replies of course that his vigor is entire and impressive; but he concedes "mon poil grisonnant" and admits, because of his increasing love of good wine and distaste for bad, that "Vray est que en moy je recongnois quelque signe indicatif de vieillesse, je diz verde vieillesse ..." — I find it striking that the greatest ado over Panurge's advancing age is made by Frère Jean, who is theoretically a generation older. Once again, Rabelais seems to be emphasizing the contrast between the two, and here, against all chronological plausibility.

To sum up, there are three marked developments —I would call them changes— in the character of Panurge between the first quarter and the last three quarters of the *Tiers Livre*: Panurge's heresy-sniffing, his cowardice, and his age. In all three respects he is placed at one time or another in rather explicit contrast with Frère Jean. Granted, Rabelais might have given Panurge all these attributes anyway, and his age is probably most directly related to his plan to marry, since an elderly suitor is a natural subject for comedy. But since one quarter of the book has passed before Frère Jean appears; since these characteristics are seen only in traces before, and are emphasized after; since Frère Jean stands in contrast with Panurge in all these respects; and since Rabelais at times seems to underline their contrast — for all these reasons, I think we may conclude that at least to a considerable degree these characteristics of Panurge in the *Tiers Livre* —and later— are aspects of the impact of Frère Jean on the character of Panurge.

CANDIDE'S QUARTERINGS

R. L. FRAUTSCHI
University of North Carolina

Surprisingly little has been written about the genealogy of Voltaire's most famous hero and the implications of Candide's illegitimacy. In his edition of *Candide* (Paris, 1913, p. 2) Morize noted that jests about quarterings were already a familiar item in Voltaire's comic baggage and cited an example (Mol., XXIII, 288) composed in 1748: "Un baron allemand n'eût pas épousé Catherine, mais Pierre le Grand ne pensait pas que le mérite eut besoin de trente-deux quartiers." Not only among the commentators, but also in English translations from Smollett to the present one finds a particular effort to emphasize the preposterous nature of the hero's lineage.

Les anciens domestiques de la maison soupçonnaient qu'il était fils de la sœur de monsieur le baron, & d'un bon & honnête gentilhomme du voisinage, que cette demoiselle ne voulut jamais épouser, parce qu'il n'avait pu prouver que soixante & onze quartiers, et que le reste de son arbre généalogique avait été perdu par l'injure du tems.

The old family servants suspected him of being the son of the baron's sister whom the lady had consistently turned down because he could trace noble descent for a mere seventy-one quarterings, the rest of his family tree having suffered the ravages of time.[1]

---

[1] R. Pomeau, ed., *Candide* (Paris, 1959), p. 83 (all subsequent quotations are taken from this edition); Joan Spencer, trans., with an introduction by T. Besterman, *Candide* (London, 1966), p. 115.

The commentaries on this extraordinary heredity tend to limit themselves to these acceptations: "Terme de genéalogie. Chaque degré de descendance dans une famille noble, tant du côté paternel que du côté maternel"; "Terme de blason. La quatrième partie d'un écusson écartelé" (Littré, 22, 23). If anything, a greater emphasis has been placed on the first of the two definitions by Littré. For example:

> Un quartier de noblesse représente une génération. En France, on était réputé de bonne noblesse quand on avait quatre quartiers du côté du père et autant du côté de la mère. En Allemagne, on était plus dfficile: mais soixante et onze quartiers feraient plus de deux mille ans de noblesse. [2]

The other line of interpretation (and the two are by no means mutually exclusive) appears, for example, in G. R. Havens' edition of *Candide* (New York, 1934, p. 114) where he describes quarterings as "divisions in heraldry indicating on a coat of arms degrees of relationships among nobility." According to Havens, who did not quote a source, sixty-four quarterings were the maximum required, while admission to knighthood was granted on the basis of sixteen. Since the quarterings progressed geometrically, according to Havens, Voltaire chose this odd number merely for "humorous" effect. [3]

Both groups, the generational and the chivalric, I would like to suggest, structure their information in order to demonstrate the comically absurd qualities of the lineage. While there can be no doubt about Voltaire's comic intent in the passage referring to seventy-one quarterings, it may be useful to interpret this detail in the light of others concerning Candide's natural parents and then to situate the hero's bastardy against practices prevailing in post-Renaisance Europe. From this perspective we can reevaluate the significance of Candide's eventual marriage with Mademoiselle Cunégonde.

When we compare the initial description of the hero's lineage with customs prevailing in Voltaire's time, a striking image of

---

[2] H. Bénac, ed., Voltaire, *Romans et contes* (Paris, 1960), p. 632, n. 210. Cf. J. E. White, ed., *Candide* (New York, 1964), p. 185.

[3] Cf. M. Bishop, ed., *Candide* (New York, 1929), p. 28 n.

Candide's condition emerges to counterpoint the prevailing exegeses of comic exaggeration. In order of presentation, the first element injected by Voltaire —"Les anciens domestiques soupçonnaient qu'il était le fils..."— provides a recognized method of legal proof. The article PREUVE in the Encyclopédie (XIII, 356) presents the example of a "preuve de commune renomée," one that is not *de visu*, but which is acceptable when grounded on "notoriété publique." This particular mode of proof sets the angle of vision for the ensuing genealogical details.

Voltaire next gives us the parentage of his hero: "...fils de la sœur de monsieur le baron, & d'un bon & honnête gentilhomme du voisinage..." He takes especial pains to emphasize the nobility, both moral as well as genealogical, of the hero's natural father, "un *bon & honnête* (my emphasis) gentilhomme." The adjectives, or derivatives, will be applied frequently to Candide himself during the course of the story, thus sustaining the identification. Although we are not given here a precise description of Candide's maternal descent, by implication it is impeccable, if not superior in ancestry to the quarterings of her lover. The mother's reluctance to marry, stated with the past definite form "voulut" as a completed action, effectively removes both parents from the scene. The presumed discrepancy in quarterings between Candide's mother and father effectively attenuates the reality that our hero is indeed the offspring, albeit illegitimate, of two extremely well born parents. Also, the fact that Voltaire did not choose to make Candide the progeny of a noblewoman and a commoner bears scrutiny vis-à-vis the condition of noble bastards in the eighteenth century.

Quite frequently Voltaire mentions examples in history of legitimized bastards. In his *Doutes sur quelques points de l'histoire de l'Empire* (1753), he cites at length these cases in Germany:

> (VII) Doit-on compter parmi les empereurs ceux qui régnèrent depuis Arnoud, bâtard de la maison de Charlemagne? Jusqu'à Othon Ier ils ne furent que rois de Germanie.
>
> (VIII) Louis IV, surnommé l'Enfant, était-il bâtard comme son père? On convient que ses frères n'étaient pas légitimes. Hübner le met au même rang que ses frères, sans aucune distinction. Il est dit dans les Annales de Fulde que

> la femme d'Arnoud vécut mal avec son mari, qu'elle fut accusée d'adultère. Il est rapporté que dans l'assemblée de Forcheim, les seigneurs statuèrent qu'un de ces frères de Louis l'Enfant serait roi, s'il ne se trouvait point d'héritier né d'un mariage légitime.
>
> Ces mêmes seigneurs, à la mort d'Arnoud, produisirent Louis, âgés de sept ans. Il faut donc le regarder comme légitime; il faut donc dire dans les vers techniques: 'Louis, le fils d'Arnoud' et non pas: 'Louis, bâtard d'Arnoud' (Mol., XXIV, 37).

The procedures for legitimacy in Carolingian times do not prevail, notes Voltaire, in contemporary Germany. The parallel with the interpretation of Candide's status by the Baron and his family is obvious.

> *Dictionnaire Philosophique*, BÂTARDS (1770)
> En Allemagne, il n'en est pas de même: on veut des races pures; *les bâtards n'héritent jamais des fiefs, et n'ont point d'état* (my emphasis).

The punctiliousness of the Germans regarding hereditary purity contrasts with the more liberal customs of France.

The discrepancy in custom singled out by Voltaire raises the broader question pertinent to Candide: what procedures for legitimization were known, if not actively used in Voltaire's day? Again the *Encyclopédie* provides some provocative examples. The article BÂTARD OU ENFANT NATUREL (II, 138-9) distinguishes two types of illegitimacy: "simples" and "adultérins ou incestueux." Candide's case falls, significantly, in the former category. And again it is no small coincidence that simplicity (or simpleness) are among the connotations of the hero's name: "Il avait le jugement assez droit, avec l'esprit le plus simple" (p. 83). The *Encyclopédie* notes that according to common law illegitimate offspring may not inherit, although they are allowed to marry and to disburse property. According to Roman law bastards born in concubinage (i. e. a kind of common law marriage) may inherit from their mother. The father however, has no lineal authority. Also, according to Roman law, continues the article: "Les bâtards pouvaient être légitimés, soit *par un mariage* (my emphasis) ou par lettres de l'empereur." In France, however, only a royal patent can sanction legitimization.

The Roman custom of uterine nobility (*partus sequitur ventrem*) applies, certainly, to Candide through his well born mother.[4] The seventy-one quarterings of his father, however, reflect the juristic precedents established during the sixteenth century in favor of male superiority: vide the dictum "le ventre affranchit et le verge anoblit." Various regional documents as well as royal edicts attest this development, which was also applied to illegitimate offspring:

> Les bâtards issus de noble génération *de par père* et leurs enfants son réputés nobles, jouissans du privilège de noblesse en toutes choses. (A. Maillard, *Coutumes d'Artois*, 1756.)[5]

Illegitimate children of a noble mother and a commoner were held to be *roturiers*: "Il leur était interdit d'invoquer à cet égard le principe que les enfants nés hors mariage suivent la condition de leur mère."[6] Thus, Voltaire's selection of a "bon et honnête gentilhomme" as the father of his hero reflects his intent to assure the nobility of Candide.

If, then, Candide enjoys the best of both worlds in so far as his noble lineage is concerned, two modes were available to him to legitimize his status. During the juristic disputes over male versus female desendance which raged in the sixteenth century J. Bacquet (*Quatriesme traité des droits du domaine de France, concernant les francs fiefs, nouveaux acquets, anoblissemens et amortissemens*, 1582) opined:

> Tout ainsi qu'en France il n'y a que deux sortes de légitimations, et que bastard ne peut estre légitimé sinon par deux moyens; ou *par mariage subséquent*, ou par rescript du prince...[7]

---

[4] See L. Verriest, *Noblesse, Chevalerie, Lignages* (Bruxelles, 1960), pp. 66-9.

[5] Cited by J.-R. Bloch, *L'Annoblissement en France au temps de François I*ᵉʳ (Paris, 1934), p. 69.

[6] H. Beaune. *La Condition des personnes* (Lyon & Paris, 1882), p. 82. Cf. Voltaire's criticism of salic law (Mol. XIX, 611).

[7] Cited by Bloch, *op. cit.*, pp. 17-8.

But the respect for Roman custom, concurrent with royal patents, as described by Bacquet gave way to the principle of royal and masculine authority in an edict by Henri IV concerning *tailles*, article 26, dated 1600, which limited ennobling authority to the monarchy.

> Pour le regard des Bâtards, encores qu'ils soient issus de pères nobles, ne se pourront attribuer le titre et qualité de gentilhomme s'ils n'obtiennent nos lettres d'annoblissement fondées sur quelque grande considération de leurs mérites ou de leurs pères, vérifiées où il appartient. [8]

Applied to Candide, the edict disqualifies him on both counts. Candide's father never appears in the tale (nor does his mother, as we have observed). And Candide himself, despite his "merits," cannot plead in his own behalf because his lord, the Baron Thunder-ten-tronck, and later the Baron's son, are prejudiced against his case. Among the judicial precedents open to Candide, the only feasible way to sanction his legitimacy as a noble is by marriage. [9]

To conclude this examination of Candide's hereditary situation at the beginning of the tale, let us return to the seventy-one quarters of his noble father. The exegesis of comic exaggeration does not adequately apply to all the levels of significance which the alert reader can eventually grasp. In their literal reality, then, what can be predicated about these quarterings? At least two strains of meaning are observable elsewhere in Voltaire's writings. He appreciated reasoned, sober genealogies, a science which had made

---

[8] In Isembert, Decrusy & Annet, *Recueil général des anciennes lois françaises de 420 à 1789* (Paris, n. d.), cited by Bloch, p. 65.

[9] A pertinent variation from the aforementioned modes of legitimization is noted by Bloch (p. 69) in Lorraine. There a practice first implimented in the sixteenth century, but well established in the eighteenth favored a system of degrees of nobility for illegitimate children of nobility and commoners. "Les bâtards avoués des gentilhommes étaient placés dans l'échelle sociale au degré immédiatement inférieur à celui de leur père; ils portaient le titre et le nom que le père voulaient leur donner, et possédaient les armes paternelles barrées transversalement de gauche à droite. En conséquence, le bâtard du seigneur était *simple* (my emphasis) gentilhomme et le bâtard de l'anobli, roturier." The nuance of inferiority prescribed by the Lorraine custom (where Voltaire for many years with Madame du Châtelet) is echoed in Candide's ambiguous status at Thunder-ten-tronckh.

great progress since the Renaissance: witness his respectful allusions to Duchesne (Best. 6254), the d'Hozier family (Best. 17404), to Ammon's restrained lineages (Best. 13999). More frequently, however, he tends to view genealogy with amused skepticism. When asked by d'Alembert to write an article on Genealogy for the *Encyclopédie* he refused politely.

> Permettez moi (*sic*) de ne traiter ni Généalogie ni Guerre littéraire; j'ai l'aversion pour la vanité des généalogies; je n'en crois pas quatre d'avérées avant la fin du treizième siècle, et je ne suis pas assez savant pour concilier les deux généalogies absolument différentes de notre divin seigneur (29 novembre 1756; Best. 6375).[10]

Given Voltaire's cautious respect for serious genealogy and his prompt ridicule of pretentious claims, the mathematical projections of the quarterings assume a new light. In the first place it is difficult if not impossible to claim with assurance what unit of generational measure Voltaire may have intended. If we apply the usual norms of thirty or thirty-three years, the descent goes back 2,160 and 2,343 years respectively. Again, we can project an alternate unit of measure, the twenty-two or twenty-three year life span cited in *L'Homme aux quarante écus* and the *Dialogue entre A. B. C.*[11] In any case these figures are quite modest when compared with the practices of Voltaire's contemporaries. For example, Voltaire questioned the figure of 174 generations from Adam and Eve to the present in Amman's *Généalogie ascendante* (Berlin, 1768) (Best. 13999). Jaucourt, who dutifully wrote the article on Genealogy, cites the fanciful example of 118 quarterings presumed between Adam and Philip II of Spain. (VIII, 549). According to the correlative, then, Voltaire's seventy-one quarterings are at once inflated and restrained. The ambiguity is heightened by the con-

---

[10] Cf. (*Histoire universelle*, 1754) "Ce n'est point ici un livre de chronologie et de généalogie. Il y en a assez. C'est le tableau des siècles (Mol., XXIV, 25); "Elles [the origin of parliaments] ressemblent assez aux généalogies des grandes maisons, qui commencent toutes par des fables" (letter to La Chatolais, 1763, Best. 10303).

[11] Bénac ed., *Romans*, op. cit., p. 291.

cluding detail which states that the father's genealogical tree has been lost in the vagaries of historical time.

A final clue to the potential significance of Candide's ambiguous bastardy appears in a reference to the genealogies of Rabelais' giants (Letter to Prince Charles,- Guillaume-Ferdinand de Brunswick-Lunebourg, 1767).

> On ne peut se méprendre à la généalogie de Gargantua: c'est une parodie très-scandaleuse de la généalogie la plus respectable (Mol., XXVI, 471). [12]

Voltaire's description of Rabelais' genealogy appears to echo Candide's initial situation. Yet, instead of seeing mere exaggeration of quaint customs in the dubious lineage of Candide, Voltaire has burdened his hero with what will only later emerge as an unjust and unnecessary inferiority. At the opening of *Candide*, then, the hero's genealogical condition is presented, not as a quantified exaggeration of known norms, as Voltaire interprets the example of Rabelais, but as a seemingly scandalous imbalance between genuine and spurious nobility. The ambiguities of Candide's nobility, let us anticipate, will never be proved by the authentification of additional quarterings or by official patents. Rather, along with his philosophical and amorous quests, the hero will eventually affirm the *"libertas originalis* of the authentic nobleman, a liberty as yet merely latent given the facts of his birth. When Candide finally understands the privileges of true nobility —freedom from authority, freedom from servitude or obligation— he will choose to submit himself to a new law, the *summum* of true liberty, the service in his garden on the Propontis.

The theme of Candide's quarters does not reappear until midway through the story in Chapter XV. There the young Baron, now a Jesuit in Paraguay, refuses Candide's request to marry his sister on the grounds that she has seventy-two quarters.

> "Vous, insolent! répondit le baron, vous auriez l'impudence d'épouser ma sœur qui a soixante & douze quartiers! je vous trouve bien effronté d'oser me parler d'un tel dessein

---

[12] Voltaire then confounds the sixty-two quarterings of Pantagruel with the more modest lineage of Gargantua.

> si téméraire!" Candide pétrifié d'un tel discours lui répondit: "Mon révérend père, tous les quartiers du monde n'y font rien; j'ai tiré votre sœur des bras d'un juif & d'un inquisiteur; elle m'a assez d'obligations, elle veut m'épouser (p. 140).

In the literal context the Baron repeats the arguments attributed in Chapter I to Candide's mother. The suitor does not have an adequate pedigree. The mention of seventy-two quarterings, however, is the first defensive reference to lineage in the Baron's family. Since Candide's father could prove seventy-one quarterings without question, and since Cunégonde herself claims only seventy-two, it would seem in terms of a generational count that Candide and Cunégonde have identical lineage. Moreover, the brother's objections are not argued as a juristic but as a moral question: "effronté," "dessein si téméraire." Nor is Candide's bastardy invoked overtly. Candide defends his claim for Cunégonde's hand in turn, not on the basis of his lineage, but according to his service to her, plus the fact that she desires the union. The argument, then, pointedly ignores the earlier objection to marriage by Candide's mother because of insufficient quarterings. Candide's remark "tous les quartiers du monde n'y font rien" removes the condition as one he recognizes. But when he persists in his scheme ("...assurément je l'épouserai!"), the Baron strikes him with the back of his sword, an insulting gesture which connotes Candide's yet inferior condition. In rebuttal Candide runs the Baron through with his sword. He no longer accepts his inferiority, but he has yet to establish positively his nobility.

The resolution of Candide's genealogical problems does not occur until the concluding chapters XXIX and XXX, during the reunion of Candide, Cunégonde and her brother in Turkey.

> Le baron pâlit à sa vue. Le tendre amant Candide voyant sa belle Cunégonde rembrunie, les yeux éraillés, la gorge sèche, les joues ridées, les bras rouges et écaillés, recula trois pas saisi d'horreur, & avança ensuite par bon procédé (XXIX, p. 217).

Candide's forward lurch, despite the shock of Cunégonde's ugliness, is depicted neither as an act of derring-do nor of personal commitment.[13] Instead, Voltaire's expression "par bon procédé" suggests an instinctive reliance upon formal procedures, that is an expression of the hero's emerging nobility.

> ...(Cunégonde) fit souvenir Candide de ses promesses d'un ton si absolu, que le bon Candide n'osa pas la refuser. Il signifia donc au baron qu'il allait se marier avec sa sœur. "Je ne souffrirai jamais, dit le baron, une telle bassesse de sa part, & une telle insolence de la vôtre: cette infamie ne me sera jamais reprochée: les enfans de ma sœur ne pourraient entrer dans les chapitres d'Allemagne. Non, jamais ma sœur n'épousera qu'un baron de l'empire. Cunégonde se jetta à ses pieds & les baigna de larmes: il fut inflexible (XXIX, p. 218).

In this final encounter with Cunégonde's brother the Baron's opposition to Candide's marriage is again predicated on skillfully ambiguous grounds. Significantly there is no mention of quarterings. Instead the argument shifts to the inferior condition of any children born of the union. They would be excluded from the noble assemblies of Germany. Hence, sums up the brother, the only suitable husband for Cunégonde is a German Baron, a highly ironic choice given Voltaire's frequent quips about the title.[14] Although not explicitly verbalized, we can guess the reason for the Baron's inflexibility: the offspring would be the issue of a bastard who had married his cousin. The insult of genealogical inferiority cedes to the injury of incest.

That Voltaire was not unaware of varying interpretations of incest can be attested, for example, by the article on the subject in the *Dictionnaire philosophique*. Comparing various legal definitions he notes that marriages with sisters were sanctioned by the

---

[13] Cf. William F. Bottiglia, *Voltaire's Candide: Analysis of a Classic* (Geneva, 1964), p. 226.

[14] The Voltaire canon is liberally sprinkled with allusions to ridiculous nobles, especially German barons:
> Les barons allemands ne remontent que jusqu'à Vitikind, et nos nouveaux marquis ne peuvent guère montrer de titres au-delà de Charlemagne (*Dict. phil.*, GÉNÉALOGIE, Mol., XIX, 222).

> On dit que les Allemans sont fort curieux de généalogies (letter to Trantzsehen, 1769, Best. 14563).

See also Best. 2814 and *Notebooks* (ed. Besterman), p. 427.

Persians, Athenians and Egyptians," "...mais le fait est que le mariage entre cousins est défendu chez les Guèbres aujourd'hui" (Mol., XIX, p. 452). In the same article he rails against the abusive punishment with which the jurist Vouglans (*Réfutation de Beccaria*, 1767) taxes sexual relations between cousins.

> Quant à l'inceste charnel, lisez l'avocat Vouglans, partie VIII, titre III, chapitre IX ; il veut absolument qu'on brûle le cousin et la cousine qui auront eu un moment de faiblesse. L'avocat Vouglans est rigoureux. Quel terrible Welche !

We can infer from this example that Voltaire has no sympathy for the final objection to Candide's marriage presented by Cunégonde's brother.

In the terminal passage relating to the genealogical theme the focus shifts from Candide's defense of his presumed inferiority to the positive demonstration of his most acceptable equality.

> Candide dans le fond de son cueur n'avait aucune envie d'épouser Cunégonde. Mais l'impertinence extrême du baron le déterminait à conclure le mariage, & Cunégonde le pressait si vivment, qu'il ne pouvait s'en dédire. ...Pangloss fit un beau mémoire, par lequel il prouvait que le baron n'avait nul droit sur sa sœur, & qu'elle pouvait selon toutes les loix de l'empire épouser Candide de la main gauche (XXX, p. 219).

The Baron's objections utterly exhausted (his "impertinence extrême"), and with Cunégonde's enduring willingness to accept Candide in matrimony, there remains only the obstacle of securing legal sanction.[15] The arguments adduced in Pangloss' brief which convince Candide to marry parody the Roman precedent of uterine nobility. Thus the Baron has no rights over his sister. As a free agent she may ennoble Candide by marriage. The marriage, argues Pangloss, is indeed sanctioned "selon toutes les lois de l'Empire," which in this context may be interpreted as Roman, a subtle counterpoint to the Baron's appeal to Germanic custom. The mas-

---

[15] Cf. *Dict. phil.*, MARIAGE, Mol. XX, 27. Voltaire defines marriage as a "contrat du droit des gens" and not as a sacrement.

sive judicial precedent is tempered, however, by the concluding detail "de la main gauche" which in the present perspective connotes a deeper meaning than that of a morganatic union between the noble Cunégonde and the commoner (or less noble) Candide. Voltaire adds this point because it counters the Baron's final objection to the marriage on the grounds of incest. The Baron was concerned that children born of an incestuous union would not be admitted to the noble German assemblies. However, children born under the morganatic contract proposed by Pangloss automatically lose all rights to noble privilege. Hence the objection is overruled. The absurd "beau mémoire" prepared by Pangloss, then, paries all previous absurd arguments. Empirically, of course, his rebuttal is irrelevant, since he appeals to customs which no longer prevail. In addition his clients plan to reside in the Ottoman Empire which has its own laws and customs.[16] But the judicial equilibrium at last effected allows Candide to get on with his marriage.

With appropriate discretion Voltaire says nothing about the marriage ceremony. He notes simply "Candide marié avec sa maîtresse" (p. 219). Since we already know that Candide does not love his wife ("Candide dans le fond de son cueur n'avait aucune envie d'épouser Cunégonde."), the significance of the marriage must be sought elsewhere. Some commentators have interpreted the union as Voltaire's "realistic" antidote to the sentimental quixoticism of courtly romances, a "constructive" solution, a "practical institution for social productivity."[17] For one thing such dreary utilitarianism belies Voltaire's debt to *Aucassin et Nicolette*, reedited by La Curne de Sainte-Pelaye in 1752.[18] In the medieval fable the idyllic marriage is consummated only when the nobility of the heroine, a Carthaginian princess, has been duly verified by the unquestionably noble Aucassin. In Voltaire's tale the reverse occurs, but with a crucial difference. Marriage is the avowed *terminus ad quem*

---

[16] C. Thacker ("The Misplaced Garden? Voltaire, Julian and *Candide*," *Stud. Volt.*, 41, p. 191) as effectively proved that Candide, a European, would have been unable to purchase property in eighteenth-century Turkey.

[17] Cited by Bottiglia, *op. cit.* See pp. 116, 217, 222.

[18] See D. D. R. Owen, "*Aucassin et Nicolette* and the Genesis of *Candide*," *Stud. Volt.*, 41, esp. p. 214. Owen also notes the denouement of *La Châtelaine de Saint-Gilles*, a again reedited by Sainte-Pelaye, and its theme of the mismatched couple.

for Aucassin alone; in *Candide* marriage marks the opening of the garden club. The legitimization of nobility through marriage helps us to understand why Candide pursues so relentlessly a formal alliance with Cunégonde. Instead of love or social usefulness, the ceremony resolves the ambiguities of his genealogy and thus proclaims Candide a noble who is unquestionably free. Only then can he willingly submit to the higher service in his garden. [19]

And finally, it has been suggested that Voltaire used, consciously or unconsciously, the Turkish garden of Emperor Julian the Apostate as a model for Candide's community. [20] The parallels between Julian and Candide can be increased in light of the significance of the latter's newly acquired nobility. We know that Voltaire relocated Julian's original garden on the southern shore of the Propontis in Bithynia to the northern shore. He transposed the nostalgic feelings about the garden in Julian's missive to his friend Evagrius to a resigned forward looking attitude toward service in Candide's garden. Also, the many references by Voltaire to Julian before and after the composition of *Candide* suggest that the noble character of the much aligned apostate was a model toward which the simple, gentle Candide could strive.

> Ainsi cet homme, qu'on a peint abominable, était peut-être le premier homme, ou du moins le second. Toujours sobre, toujours tempérent, n'ayant jamais eu de maîtresses, couchant sur une peau d'ours, en y donnant, à regret encore, peu d'heures au sommeil, partageant son temps entre l'étude et les affaires, généreux, capable d'amitié, ennemi du faste, on l'eût admiré s'il n'eut été particulier (*Dictionnaire philo.*, Mol. XIX, 542).

Moreover, the incest element in *Candide* is echoed in the biography of Julian who married, in accordance with legal sanctions, his sister. And Julian's militantly Christian cousin Constance receives a frown from Voltaire for having forbidden marriage between sects. (*Lettres philo.*, Mol. XX, 27). Julian, let us not forget, suc-

---

[19] For a description of the privileges of the nobility, the *franci homines*, see Verriest, *op. cit.* pp. 155-6
[20] Thacker, *op. cit.* Voltaire writes copiously on Julian. See, for example, Mol. XXX, pp. 574-5.

ceeded Constance as Emperor just as Candide replaced the Baron. And again Julian opposed Constance's Christianity as Candide opposed the Baron's haughty claims to nobility.

The resolution through marriage of Candide's uncertain nobility functions, we have suggested, as a condition for his freely consented service in the garden. In retrospect the theme of Candide's genealogy is developed by Voltaire in a highly formal arrangement. It is posited at the beginning of Chapter I as an amusing irregularity of birth and quarterings. In the median Chapter XV, the revelation of Cunégonde's equal number of quarterings subtly resolves the linear ambiguity, but the hero's efforts to legitimize his bastardy through marriage are frustrated. In the concluding Chapters XXIX and XXX, the last objections of the Baron, the defective nobility of children born of an incestuous union, are overcome by Pangloss's brief and Cunégonde's uterine cooperation.

Such a deliberately ordered introduction, development and resolution of Candide's ambiguous condition suggests that the theme has greater import than just another example of Voltaire's wit. Of course we chuckle at the grotesque union of Candide and ugly Cunégonde. Yet the loss of desire for his beloved and the concurrent disenchantment with Panglossian philosophy are perhaps a small price to pay for the privileges of consanguinity, even in the embourgeoised garden of the Emperor Julian. By his marriage with Cunégonde and the cultivation of his garden fief, the pretentions of love, optimism, and also genealogy have been reduced to their rightful proportions.

AFFINITY AND ANTITHESIS IN THE VOCABULARY OF *PHÈDRE*

Stirling Haig
University of North Carolina

No one would deny that the relationships between the gods and the characters of *Phèdre* are important functions of the play's structure. The references to Venus, Neptune, and the Sun create a web of allusions that explicitly and inextricably envelops the characters in their fate. These relationships, which we might call "vertical," inasmusch as they oppose the earth and the heavens, are translated into a pattern of terrestrial, or "horizontal" antitheses. Thus Phèdre's effort to repress her illicit passion, which sets her against Venus on one plane ("C'est Vénus toute entière à sa proie attachée"), is expressed by the antithetical images of night and day: [1] "Fuyons dans la nuit infernale" evokes Phèdre's love and its overtones of incest and adultery, while her final lines, "Et la mort, à mes yeux dérobant la clarté,/ Rend au jour qu'ils souillaient, toute sa pureté" call forth the image of the Sun, associated with her longing for reason, calm, and innocence.

The imagery is then linked in every direction; many images are antithetical, but also complementary, in that all reflect, to some degree, every aspect of the agon. The purely human struggle conforms to a similar pattern, presenting several pairs of antagonists which are constantly regrouping themselves. At different points in the play, we find each character at odds with the others. Phèdre's

---

[1] See John Lapp, *Aspects of Racinian Tragedy* (Toronto, 1955), pp. 75, 132.

chief "enemy" is Hippolyte, but it is certainly Thésée too, and Aricie (whom Hippolyte loves). Thésée is at odds with Aricie because of her lineage, with Hippolyte because of his supposed betrayal, and with Phèdre for obvious reasons. Aricie's concept of *amour-conquête* leads her at one moment to regard even Hippolyte as an antagonist:

>   Mais de faire fléchir un courage inflexible,
>   De porter la douleur dans une âme insensible,
>   D'enchaîner un captif de ses fers étonné,
>   Contre un joug qui lui plaît vainement mutiné:
>   C'est là ce que je veux, c'est là ce qui m'irrite
>   (vv. 449-453).

And Hippolyte says of her: "Hippolyte en partant fuit une autre ennemie:/ Je fuis, je l'avouerai, cette jeune Aricie" (vv. 49-50).

All this says a good deal about Racine's concept of love, but it is only to point up the struggles of *Phèdre* that these lines are quoted. If the contrast that sets the characters against one another seems to be as sharp as that of black and white, the true relationship, especially that of Phèdre and Hippolyte, bears a closer analogy to that of photographic print and negative. Where the one is black, the other is indeed white, but both are essentially the same, presenting as they do the same image.[2] The vocabulary of the play strongly suggests that *Phèdre* is a tragedy of the antagonists' unwitting complicity.

At first, Hippolyte and Phèdre's opening lines seem to set them apart:

> HIPPOLYTE   Le dessein en est pris: je pars, cher Théra-
> [mène,
>   Et quitte le séjour de l'aimable Trézène
>   (vv. 1-2).
> PHÈDRE   N'allons plus avant. Demeurons, chère Œnone
>   (v. 153).

---

[2] This meeting of opposing elements strengthens the baroque reading of the play. Spitzer, basing his interpretation to a large extent on the oxymora of *Phèdre*, called it "the ideal type of a baroque tragedy..." (*Linguistics and Literary History* [Princeton, 1948], p. 119.)

Hippolyte is cast in the rôle of the oppressed, the pursued, the innocent, and Phèdre in that of oppressor, pursuer, and sinner. But the distance that separates them is that between huntress and hunted. The epithet most commonly applied to Hippolyte is *farouche* or *sauvage*, suggesting the timorous fugacity of the prey, and every mention of the verb *partir* is reserved for Hippolyte, or applied to him.[3] The counterpart of these terms would appear to be the verb *oser*. Where Hippolyte tries to avoid, to circumvent, to elude, Phèdre dares: "Contre moi-même enfin j'osai me révolter: / J'excitai mon courage à le persécuter" (vv. 291-292). Again and again, *oser* evokes a shudder of horror: "La veuve de Thésée *ose* aimer Hippolyte!" (v. 702) —"Mes fureurs au dehors ont *osé* se répandre" (v. 741)— "Moi, que j'*ose* opprimer et noircir l'innocence?" (v. 893) —"C'est moi qui sur ce fils chaste et respectueux / *Osai* jeter un œil profane, incestueux" (vv. 1623-24).

Conversely, terms that are remarkably similar hold opposite connotations for Phèdre and Hippolyte. Thus *nœud*, for Phèdre, designates entanglement:

> Quelle importune main, en formant tous ces nœuds,
> A pris soin sur mon front d'assembler mes cheveux?
> Tout m'afflige et me nuit, et conspire à me nuire
> (vv. 159-161).

Phèdre is unwillingly bound to her fate, and seeks to dissolve the knot of guilt. Thus Œnone is led to suggest that "Thésée en expirant vient de rompre les nœuds / Qui faisaient tout le crime et l'horreur de vos feux" (vv. 351-352). On the other hand, Thésée speaks of the noble "liens du sang" (v. 1011), while Hippolyte and Aricie constantly make use of the term *lien* to refer to their "innocent" love: "un si beau lien" (v. 556); "Dans quels ravissements, à votre sort liée" (v. 1377); "un lien si doux" (v. 1379).

Still other terms seem to polarize the struggle between Hippolyte and Phèdre, such as the antipodal images of the labyrinth and the forest. In the famous scene of Act II, Phèdre's confession of love for

---

[3] Even secondary characters use a vocabulary peculiar to the main ones. Thus Panope, in the same speech, uses *partir* for Hippolyte (v. 332) and *cacher* for Phèdre (v. 317).

Hippolyte, the labyrinth is laden with sexual overtones ("C'est moi, prince, c'est moi, dont l'utile secours/ Vous eût du labyrinthe enseigné les détours" (vv. 655-656),[4] and conveys the metaphorical imprisonment of Phèdre, captive in the maze of her passions. At the center of the labyrinth lies the bestial minotaur, symbol of her monstrous ascendancy. Every reference to paths and descent into the underworld suggests the sinuous topography of the labyrinth.[5] Every avenue of escape is a *cul-de-sac,* and this infernal impasse is echoed upon earth:

> Il me semble déjà que ces *murs,* que ces *voûtes*
> Vont prendre la parole, et prêts à m'accuser,
> Attendent mon époux pour le désabuser
> (vv. 854-856).

The very palace, symbol of royal mandate, damns Phèdre to immurement. Within this terrestrial prison, she can only stalk her fleeing prey, pursued in turn by the implacable Venus.

The counterpart of Phèdre's labyrinth is Hippolyte's forest. To recall happier days of carefree roaming, Théramène reminds Hippolyte that "Les forêts de nos cris moins souvent retentissent" (v. 133), and the latter also speaks of those halcyon times: "dans les forêts mon oisive jeunesse" (v. 933). The incarcerated Phèdre cries out "Dieux! que ne suis-je assise à l'ombre des forêts!" (v. 176) and upon learning that Hippolyte loves Aricie, she is tortured by the thought of their freedom: "Dans le fond des forêts allaient-ils se cacher?/ Hélas! ils se voyaient avec pleine licence" (vv. 1236-37). But these quotations illustrate either what the forest formerly stood for, or how characters other than Hippolyte conceive of it. As Hippolyte reveals to Aricie, one can hunt and also be hunted in this forest:

> Contre vous, contre moi, vainement je m'éprouve:
> Présente, je vous fuis; absente, je vous trouve;
> Dans le fond des forêts votre image me suit;
> ....
> Mon arc, mes javelots, mon char, tout m'importune;

---

[4] See J. D. Hubert, *Essai d'exégèse racinienne* (Paris, 1956), p. 208.

[5] In the *récit de Théramène,* the sea monster's "replis tortueux" again evoke the labyrinth. See Hubert, p. 205.

Je ne me souviens plus des leçons de Neptune;
Mes seuls gémissements font retentir les *bois*
(vv. 542-551).

As I have indicated, this pair of images is both antithetical and complementary. From a special point of view it sets Phèdre and Hippolyte apart, but beyond the individualized consciousness of the characters, it unites them, inasmuch as the forest is the equivalent of the labyrinth, transposed from the underworld to the earth, from the "inside" to the "outside." It suggests that *Phèdre* is a drama of hidden complicity, whose outlines can be traced throughout certain key words. As well as images and terms that oppose Phèdre to Hippolyte, we should seek those that unite them.

In Act I, the only link between Hippolyte and Phèdre would seem to be their culpability. Hippolyte's love for Aricie is illicit because it is forbidden by reasons of state, embodied in his father: "D'une tige coupable il craint un rejeton" (v. 107). Phèdre is only too aware of her transgression; speaking of her life, she says: "J'en ai trop prolongé la coupable durée" (v. 217).[6]

The aura of furtiveness that envelops the two antagonists is translated in their wary and devious references to one another. Hippolyte's oblique phrase "la fille de Minos et de Pasiphaé" finds its counterpart in Phèdre's "ce fils de l'Amazone." Both circumlocutions inscribe the characters within the circle of their ancestry, indicating the weight of heredity and the range of emotions that are crystallized in the *nom propre,* too overpowering to pronounce: "C'est toi qui l'as nommé" is Phèdre's famous reply to Œnone's direct mention of Hippolyte's name. *Nomina numina.* Hence, after the professions of guilty love, Hippolyte to Aricie, and Phèdre to Hippolyte, the nearly frenzied use of *cacher* and *silence,* words that unite the antagonists behind a common veil of secrecy.

Œnone's lies to Thésée are seconded by Hippolyte's refusal to enlighten his father as to the true nature of events that have transpired in the ironically "aimable Trézène": "je supprime un secret qui vous touche" (v. 1089). Phèdre ("Je me cachais au jour, je fuyais la lumière") and Hippolyte ("Ai-je dû mettre au jour l'opprobre

---

[6] A rapid survey reveals that *coupable* is equally applied to Phèdre and Hippolyte: to the former six times, to the latter five.

de son lit?") contract a bond of silence that links them in a shared guilt with respect to Thésée. They will share the same punishment, for Phèdre's metaphorical wound ("Ma blessure trop vive aussitôt a saigné") will be literally inflicted upon Hippolyte in the *récit de Théramène* ("Tout son corps n'est bientôt qu'une plaie"). Their complicity consists of an unconscious entente that draws them toward a common fate.

This concord is based upon a coincidence of excesses, first of action,[7] then of inaction (when confronted by Thésée). This is not the ominous silence of Nero listening to Agrippine; it is an infringement of legitimacy. The guilt of Phèdre and Hippolyte is at first the transgression of silence: "Tu frémiras d'horreur si je romps le silence," says Phèdre to Œnone. And Hippolyte to Aricie: "Puisque j'ai commencé de rompre le silence,/ Madame, il faut poursuivre." But later, silence observed anew becomes the tacit lie of omission that, unnatural as a vacuum, summons forth the physical presence of the sea monster, symbol of devouring passions, and precipitates the dénouement. The overzealous Œnone needs only her mistress's silence to deceive Thésée, who hastily misinterprets the unspeakable: "Traître, tu prétendais qu'en un lâche silence/ Phèdre ensevelirait ta brutale insolence" (vv. 1081-82). The use of the verb *ensevelir* in conjunction with *silence* is particularly inauspicious: silence prefigures death, whose monstrous cry will consume hero and heroine; and that shriek will be all the more frightening for the silence that precedes it. The symbolic irruption of the monster, ripping through Hippolyte's veil of silence ("ses gardes affligés / Imitaient son silence") is a din of "gémissements," "cris effroyables" and "mugissements." And once infringed, Phèdre's silence, literally an interdiction, inexorably leads to her death. As she comes to "rompre un injuste silence" (v. 1617), death, in the form of a Medean poison, is already coursing through her veins.[8] Silence unites Phèdre and Hippolyte in life and in death.

---

[7] As revealed in the insistent repetition of *trop*. Phèdre "laisse trop voir [ses] honteuses douleurs;" she has "un cœur trop plein," a "sang trop vil" and is "trop coupable;" similarly, she cries out to Hippolyte: "Ah! cruel, tu m'as trop entendue." Hippolyte avows to Aricie that he is "engagé trop avant," and his father tells him "à te condamner tu m'as trop engagé."

[8] This poison is of course the literal echo of an earlier, figurative use of *poison:*

In the end the monster of passion, weaving fateful strands that only Atropos can sever, ensnares both characters. The progressively significant use of the word *monstre* (descriptive, then moral, and finally symbolic) approximates the unwitting collusion and its advance. In *Phèdre*, *monstre* is a terrifyingly mysterious vocable that ought never to be uttered, lest its very articulation conjure the presence of some tenebrous god. Thus the double-edged irony of Phèdre's "Délivre l'univers d'un monstre qui t'irrite" (v. 701) or Hippolyte's "Souffrez, si quelque monstre a pu vous échapper,/ Que j'apporte à vos pieds sa dépouille honorable" (vv. 948-949).

The growing dramatic intensity of *Phèdre* is in large measure the result of the multiple uses of terms such as the ones I have examined. Some of them, apparently antithetical, are seen to be complementary upon closer scrutiny. Still others reveal a hidden identity of fate. The graveyard temple at the gates of Trézène stands as a symbol of Phèdre's and Hippolyte's common destiny, where the characters expiate their trespasses and find release in death:

> Aux portes de Trézène, et parmi ces tombeaux,
> Des princes de ma race antiques sépultures,
> Est un temple sacré formidable aux parjures.
> C'est là que les mortels n'osent jurer en vain.
> Le perfide y reçoit un châtiment soudain;
> Et craignant d'y trouver la mort inévitable,
> Le mensonge n'a point de frein plus redoutable
> (vv. 1392-98).

The homologous usage of *monstre, silence, coupable* and other terms constitutes a pattern of lexical analogies structuring the play's movement along parallels that merge into the infinity of death.

> J'aime. Ne pense pas qu'au moment que je t'aime,
> Innocente à mes yeux, je m'approuve moi-même,
> Ni que du fol amour qui trouble ma raison
> Ma lâche complaisance ait nourri le poison (vv. 673-676).

LES COMMENTAIRES DE CHARLES PÉGUY SUR *POLYEUCTE*

Jacques Hardré
University of North Carolina

L'oeuvre en prose de Charles Péguy contient d'innombrables références à la littérature classique, celle de l'antiquité grecque et celle de la France. Dès son entrée au lycée de la ville d'Orléans, Péguy avait découvert chez Homère, Sophocle et Eschyle, mais aussi chez Corneille, Racine et Pascal, un monde jeune et neuf qui l'avait ébloui. Sa vie durant, il se tournera tout naturellement vers les sources antiques soit pour nourrir sa haine du monde moderne,[1] soit pour comparer à un événement contemporain son répondant ancien.[2] Lorsqu'il tombe malade, en 1908, il en profite pour relire Pascal et lorsqu'il se met à méditer sur la grâce c'est dans *Polyeucte*, plutôt que dans un traité de théologie, qu'il cherche son inspiration.

De tous les classiques c'est Corneille qui a retenu le plus l'attention de Péguy:

> "Quoi qu'ils en disent, quoi qu'ils en pensent même peut-être, les Français sont généralement cornéliens. Et d'autre part comme il n'y a que les Français qui soient assez fins

---

[1] "Ces modernes manquent d'âme... Le monde antique ne manquait point d'âme... Il était plein, il était nourri de l'âme la plus pieuse, la plus pure, il faut dire le mot, la plus sacrée." (*Clio, dialogue de l'histoire et de l'âme païenne*, dans *Œuvres en prose, 1909-1914*, Paris: Bibliothèque de la Pléiade, 1957). Les citations dans le texte prises dans cette édition seront dorénavant indiquées par le sigle *O.E.P.*

[2] Voir, par exemple *Les suppliants parallèles*, Cahiers de la Quinzaine, VII, 7, 17 décembre 1905, où Péguy fait le rapprochement entre les événements de la révolution russe et *Œdipe-Roi*.

pour être raciniens, il suit qu'en réalité il y a beaucoup moins de raciniens que de cornéliens" (*Victor-Marie, Comte Hugo, O. E. P.*, p. 770).

À maintes reprises, que ce soit dans *de Jean Coste* ou dans *Clio*, dans *Victor-Marie, Comte Hugo* ou dans la *Note conjointe sur M. Descartes et la philosophie cartésienne*, Péguy revient inlassablement sur la grandeur de Corneille et célèbre en particulier l'auteur de *Polyeucte*.[3]

Pour comprendre cette prédilection, il faut se rappeler d'abord la conception péguyste de l'héroïsme. Bien que Péguy n'ait jamais donné une définition de l'héroïsme mais plutôt des définitions multiples, on peut, en se rappelant les incarnations de héros qu'il étudie dans son œuvre, dégager les traits saillants de ce qu'il entendait par cette qualité. Comme nous le fait remarquer Rosemary Goldie:

"Âme cornélienne, accordée naturellement à la 'cité harmonieuse', mais profondément racinée dans une réalité concrète et actuelle, fils de la France chrétienne —de sa terre laborieuse, de son peuple fidèle et de son âme ardente— Péguy vit entouré d'héroïsmes incarnés qui sont pour lui au moins aussi réels que tout ce qu'il flétrit du nom de 'monde moderne'. Son 'héros', c'est le républicain qui ne se paie pas de mots, qui vient respirer à pleins poumons l'air de la liberté; c'est le citoyen fidèle à sa 'mystique' — le dreyfusard de la première et de la dernière heure; c'est le soldat, Psichari, qui 'joue sa vie' pour la France, pour la paix, par les armes; c'est Rodrigue, Horace, Sévère et, au-dessus d'eux, c'est Polyeucte, le 'saint' qui ne leur cède en aucune des vertus héroïques de l''honnête homme'. C'est Saint Louis. C'est avant tout Jeanne d'Arc ...Enfin, au-dessus de toutes ces fidélités, de tous ces héroïsmes vécus que Péguy a célébrés, Celui que l'on entrevoit, c'est le Christ, leur source à tous: Vérité, Justice, Amour et Vie.

---

[3] Péguy aurait approuvé le jugement du critique anglais Edmund Gosse: "the profoundest of all religious tragedies... that *Polyeucte* which we English have enviously to admire in the literature of France." (R. Garnett and E. Gosse, *An Illustrated History of English Literature*, N.Y., MacMillan, 1935, Vol. III, p. 7.)

L'héroïsme —un héroïsme pleinement humain— c'est bien ici le point de départ, mais il s'agit toujours d'un héroïsme qui ne demande qu'à être 'porté à l'éternel'." [4]

Il faut se rappeler également que Péguy admirait dans le héros cornélien l'absence de cruauté (cette cruauté qu'il trouve par contre dans tous les héros et dans toutes les héroïnes du théâtre racinien), leur libéralité de cœur, et ce qu'il nomme leur "impotence de mal." Ce sont ces qualités, dit-il, qui expliquent que "Corneille était tiré de toutes parts vers *Polyeucte*. Il était conduit, il montait de toutes parts vers *Polyeucte*. Par toute cette grâce dont son œuvre est pleine; par tout son héroïsme; par vingt autres montées." (*O. E. P.*, p. 778.)

Dans *Victor-Marie, Comte Hugo*, [5] Péguy développe, à son tour, le parallèle de Corneille et de Racine. Il constate que "Corneille ne travaille jamais que dans le domaine de la grâce et que Racine ne travaille jamais que dans le domaine de la disgrâce." Puis, se tournant vers l'ordonnance des pièces de ces deux auteurs, il nous fait remarquer que l'ordonnance "impeccable," "intelligente," "harmonieuse" de Racine recouvre souvent "les pires désordres organiques"; tandis que chez Corneille on trouve "un ordre profond, un ordre de race, un ordre de chair même."

De plus, Racine faisait toujours "la même tragédie, qui était toujours un pur chef-d'œuvre ... qui est proprement *la* tragédie racinienne." Ainsi la tragédie racinienne n'est nullement "une construction, une structure organique ... Toutes les tragédies de Racine se couronnent chacune d'elle-même ... sont des sœurs alignées qui se ressemblent." Par contre, les tragédies de Corneille, et notamment *Le Cid, Horace* et *Cinna*: "d'un seul et même et triple geste comme des cariatides se couronnent en *Polyeucte*."

Selon Péguy, en effet, ces quatre pièces traduisent une accélération intérieure qui, prenant son point de départ dans *Le Cid*, s'achève et culmine en *Polyeucte*. L'héroïsme chrétien et chevaleresque de Rodrigue se trouve promu en l'héroïsme, et en la chevalerie, de sainteté de Polyeucte. Aux stances du *Cid* répondent, mais à un degré supérieur, en passant du registre héroïque au registre sacré, les stances de *Polyeucte*.

---

[4] *Vers un héroïsme intégal: Dans la lignée de Péguy*, Cahiers de l'Amitié Charles Péguy, 1951, pp. 24-25.
[5] *O.E.P.* pp. 770 passim.

Horace, d'autre part, apporte l'héroïsme civique; non plus l'honneur chevaleresque et guerrier, mais l'héroïsme militaire civique. Et ceci, dans *Polyeucte,* sera promu en héroïsme de la cité céleste. De même que Rome est l'origine et le germe de l'Empire romain, ainsi celui-ci est la charpente charnelle du monde chrétien. De même donc, l'héroïsme civique de *Horace* prépare celui de *Polyeucte* qui s'applique non plus à la charnelle cité, mais à la Cité intemporelle.

Finalement, *Cinna* pose les principes de la paix romaine, de la clémence romaine, de la force, de la loi et du droit romains, principes qui seront repris dans *Polyeucte* et qui serviront de soubassements au spirituel et à l'éternel de *Polyeucte.* L'Empire romain, encore une fois, fournissant la charpente matérielle du monde chrétien.

Ainsi, au lieu de trouver comme dans le théâtre de Racine, une suite de pièces alignées les unes après les autres, Péguy trouve dans le théâtre de Corneille une merveilleuse progression dans les pièces majeures, chacune apportant sa contribution à celle qui les couronne, à la tragédie chrétienne de *Polyeucte.*

Dans la *Note conjointe sur M. Descartes et la philosophie cartésienne,*[6] Péguy a consacré plusieurs pages à un nouvel examen de Corneille et, en particulier, à une nouvelle appréciation de *Polyeucte.* Dans les pages qui précèdent cette étude, Péguy s'était livré à une comparaison entre Saint-Louis et Philippe le Bel, le premier représentant la sainteté et la probité, le second le commerce et la politique; le premier ayant joué "un noble jeu," le second "un jeu de bassesse." Cette considération mène Péguy, par une association d'idées qui ne surprend nullement ceux habitués à sa pensée, à déclarer:

> "Tant que l'on parlera le langage français Corneille demeurera le poète de ce noble jeu... Tant que le français sera parlé et plus tard peut-être aussi longtemps que le français sera lu et sera la troisième langue classique Corneille sera et le théoricien et le philosophe autant que le poète du noble jeu."[7]

---

[6] *O.E.P.,* pp. 1301-1496.
[7] Ibid., p. 1380.

D'abord, continue Péguy, il ne faut pas faire l'erreur de croire que le théâtre de Corneille soit uniquement celui d'un conflit entre le devoir et la passion, où le premier, représentant la grandeur et la noblesse, triomphe de la seconde qui représente la faiblesse et la bassesse. Car l'amour de Rodrigue et de Chimène, pas plus que l'amour de Polyeucte et de Pauline, n'est ni une faiblesse ni une bassesse. C'est plutôt "un débat tragique ... entre une grandeur et une autre grandeur, entre une noblesse et une autre noblesse, entre l'honneur et l'amour." En plus, ce "débat tragique" n'est pas un combat inégal puisqu'il a lieu entre deux grandeurs de même ordre. C'est en ce sens donc, dit Péguy, que la poétique de Corneille "est essentiellement une poétique du noble jeu." Tandis que le romantisme repose sur l'impair, le décalé et le porte à faux, le classicisme (et le cornélien) repose sur le pair, le comparable et le loyal. Le débat tragique est bien entre l'honneur et l'amour mais "c'est un débat pénétré et compénétré." Et Péguy continue par cette affirmation qui nous fait mieux comprendre son admiration pour *Polyeucte:*

> "Car, et nous atteignons ici au secret même, au point de secret de la poétique et du génie de Corneille: l'honneur est aimé d'amour, l'amour est honoré d'honneur." [8]

Ainsi, dans le théâtre de Corneille le combat constant se livre à égalité, et le seul ennemi véritable c'est la fraude. "Ce qu'il y a de plus fort et de plus grand dans *Polyeucte,* c'est certainement l'absence totale de fraude pieuse; et de cette exécrable dévotion frauduleuse." [9]

Dans cette tragédie, Péguy nous fait remarquer, Corneille n'a pas cherché à rehausser celui (Polyeucte) qui soutient la bonne cause, en rabaissant ceux qui soutiennent la cause adverse. "Nul ne sera diminué pour que les autres paraissent plus grands... Le saint, le martyr s'élèvera de toute sa hauteur au-dessus de l'homme et ce n'est pas l'homme qui aura baissé."

Ceci explique l'humanité profonde de *Polyeucte* ainsi que la bonté et la tendresse qu'on y trouve. Car il n'y a pas seulement

---

[8] *O.E.P.,* p. 1382.
[9] Ibid., p. 1385-1386.

la tragédie sacrée, mais il y a aussi la tragédie profane, celle de Pauline et de Sévère, dans *Polyeucte*. Et le génie de Corneille est tel que cette tragédie sous-jacente qui, pour Péguy, représente encore mieux que *Le Cid* la grande tragédie profane cornélienne, est masquée par la tragédie sacrée. Si cette dernière était ôtée on s'apercevrait alors que la tragédie de Pauline et de Sévère est "la plus gracieuse et la plus grave et la plus sacrée tragédie profane de l'amour que nous ayons."

Péguy admire ainsi que dans cinq actes Corneille ait réussi à présenter deux mondes superposés, à développer simultanément deux tragédies, l'une profane, l'autre sacrée, et toutes deux également profondes; mais l'une, comme il se devait, reposant et s'élevant sur l'autre. Et toutes deux également légitimes, c'est-à-dire, fondées sur l'honneur. Sévère est un stoïcien, un chevalier et un galant homme. Polyeucte se doit donc de le traiter comme tel et de ne point lui céder en honneur. Selon Pascal, Péguy nous le rappelle, le stoïcisme était "le pôle de pensée et de système de l'héroïque et du sacré dans un monde profane... de lui étaient sortis ce qui dans le registre antique répondait à ce que sont dans le registre chrétien les saints et les martyrs: les héros et peut-être faut-il aussi dire les martyrs." Sévère est donc un stoïcien et est estimé, honoré et admiré en tant que tel par Polyeucte. Péguy commente longuement cette attitude de Polyeucte envers Sévère, en insistant sur le fait que la grandeur du premier repose "sur le dépassement et non sur l'ignorance de la grandeur païenne." Polyeucte voit en Sévère non point un rival, mais un combattant, un "partenaire digne de lui." Étant lui-même un chevalier chrétien, il voit en Sévère un chevalier romain et le combat qui les engage comme un combat "intégralement loyal." Or, dans ce combat il importe que Polyeucte vainque non pas devant Dieu, ou devant les saints et les martyrs, mais bien devant Sévère lui-même; qu'il agisse de telle sorte que Sévère arrive à regretter "que Polyeucte ne soit pas demeuré païen." Il faut que Sévère qui est habitué au païen soit atteint dans son seul point vulnérable: le point d'inhabitude à considérer que Polyeucte soit chrétien. Car, en termes bergsoniens, c'est ce point d'inhabitude qui est le seul point d'entrée "par lequel nous puissions espérer que la grâce puisse passer jamais." Il importe donc que Polyeucte vainque de telle sorte que Sévère soit touché par l'image de Polyeucte, une image païenne, puisque c'est la seule que Sévère puisse comprendre, une image de grandeur et une image d'honneur, mais qu'en même temps Sévère soit frappé par la pensée qu'un homme qui projette une telle image soit devenu chrétien. C'est par ce point de scandale que Sévère est vulnérable, et c'est par cette blessure que pourra pénétrer la grâce.

Et ainsi l'argument de Péguy rejoint son point de départ. Car il retrouve ce système et cette politique de Polyeucte chez Saint-Louis, pour qui il ne suffisait pas d'être roi de France devant ses barons, ou devant Dieu, mais aussi devant les infidèles, et chez Jeanne d'Arc à qui il ne suffisait pas d'avoir raison devant son Roi et devant Dieu, mais aussi devant l'ennemi. De même que Sévère voulait imposer une image à Sévère dans les termes que ce dernier pouvait comprendre, ainsi Saint-Louis et Jeanne d'Arc voulaient mener leur combat dans "les règles de l'honneur et du combat courtois." C'est encore une fois le "noble jeu" que Péguy salue et qu'il admire tellement dans le théâtre de Corneille.

Que Péguy ait souhaité, hanté comme il l'était par cet exemple, écrire lui-même un *Polyeucte* ne saurait nous étonner. Au début de sa carrière d'éditeur des *Cahiers de la Quinzaine*, il avait conçu l'idée de préparer une édition de luxe de *Polyeucte*, mais, faute de souscripteurs, avait dû abandonner ce projet. Plus tard, dans *Victor-Marie, Comte Hugo*, il écrit: "Quand nous ferons notre *Polyeucte* (vous n'avez jamais douté que nous le ferons)..." Ceci date de 1910. En 1913, quand Péguy écrit *Ève*, il a constamment devant lui l'exemple de *Polyeucte*, et la première ligne dictée à Joseph Lotte pour l'article que celui-ci allait consacrer à *Ève* commence ainsi: "*Polyeucte* excepté, que Péguy nous a enseigné à mettre au-dessus de tout...".

Le sort a voulu que Péguy n'écrive jamais *son Polyeucte*; du moins nous a-t-il laissé ses commentaires sur la tragédie cornélienne, commentaires profonds et perspicaces qui nous aident à mieux mesurer et apprécier le génie de Pierre Corneille.

BONAVENTURE DES PÉRIERS ABROAD [*]

J. WOODROW HASSELL, JR.
University of Georgia

Born around 1510, it is believed, Bonaventure des Périers died at an undetermined date between May 1, 1543, and August 31, 1544. After assisting in the preparation of Olivetan's translation of the Bible (1535) and of the first volume of Estienne Dolet's *Commentarii linguae latinae* (1536), he was employed by Marguerite de Navarre, whom he served as a *valet de chambre*. He left to posterity a number of poems, a translation of the *Lysis* of Plato, four philosophic dialogues after the manner of Lucian entitled the *Cymbalum mundi*, and a collection of short stories published under the title of *Les nouvelles Récréations et joyeux devis*.

We are reasonably well informed about the popularity and influence in France of Des Périers' works, although, to be sure, the last word has certainly not yet been said on this subject. However, the problem of his popularity and influence abroad, that is to say outside France, has been almost completely neglected until relatively recently, and even now much remains to be learned. It is the purpose of this essay to present the principal facts that are known, adding a few data which have not previously been noted.

It should be made clear at the outset that we are concerned here primarily with the questions of how widely Des Périers' writings have been read by people of other than French origin, of the influence that his works have exerted upon foreign authors,

---

[*] This is a revised and expanded form of a paper that was presented November 11, 1966, before the French I Section of the South Atlantic Modern Language Association.

and of the reputation that he has enjoyed abroad. Such peripheral matters as the use of Des Périers' writings as source materials for scholarly compositions and the contributions made by non-French nationals to Des Périers scholarship are beyond the scope of this paper.

It will be helpful as we proceed with this discussion to bear in mind what happened in France to Des Périers' works during the sixteenth and early seventeenth centuries. The *Recueil des œuvres*, which includes the *Lysis* translation and most of the preserved poems, was published in Lyon by Jean de Tournes in 1544 but was not republished until much later; a few poems were published separately during the sixteenth century, and one is preserved in a manuscript of that period, BN ms. fonds fr. 1667, ff. 252-54. The *Cymbalum mundi* was suppressed so rigorously that for all practical purposes it did not exist until the eighteenth century; one copy of the first (1537) edition, preserved at the Bibliothèque de Versailles, a very few copies of the second (1538), such as those owned by the Bibliothèque nationale and the Musée Condé at Chantilly, and a sixteenth century manuscript copy apparently made from the first edition (see Domenico Ciàmpoli, *I Codici francesi della R. Biblioteca nazionale di S. Marco in Venezia.* ...[Venice, 1897], pp. 177-78, no. LXVII) appear to be all that survive of the *Cymbalum mundi* from the centuries preceding the eighteenth. The short stories, on the other hand, were in the best seller category during the second half of the sixteenth century and the first decades of the seventeenth.

On the basis of the data currently available to us we must conclude that Des Périers' works have been more widely read and more influential in the English-speaking world, and particularly in England, than elsewhere.

In 1581 George North published ([London]: Henry Binneman, 1581) an anti-Catholic propaganda work entitled *The Stage of Popish Toyes*. Derived for the most part from Henri Estienne's *Apologie pour Hérodote*, this little book contains two passages which almost certainly were adapted from Des Périers' tale collection; one (p. 15 of *The Stage of Popish Toyes*) is a version of the French writer's *nouvelle* VII, an anecdote about an ignorant Norman who seeks ordination into the priesthood at the hands of the Pope; the other (pp. 16-17 of *The Stage*) is a free translation of the first two anecdotes of *nouvelle* XL. (Curiously enough, notes in the margin of *The Stage* attribute both these passages to Straparola, among whose tales these anecdotes do not appear.)

Two years after the publication of *The Stage of Popish Toyes*, i.e., in 1583, there appeared from the London presses of Roger Warde a translation into English of thirty-nine of Des Périers' tales, bearing the title of *The Mirrour of Mirth and Pleasant Conceits*. There is some evidence to indicate that the translator may have been the ballad writer and novelist Thomas Deloney. Under the same title but in abbreviated and slightly edited form, this translation was reprinted in London by John Danter in 1592. Today only one copy of each of these Elizabethan editions survives, but a critical edition of *The Mirrour* was published by the University of South Carolina Press in 1959.

In almost identical language the title pages of the two sixteenth century editions of *The Mirrour* credit Des Périers with its authorship and, indeed, refer to him as "that Worshipfull and learned Gentleman Bonaduenture de Periers, Groom to the right excellent and vertuous Princesse, the Queene of Nauara."

Evidence of the popularity of *The Mirrour* and further evidence of Des Périers' appeal to English readers is found in the jestbook published in London by R. Blower in 1613 and bearing the title of *Scoggins Iestes*. Ten of the stories in this collection were lifted almost word for word from *The Mirrour of Mirth*, without any acknowledgment of the source (see *Mediaeval Studies in Honor of Urban Tigner Holmes, Jr.*, [Chapel Hill, 1965], pp. 79-88).

Des Périers seems to have enjoyed a rather "mixed press" in Elizabethan and Jacobean England. If, as we have seen, he is referred to deferentially on the title page of *The Mirrour*, he was also the object of less generous comment from such writers as Thomas Lodge and Thomas Beard. The former in his *Wit's Miserie* (1596) violently condemns Des Périers, along with Bouchet and Rabelais, as follows:

> ... hée that longs to know more of him [*i. e.* of "Scurilitie"] let him read Bouchets *Serees*, and if hée find a leafe without a grosse ieast hée may burne the Book I warrant him. And if he require further insight into the filthy nature of this fiend, in Artine in his mother Nana, Rabelais in

his Legend of Ribaudrie, and Bonauenture de Perriers in his Nouels, he shall be sure to loose his time, and no doubt, corrupt his soule.[1]

And in Thomas Beard's *The Theatre of God's Judgements* (1597, reprinted in 1612), we find the following passage:

> How miserable was the end of *Periers*, the author of that detestable book intituled *Symbalum mundi*, wherein he openly mocked at God and his religion: euen hee fell finally into despaire, and notwithstanding all that guarded him killed himselfe.[2]

That this is simply a paraphrase of the two passages in the *Apologie pour Hérodote* in which Estienne tells of Des Périers' death [3] confirms what we had every reason to suspect, namely, that Beard had not seen a copy of the *Cymbalum mundi* and had no direct knowledge of the circumstances of Des Périers' decease. However, valid or not, Beard's statement certainly helped to disseminate Estienne's uncharitable opinions about Des Périers.

In evaluating Lodge's observations quoted above, we must recognize that he could have read Des Périers' "novels." However, the intemperate language of the Englishman's remarks is certainly not warranted by the innocuous character of the tales, particularly when judged by Elizabethan standards, and I think we must see in the Englishman's attitude a reflection of the violent hostility to Des Périers that prevailed among continental Calvinists.

In 1607 the London printer John Norton published under the title of *A World of Wonders* a translation of Henri Estienne's *Apologie pour Hérodote*, and this translation was reissued the following year (1608) in Edinburgh. Included were, to be sure, the passages in which Estienne vents his spleen upon the deceased Des Périers (chapters XVIII and XXVI).

For the period of almost a hundred years bounded by 1613 and 1712 I have found nothing to indicate that Des Périers was known

---

[1] Thomas Lodge, *The Complete Works...* (New York, 1963), IV, 88-89.
[2] Thomas Beard, *The Theatre of God's Judgements* (London, 1597), pp. 143-44.
[3] Chapters XVIII and XXVI.

or his works read in England. This circumstance can be explained in part by the fact that while Des Périers seems never to have fallen into complete oblivion in France, there was a significant decrease in his popularity with the French reading public of the last three quarters of the seventeenth century and the first decade of the eighteenth; this situation certainly did not stimulate British interest in our author. Moreover, the political, religious and social conditions prevailing under the Stuart rulers and during the Protectorate were not favorable for the dissemination of Des Périers' works. It is therefore probable that he was in fact little known and his works generally ignored in seventeenth century England. However, it is distinctly possible that as in the France of this time so in England Des Périers was read and appreciated by a limited group of discriminating readers. It is to be hoped that further research will shed light upon this question.

Early in the eighteenth century there was in France a notable revival of interest in Des Périers. Editions of his short stories were issued in 1711 and 1735, and of the *Cymbalum mundi* in 1711, 1732, and 1753; moreover, four of his poems were included in Sautreau de Marsy's *Annales poétiques* (Paris, 1778-88), III, 221-30. Des Périers and his works were also fairly frequently mentioned by French intellectuals.

This renewed interest spread quickly across the Channel. In 1712 a translation of the Prosper Marchand edition of the *Cymbalum mundi* was published in London; a copy could be purchased for one shilling. Apparently the venture was a financial success, for another translation appeared in London in 1723. According to Professor Nurse, who published a brief study of these translations in 1959, the work of the two anonymous translators was generally accurate, "mais ils n'ont su transmettre toute l'animation et la verve qui font la gloire des dialogues français, écrits dans ce qu'on a justement appelé 'cette bonne et luxuriante et fringante langue française d'avant les Vaugelas et les Boileau-Despréaux'." [4]

---

[4] Peter H. Nurse, "Le *Cymbalum mundi* en Angleterre." *Bibliothèque d'humanisme et Renaissance* 21: 206, 1959.

Perhaps of greater interest to students of Anglo-French literary relations is Horace Walpole's poetic adaptation of Des Périers' *nouvelle* LXXXVII, "De la pie et de ses piauz." In his "Short Notes" for 1764, Walpole included the following entry:

> Oct. 15, wrote the 'Fable of the Magpie and her Brood' for Miss Hotham, then near eleven years old, great-niece of Henrietta Hobart Countess Dowager of Suffolk. It was taken from *Les nouvelles ré[c]réations de Bonaventure des Périers,* valet-de-chambre to the Queen of Navarre. [5]

According to the *Journal of the Printing-Office at Strawberry Hill* (London, 1923), p. 13, two hundred copies of the "Fable" were printed on Oct. 17, 1764. There was also a nineteenth-century reprint of uncertain date. [6]

On Oct. 30, 1764, Walpole sent from Strawberry Hill to his friend the Rev. William Cole a brief note with which he enclosed a copy of the newly printed "Fable." On November 4 Cole replied; included in his letter is the following paragraph:

> I heartily thank you for that elegant pretty piece of poetry you was [sic] so kind to send me in your last. Bonaventure des Periers [sic] will be obliged to you for introducing him to so much advantage into our language. Your introduction is elegant beyond expression, and the tale is told in words the most natural and numbers the most harmonious, easy and spirited that can be conceived. I shall never see a magpie but I shall think of
>
> Go, cater where you list. [7]

A few years later Edward Capell reprinted in incomplete form the English translation of *nouvelle* XII which appears in *The Mirrour of Mirth,* [8] and roughly a century and a half afterwards F. P. Wilson published the same text in a scholarly article. [9]

---

[5] *The Yale Edition of Horace Walpole's Correspondence,* ed. W. S. Lewis (New Haven, 1937—), XIII, 41.

[6] See A. T. Hazen, *A Bibliography of the Strawberry Hill Press* (New Haven, 1942), p. 194.

[7] *The Yale Edition of Horace Walpole's Correspondence,* I, 79-82.

[8] E. Capell, *Notes and Various Readings to Shakespeare* (London, 1779-83[?]), III, 77.

[9] F. P. Wilson, "The English Jestbooks of the Sixteenth and Early Seventeenth Centuries." *The Huntington Library Quarterly* 2: 139-40, 1938-39.

More recently, John A. Rea's translation of *nouvelle* XXXII appeared under the title of "Cock of the Walk" in the popular American magazine *Playboy* (6:63, 1959).

Soon afterwards *nouvelle* XIX, the amusing account of the troubles of the "savetier Blondeau," found a place in a textbook for American students of French, the *Contes de plusieurs siècles*, ed. R. W. Linker and G. B. Daniel (New York, 1964), pp. 26-29. Fifteen of Des Périers' *nouvelles* (I, III, IV, V, VII, X, XVI, XX, XXI, XXII, XXIII, XXIV, XLI, XLV, and XLIX) appear in the anthology edited by A. J. Krailsheimer for the Oxford University Press and published in 1966 under the title *Three Sixteenth-Century Conteurs*. (While in these school texts the tales are presented in the French language, the purpose of the editors is obviously to introduce the stories and their authors to readers of other nationalities; consequently, these collections deserve mention here.)

Finally, mention must be made of the English translation of the *Cymbalum mundi* recently published by Bettina L. Knapp (New York, 1965).

Except for Holland and Germany I have found nothing of significance to report on Des Périers' popularity and influence outside the countries that we have been considering. Four of his *nouvelles* (V, X, LXVIII, and LXXII) and one of those that have been incorrectly attributed to him (CXXII) were translated into Dutch and published in Franz Loockman's *LXXI lustige Historien* (Antwerp, 1589).[10]

In 1906 Jakob Ulrich published in Leipzig the first volume of a projected two volume critical anthology of French Renaissance narrative literature entitled *Proben der französischen Novellistik des sechzehnten Jahrhunderts*. Included are selections from the works of eleven French authors; Des Périers is represented by twenty-eighth *nouvelles*, nine of which are, however, spurious. As I recall, the texts are all in French, but since the work clearly represents an attempt to introduce to German readers the authors whose

---

[10] Johannes Bolte, "Beiträge zur Geschichte der erzählenden Litteratur des 16. Jahrhunderts." *Tijdschrift voor nederlandsche Taal- en Letterkunde* 13: 2-3, 7-8, 1894.

writings appear in this anthology, I have judged it worthy of mention here.

Four years later there appeared what is to my knowledge the only complete translation into a foreign language of Des Périers' tales. Under the title of *Die neuen Schwänke und lustigen Unterhaltungen gefolgt von der Weltbimmel,* Hanns Floerke published in 1910 in Munich and Leipzig a translation of both the *nouvelles* and the *Cymbalum mundi.* The accompanying relatively elaborate critical apparatus renders this translation an excellent edition.

The data which have just been presented warrant certain conclusions, some of which are well established, while others must necessarily be considered tentative:

1. Des Périers' poetry and the *Lysis* translation have been almost totally unknown outside France, except to academicians.

2. The short stories became known in England and Holland during or before the 1580's, when some of them were translated into the languages of these countries. That they found better fortune in England than in Holland is indicated by the appearance of the two editions of *The Mirrour of Mirth* and by the borrowings from it that we find in the *Scoggin's Iestes* of 1613. Later, in the twentieth century, the *nouvelles* were presented to the general reading public of Germany.

3. Continental Calvinist influence in general and that of Henri Estienne in particular gave Des Périers a dubious reputation in England. While we find the title *Cymbalum mundi* mentioned by a few Elizabethan authors, it may be considered certain that the work itself remained unknown in the British Isles until the eighteenth century.

4. Des Périers seems to have been forgotten in England between 1613 and 1712 but enjoyed a renewed popularity during the Age of Enlightenment. Interestingly enough, the *Cymbalum mundi* was a greater commercial success than any of Des Périers' other works; from an artistic standpoint, the compliment that Walpole paid Des Périers by adapting one of his *nouvelles* is significant.

5. The great enthusiasm for Des Périers' works that developed in France during the nineteenth century found no significant echo abroad. While meritorious attempts have been made in our own century to present the *Nouvelles Récréations* and the *Cymbalum mundi* to the general reading public of England, Germany, and the United States, it would appear that since the eighteenth century Des Périers' non-French readers have been primarily academicians.

MONTAIGNE'S SPAS

URBAN T. HOLMES
University of North Carolina

The late Erich Auerbach suggested in his book *Mimesis* that the essayist Montaigne may have been seeking to create a *Person* —in the way that Plato fashioned his image of Socrates— and that he was not always portraying a frank image of himself in the frank and homey admissions which we delight in reading.[1] It is difficult for some to give much credence to this. In any case we can be certain that in the description of his suffering from the stone Montaigne meant what he said.

It is in his Essay 37 of Bk. II: "Of the Resemblance of children to Fathers" that Montaigne becomes most eloquent on the subject of his malady.[2] He asserts that he began his Essays some eight years before and that it was then eighteen months since he was afflicted with his "colicky ailment." This was in 1578 when he was forty-five years of age. "And moreover, how did it remain so concealed that I began to feel it forty-five years later, the only one to this hour out of so many brothers and sisters, and all of the same mother?" He goes on to say that he has an antipathy to doctors — perhaps inherited from his father; but he does not despise medicines. The physicians are full of contradictions. On almost any point of remedies and health they argue from opposite camps. "They go juggling and trifling at our expense in all their reasonings. And they could not provide me with one proposition to which I

---

[1] Ch. 11. Willard Trask tr. (Anchor Books), p. 246.
[2] I am quoting from the translation by Donald M. Frame (Stanford University Press, 1958).

could not construct a contrary one of equal force. So let people no longer cry out at those who, in this confusion let themselves be gently led by their appetite and the advice of nature, and commit themselves to the common lot." And then in his final Essay ("Of Experience") Montaigne adds "We should give free passage to diseases. Let us give Nature a chance... Why cannot the heat of my kidneys be... weakened; so that they can no longer petrify my phlegm, and nature may take steps to find some other way of purgation?... It is only fools that let themselves be persuaded that this hard, solid body that is baked in our kidneys can be dissolved by potions."

To return to the Essay of "Resemblance of Children to Fathers":

> As for drinking the waters, it is natural and simple, and at least is not dangerous, even if it is useless. I take as warrant for this the infinite number of people of all sorts and constitutions who assemble there... I have hardly seen any people whom these waters make worse, and it cannot without malice be denied that they arouse the appetite, facilitate digestion and lend us some new blitheness, if we do not go there beaten down in strength, which I advise against doing. They are not able to restore a ponderous ruin; they can prop up a slight leaning or provide against the threat of some deterioration... For this reason I have up to now chosen to stay in and make use of those which are most pleasantly situated and which offer the most advantages in lodging, food and company. Such are in France the baths of Bagnères; on the frontier of Germany and Lorraine, those of Plombières; in Switzerland those of Baden; in Tuscany, those of Lucca, especially those of La Villa — which I have used most often and at different seasons.

Indeed, and now I am using my own words, it was the very next year after the penning of these remarks just quoted that Montaigne made an extensive journey to three of these baths. As M. Piéry has written in the *Histoire Générale de la Médecine* of Laignel-Lavastine: "Le récit de ce voyage, qui nous apporte son aperçu pittoresque et fidèle des stations balnéaires et des mœurs thermales, nous montre le célèbre philosophe promenant sa gravelle de Plombières à Bade, de Lucques aux bains d'Albano, en donnant sa préférence aux eaux où se trouve le plus d'aménité, de bien, de commodité, de loges, de vivres, et de compagnie."

This "récit où il promène sa gravelle" is, of course, the famous *Travel Journey* which is read less often by devotees of Montaigne — which gives a fascinating account of his thoughts and habits when in direct contact with the world. For one concerned with daily life in the Sixteenth Century this particular narrative is a gem. Thomas Giunta in his volume called *Collectio de Balneis* (Venice 1553), which lists over one hundred spas (within a thousand pages), mentions that many of these health centers were first opened by the Romans. The one at Baden is supposed to go back to the year 61 B. C. Ancient physicians were not unanimous as to what is the cause of disease. (Montaigne cites Hierophilus, Erasistratus, Asclepiades, Alcmaeon, Diocles, Strato, and Hippocrates on this controversy.) The two more prominent theories were that of the Methodists (in medicine not religion) who believed that disease meant a part of the body had undue tension or relaxation, and the followers of Hierophilus and Galen who attributed illness to a lack of balance in the four humors. It is easy to believe that the ancient Methodists saw great virtue in the hot and tepid waters of the springs. Prolonged bathing was a means for easing tension. The Galenists required the strange smelling water to be taken internally, believing that a natural medicinal compound would bring erring humors back into line. Even so in Montaigne's time, and till the present day, these uses for the waters have continued. In Montaigne's period the relief of tension was heightened by the practice of scarification. While sitting in the bath a number of small cuts would be made together on the arm or leg and be cupped. Montaigne says of Baden: "The people of the region use it principally for bathing, during which they have themselves cupped and bled so heavily that I have sometimes seen the two public baths [at Baden] look like pure blood." [3] But many drank. Montaigne goes on to say that he drank seven little glasses from this spa, the day after arrival; the next day five big glasses "which amounted to ten of the little ones and might make a pint."

---

[3] Travel Journal. Frame tr., p. 883.

This same Tuesday morning at nine o'clock, while the others were dining, he got into the bath and after coming out sweated very hard in bed. He stayed in the bath only a half hour; for the people of the country who are in it all day long playing and drinking are in the water only up to the loins; he stayed in up to the neck, stretched out the full length of the bath.

Montaigne describes his kidney stones and gravel as being reddish. This means that he suffered from uric or urate *calculi* which are reddish yellow in color.[4] The best present-day source of information on the efficiency of the European spas is a volume published in 1963 entitled *Medical Hydrology*, edited by Sidney Licht. In this the article on treatment for the stone was written by John Mates, a Hungarian specialist (pp. 384-89). All the spas, with the chemical analysis of their waters, are discussed in this book. Dr. Mates says that there are several phases in the treatment of urate stones at a spa. Such stones respond to alkaline gas and minerals, particularly to calcium in the waters. Secondly *any* water, if taken in great quantity, has a diuretic effect which flushes stones out of the system —BUT— when there is Sodium present in the water this diuresis is slowed down considerably. Thirdly, Carbon dioxide gas has an effect through the skin when people bathe in it. The capillaries of the skin are dilated by this and the relaxation of tension is good for the heart and general well being. Heat when applied also relaxes the capillaries; but heat causes the heart to beat faster. In a quotation which we gave above, Montaigne mentions that at Baden the people drink the water little but bathe and have themselves scarified and cupped. Scarifying means that numerous small shallow cuts are made on a limited area. This bleeding added to the dilation and relaxation. The instrument for scarifying is a small block of wood with about eight little knives which operate when a spring is released. The spring is triggered and the blades make a series of shallow cuts. At Plombières too the bathers

---

[4] Our chief informant has been Dr. William Stewart McClellan who was for twenty-three years head of the Medical Department at Saratoga Springs, (N. Y.).

did little drinking. They frolicked in the water mostly and had themselves scarified.

There are, chemically speaking, six types of spas in Europe: Choride or saline, sulfate or purgative, Chalybeate (iron and arsenic in tonic qualities), sulphide waters, and Hot Springs. In this last the mineral substance is very low. Finally there is the Alkaline chalcic type wich has the bicarbonates and Carbon dioxide gas. This last is the kind that would benefit the stone best. The spas at Contrexévile and Vittel are excellent examples of this.

Montaigne, in his Italian Voyage, went first to Plombières-les-Bains (Vosges), near Remiremont and Epinal, and remained there eleven days (September 16 to 27). He excited amusement when he insisted upon drinking while the others merely bathed. He remarked that the water was hot but without taste, although water which came from a certain spring had a faint iron taste; another spring had a slight mineral content which he described as alum. Plombières has plenty of Carbon dioxide gas but only infinitesimal quantities of sodium bicarbonate, potassium, bicarbonate of lime, and magnesium bicarbonate. In addition this hot spring because of its small alkaline content had some slight value against the stone. This was from the Carbon dioxide which is alkaline — although quickly evaporated. It cannot have the stronger effect which comes from Calcium. Fortunately for the sufferers from the stone there is little Sodium at Plombières.

Montaigne used the Roman bath building there which has stone steps along the sides of the main pool like those of a theater. He had an affection for the place. "But he left the said baths judging that he still had in the bladder both the stone of the aforesaid colic and some other small ones whose descent he thought he had felt." [5] The waters had not been strong enough. His next thermal stop was at Baden near Zurich in Switzerland. Here he remained only five days (October 2-7). He discovers here that "he does not pass the water he has drunk" which he attributes to excessive sweating in the bath. You and I know better. There was too much Sodium — for this spring has Sodium, Calcium, Sulfate, and Chloride totalling

---

[5] Frame tr., pp. 872-5.

4.4 gr. to the liter. It has also Carbon dioxide and Hydrogen sulphide. He remarks that "The water of the baths gives off a smell of sulphur" — from the sulphate. The pH is only 6.36 which means that the alkalinity and acidity are about neutral; so Baden could have halped Montaigne not at all, and he stayed there less than a fortnight. The amenities *were* pleasant! [6]

The spa that interested him most was that of the Bagni di Lucca —which is an area 14 miles to the north of Lucca— its central spring is at La Villa. [7] Montaigne was there May 7-June 21, and then again August 14 to September 12, 1581 —a total of seventy-two days. With the medical information we have been giving you can guess from the content of the water why he stayed: alkaline earth salts (magnesium, calcium and sulfate) as high as 7.6 to the liter — and NO SODIUM. This meant a maximum of diuresis — which was sometimes painful and even a little bloody; but the stones were passed freely and, of course, there was plenty of alkalinity. Montaigne remarks, "Since at other times I have repented of not having written more in detail on the subject of the other baths, so that I could derive rules and examples for those I used later, this time I want to expatiate." He noted that the stones he was passing "seemed much rougher than usual"; they appeared from their size to be bladder rather than kidney calculi. After he arrived for his second visit he voided a very large stone. The strong diuretic effect was even becoming painfully unpleasant. [8] He talked with a local man on September 10 and this individual indicated that

> ...he was very sorry about one thing, that for a number of years he had observed the baths did more harm than good to those who used them ... those people who consider their own profit have spread the notion that the baths are of no value unless you take medicine, not only after and before the bath, but even mixing it with the operation of the waters; and they would not readily consent to your taking the waters pure. From this ... there followed this very evident result, that more people died from these baths

---

[6] *Ibid.*, pp. 882-6.

[7] *Ibid.*, pp. 1016 ff. A. Bonaventura, *I Bagni di Lucca, Careglia, e Barga* (Bergamo, 1914).

[8] p. 1019.

than were cured by them. An he held it for certain that in a little while they would fall into universal disrepute and be abandoned.

To sum up: the Lucca baths were extremely diuretic; but they had no soothing Carbon dioxide for the skin. Montaigne was a scientist at heart, even though chemistry had not yet been invented. He was certainly much interested in the baths at Lucca — their violence and their strangeness. They hurt even his jaw and gave him a headache. "I do believe that the fumes of this water, from drinking and from bathing...are very bad for the head, and I can say with assurance, even worse for the stomach." — and yet he stayed on-and on-and on.

There was one gas which was especially prominent at Plombières and then less so at Baden, and even less at Lucca. This is Radon, the Alpha emanation from radium. All three of these springs, and many others, are radioactive. Most medical experts in the United States would say that this could only be harmful to the digestive tract. If Montaigne indulged too vigorously in such waters he could have suffered eventually from something more deadly than the stone, which they could not diagnose. But European specialists are more inclined to believe that small doses of radium are beneficial.

One can only wonder why, in the face of unpleasant results, Montaigne spent so much more time at La Villa and Corsena (Lucca) than he did at Plombières, where the waters were more beneficial. The answer is twofold. Montaigne certainly liked Italy more than he did the northern area, despite the china stoves. He wanted to speak Italian, and then the people in the north were not so fond of drinking the waters as they were of bathing and cupping. Secondly, Montaigne was at heart an experimenter. The strange results at La Villa excited his curiosity and he stated frankly that he kept close notes. It is a shame that he lived before the new science, chemistry, which was to be developed two hundred years later. Elementary chemistry could have satisfied his curiosity about the waters. Montaigne should have remained at Plombières and avoided Baden at all costs. The Lucca baths were diuretic and caused him to discharge the calculi in large, rough sizes; they did not dissolve. Montaigne could have spared himself his arduous journey through Switzerland and Italy if he had only had a good supply of Vittel water in his cellar, for Vittel was the best spa he could have visited! But then we would have lost the newsy details of his *Travel Journal*.

It is with great pleasure that I present this paper to William Leon Wiley who has been my colleague for forty-two years. Perhaps when we are retired we may take this journey with Montaigne, from place to place, noting how details have changed.

DRAMATIC TECHNIQUES IN *LES PRÉCIEUSES RIDICULES*

QUENTIN M. HOPE
Indiana University

After two five-act comedies in verse based on Italian models, Molière struck out in a wholly new direction with a one-act satirical farce in prose, *Les Précieuses ridicules*. The action moves indoors, from the street-corner of a vaguely Mediterranean seaport to the *salle basse* of a specifically Parisian town house. The season, which in *L'Etourdi* and *Le Dépit amoureux* is the eternal love-season, a springtime offering suitable weather for serenades, duels, and abductions, becomes in *Les Précieuses* the winter social season, the season of theatrical openings, dances, and receptions, where it is heaven to be an insider and hell to be left out. The ridiculous characters in *Les Précieuses* are subjected to a wintry blast of satire. Mascarille and Jodelet, stripped of their borrowed feathers and reduced to their natural condition, are cast out to face "les insultes de la boue et du mauvais temps" with scant protection against the elements. Cathos and Madelon, when their misadventure becomes known, will have to face the far more mortifying insults of ridicule and contempt, with no way of hiding their shame. This contrasts with the denouements of the two Italianate comedies with their miraculous discoveries and reconciliations where the removal of disguise brings bliss rather than shame.

The move from the stock situations of comedy in the Italian tradition to topical satire brought with it fruitful innovations in Molière's dramatic technique and additions to his gallery of dramatic types. Mascarille is essentially the first of the *marquis*, and is more closely related to Acaste and Clitandre than he is to his namesake in the two previous plays. Cathos and Madelon are followed by a series of prudes and *précieuses* and prefigure all characters in Molière from Orgon to Argan who are enchanted with the magical power of words, long to inhabit a dream world, and feel a deep aversion for common sense. Some of the less obvious ways in which *Les Précieuses* foretells Molière's later practice deserve attention: the use he makes of the minor roles, the timing and rhythm of the central scene, the recurrence of certain phrases and themes.

From the very beginning La Grange and du Croisy strike a fresh note. They are the first detached, worldly, satirical observers in Molière comedy. They are *honnêtes hommes,* and given a little more talking room could easily become *raisonneurs*. To be sure, the *pièce sanglante* which they play on the two girls is primarily a vengeance, and La Grange seems to take almost as much delight as Scapin in repaying a minor humiliation with a major one. Nonetheless, there is a point to the prank: the trick he proposes "pourra leur apprendre à connaître leur monde." His explanation of how Cathos and Madelon got to be the way they are shows him to be a sharp observer of the contemporary scene with a critical awareness of fashions and foibles: "L'air précieux n'a pas seulement infecté Paris, il s'est aussi répandu dans les provinces, et nos donzelles ridicules en ont humé leur bonne part." La Grange is spirited, aggressive, intolerant of fools, and given to exaggeration. He foreshadows such satirists in subsequent Molière plays as Eraste, the victim of *Les Fâcheux,* the *vicomte* in *La Comtesse d'Escarbagnas,* and Clitandre in *Les Femmes savantes*. His indignation, like Alceste's in *Le Misanthrope* or Madame Pernelle's in *Tartuffe,* gives the play a lively start and orients the audience. The contrast between La Grange's indignation and du Croisy's more detached amusement is the kernel of many Molière scenes in which a phlegmatic character offsets a sanguine one. The reappearance of the two characters close to the end of the play provides a frame for the action. Similarly Chrysalde in *L'Ecole des femmes,* Ariste in *L'Ecole des maris,* and Madame Pernelle in *Tartuffe* appear in the opening scene and again close to the end. Such reappearances recall the opening, herald the denouement, and underline the reversal of the situation which has occurred during the absence of the frame characters or measure the distance a central character has travelled. The frame character reappears to voice the same sentiment he expressed in the opening scene. Thus La Grange's determination at the start to teach the girls a lesson is echoed when du Croisy says to the valets who are being beaten, "Voilà qui vous apprendra à vous connaître."

Gorgibus, like du Croisy and La Grange, appears early in the play (scenes 2-4) and reappears only at the end (scenes 16-17). It is a short part —he has only eighteen cues— but it is a significant one. It is the grossness of Gorgibus rather than the polish and true wit of du Croisy and La Grange which sets off the affectation of the *précieuses*. Here Molière explores for the first time the comic effects and the powers of illumination of the scene which brings extremely incompatible characters into conflict with one another. Misunderstanding reigns from the very beginning. Gorgibus asks what the girls are doing: "Que font-elles?" Marotte who takes him to mean what are they making replies, "De la pommade pour les lèvres," and this prompts an irate outburst from Gorgibus:

> "C'est trop pommadé: dites-leur qu'elles descendent. (*Seul*.) Ces pendardes-là avec leur pommade, ont, je pense, envie de me ruiner. Je ne vois partout que blancs d'œufs, lait virginal, et mille autres brimborions que je ne connais point. Elles ont usé, depuis que nous sommes ici, le lard d'une douzaine de cochons, pour le moins; et quatre valets vivraient tous les jours des pieds de mouton qu'elles emploient."

Gorgibus has stumbled on the subject of cosmetics inadvertently. It is really not what he had intended to get angry about for the moment. His intention was to find out what went wrong with the visit he had arranged between Cathos and Madelon and their two suitors. Repeatedly in later plays Molière uses the device of setting an obstruction in the path of an irritated character which doubles his irritation and gives rise to a particularly characteristic outburst. The unexpected obstacle produces a spontaneous and instinctive response.

Gorgibus' annoyance at the girls for spending so much on cosmetics spills over into the next scene, launches it with promising vigor, and neatly underlines the entrance of the two title-characters, calling attention to their make-up which is no doubt as extravagant as Mascarille's costume: "Il est bien nécessaire vraiment de faire tant de dépense pour vous graisser le museau!" Soon Gorgibus goes on to express his bewilderment and annoyance at the girls' language and behavior, but it is typical of him —and of Molière— to begin with the physical. *Pommade, blancs d'œufs, lait virginal* give him something concrete to be annoyed at, something he can lay his hands on. Like most fathers in Molière he is obsessively aware of material things. Cathos' exclamation to Madelon, "Que ton père a la forme enfoncée dans la matière!" is a parody of *portrait* phraseology, marvelously pretentious and infelicitous, but it does characterize the old man. He reduces everything to the lowest and most concrete terms. To put on rouge and lipstick is "se graisser le museau." Pommade is lard and sheepsfoot. The girls' cosmetics are his comestibles, and he is clearly a man to whom food is important. "Il faut manger pour vivre" and "Je vis de bonne soupe" are maxims he can understand. He and the two girls are at polar extremities. His *douzaine de cochons* would be as incongruous in their ethereal world as the *trompette marine* in Monsieur Jourdain's house orchestra.

It is talk more than anything else that makes *Les Précieuses* funny, and the lines that audiences remember are the absurd metaphors of the *précieuses*. But it is Gorgibus who has the first and last word. His short, vigorous, irate statements near the beginning and at the end of the play provide a frame for the central scenes and a contrast. Gorgibus makes his heavy physical presence felt in metaphors which picture him in various uncomfortable postures: "Je me lasse de vous avoir sur les bras... Vous nous mettez dans de beaux draps blancs... Il faut que je boive l'affront." Generally speaking, the metaphors of Cathos and Madelon transform the substantial into the unreal. Violins are *les âmes des pieds,* mirrors are *les conseillers des grâces,* chairs are *les commodités de la conversation.* Gorgibus, who speaks not to display his cleverness but to vent his wrath, reaches instinctively for a concrete image as his anger rises. He transforms money —something real and palpable to begin with— into something even more palpable: a beating. When the violinists ask him for payment he sets upon them exclaiming, "Voici la monnaie dont je veux vous payer."

Between Gorgibus and the two girls there is the radical failure of communication on which much subsequent Molière dialogue is based. Gorgibus does not understand what the girls say and do, and he makes the fact plain repeatedly: "mille brimborions que je ne connais pas... quel diable de jargon entends-je ici... je n'entends rien à toutes ces balivernes... je ne puis rien comprendre à ce baragouin." This recalls the Molière scenes in which characters express the same idea repeatedly in different words (a device sometimes called *répétition molièresque*). There is something unmistakably *molièresque* also about such energetic, scornful, and mouth-filling expressions as *brimborions, balivernes, billevisées*. They are as far from the normal speech of the *honnête homme* in one direction as Mascarille's contrived phrases are in the other. Such coinages as *pommadé*, a word which according to Furetière is to be found only in *Les Précieuses ridicules*, are also typical of Molière. The character, impatient with the restraint that language puts upon the expression of his wrath or indignation bursts forth with an ejaculation (*ouf!*), or even an onomatopoeia (*drelin, drelin, drelin*). Gorgibus' exclamation "C'est trop pommadé!" expresses his annoyance at the thing signified by recoining the word itself. In his final diatribe against the pernicious causes of preciosity he does similar violence to the word *sonnet* to which he adds, whether in denigratory wordplay or out of honest ignorance, the feminine form *sonnette*, and with which his curse reaches its climax:

> "Et vous qui êtes cause de leur folie, sottes billevisées, pernicieux amusements des esprits oisifs, romans, vers, chansons, sonnets et sonnettes, puissiez vous être à tous les diables!"

There are structural as well as stylistic elements in *Les Précieuses* which foretell Molière's practice in later and longer plays. The play falls into three parts, approximately equal in length. Scene Nine between Cathos, Madelon, and Mascarille occupies the center of the play. Eight scenes lead up to it, seven follow it. If we can accept the number of lines in a scene as a crude measure of its duration, it is also the longest part of the play: 290 lines in the Despois et Mesnard edition. The first eight scenes taken together are 265 lines long, the last seven are 240 lines long. This partly indicates the acceleration which occurs after Scene Nine, particularly if one takes note that the number of cues, that is individual speeches, actually increases. There are 79 in the first eight scenes, 111 in Scene Nine, and 119 in the last seven scenes. Structurally the long scene between Cathos, Madelon, and Mascarille resembles the portrait scene in *Le Misanthrope,* or the scene in *Le Malade imaginaire* in which Diafoirus father and son pay a formal call upon Argan and his household. That is to say, it is a long scene towards the middle of the play in which the characters, uninterrupted by new entrances bringing new developments in the plot are engaged as participants in a social occasion. *Les Femmes savantes* is particularly close to *Les Précieuses ridicules,* and its Act III, scene 2, in which Trissotin reads a sonnet and then an epigram to the learned ladies is closely analogous with the corresponding scene in *Les Précieuses. Les Femmes savantes* is 1778 lines long. The two hundred lines of its central scene (ll. 726-926) come right in the middle of the play. Thirteen scenes precede it and thirteen follow. Whether such scenes are on dead center or not the important thing is that in them the action reaches a plateau. They offer the central character more breadth and elbow-room for self-expression and self-display than he could find in a scene where the dialogue is rooted in conflict or misunderstanding. The conversation moves freely from one topic to the other and the central character, seizing the opportunity to perform before an audience composed (at least in part) of admirers spreads out as he could not in more constricting circumstances. The fatuousness of Mascarille, Trissotin, and Diafoirus, and the wit of Célimène take on a special glow in such hospitable surroundings. Scene Nine of *Les Précieuses* gives the same sense of free but not random movement as the scenes from the later plays. In fact it offers a particularly clear example of how Molière gives both an impression of spontaneity and a sense of shape to a scene. This one scene carries most of the weight of the satire. In the following scenes the pace accelerates, the satirical elements become more scattered, the buffoonery more prominent, violins enter, a dance begins, there is a beating, a disrobing, and another beating, and like a *comédie-ballet* the play ends in a whirl of movement and animation on stage. Molière reserves his strongest attack on preciosity for the central scene, and since preciosity is primarily a literary phenomenon, literary talk forms the heart of the play. The conversation has a spirited, impromptu quality, but there is a calculated progression and an increase in intensity of feeling as the talk moves from the pleasures of being part of the literary in-group through Mascarille's song and the *explication de texte* following it to the subject closest to Molière's heart, the theatre. Here he boldly attacks his rivals at the hôtel de Bourgogne by having Mascarille express his admiration for them and his contempt for "les autres... des ignorants qui récitent comme l'on parle." With this reference to Molière, the first of many in Molière's comedies, the sharpest part of the satire ends, and more lively, farcical action takes over. Mascarille suddenly asks the girls their opinion of his costume and after having them admire it returns to a gallant and metaphoric compliment. The scene ends as it began with Mascarille's compliment to the young ladies.

A comparison of these two compliments reveals the extent to which the second one parallels and contrasts with the first. The words from the first compliment which are repeated in the second are italicized.

Opening Compliment	Closing Compliment
MASCARILLE: Mais, au moins, y a-t-il sureté ici pour moi?	MASCARILLE: Ahi, ahi, ahi, doucement! Dieu me damne, Mesdames, c'est fort mal en user; j'ai à me plaindre de votre procédé; cela n'est pas honnête.
CATHOS: Que craignez-vous?	CATHOS: Qu'est-ce donc? qu'avez vous?
MASCARILLE: Quelque vol de *mon cœur*, quelque assassinat de ma franchise. Je vois ici des yeux qui ont la mine d'être de fort mauvais garçons, de faire insulte aux libertés, et de traiter une âme de Turc à More. Comment, diable! d'abord qu'on les approche ils se mettent sur leur garde meurtrière.	MASCARILLE: Quoi? toutes deux contre *mon cœur* en même temps! m'attaquer à droite et à gauche!

Ah! par ma foi, je m'en défie !
    et je m'en vais gagner au pied, ou je veux caution bourgeoise qu'ils ne me feront point de mal.

MADELON :

    Ma chère, c'est le caractère enjoué.

CATHOS :

    Je vois bien que c'est un Amilcar.

MADELON :

    Ne craignez rien, nos yeux n'ont point de mauvais desseins,
    et votre cœur peut dormir en assurance sur leur prud'homie.

Ah! c'est contre le droit des gens ; la partie n'est pas égale ;
    et je m'en vais crier au meurtre.

CATHOS :

    Il faut avouer qu'il dit les choses d'une manière particulière.

MADELON :

    Il a un tour admirable dans l'esprit.

CATHOS :

    Vous avez plus de peur que de mal,
    et votre cœur crie avant qu'on l'écorche.

The device of beginning a scene with a motif which is then repeated at the close of the scene is one Molière uses in later plays. An example is the first scene of *Tartuffe* which begins with Madame Pernelle's "Allons, Flipote, allons," and ends with her delivering the same message in the same rhythm and with even greater exasperation, "Marchons, gaupe, marchons." All of the first scene is an interruption of her exit included between the two brackets of the opening and closing hemistich. The reprise upon the opening compliment in the scene from *Les Précieuses* is more prolonged and elaborate, but it has a similar function. There is more feeling and warmth in the return to the opening motif than in its first appearance. Madame Pernelle has grown angrier during the scene and now punctuates her exit line by giving Flipote a box on the ear. As for Mascarille, he has grown bolder and more amorous. The parallelism serves to underline the differences between the two compliments as much as it calls attention to their similarity. "Je m'en vais gagner au pied" becomes "Je m'en vais crier au meurtre." The repetitive elements in Molière dialogue serve a function similar to the repetitive mannerisms and pieces of business the actor uses to establish a part. The comic actor must repeat and yet he must continue to surprise. Here he surprises his audience on both sides of the footlights with the extravagant exclamation of alarm at the beginning, "Ahi, ahi, ahi, doucement!," then dazzles them by blatantly returning to the metaphor of the heart under attack which had begun the whole conversation, now warmed over and served up with new gusto. The analogy may be pushed a little further: in the technique of the comic dramatist as in the technique of the comic actor it is the cumulative effect of such minutiae as the rhythm of a scene or the timing of a gesture that makes the difference between inspiration or banality. One can point out a specific dramatic technique such as the parallelism at the beginning and end of Scene Nine, as one might point out a certain intonation or stance on the part of an actor, but in an art which depends on accumulation and, as Molière himself often pointed out, upon the response of an audience, one must be careful not to overstress any single feature.

One can be certain, however, that any device that can serve to mark off one scene from another has an aesthetic function in Molière farce. *Les Précieuses* presents an apparently fortuitous succession rather than an inevitable chain of events. It cannot derive its unity from the necessity of its action. Any of its separate topics of conversation or gags could be omitted without in any way diminishing its comprehensibility. But there is a dynamic interrelationship between them. They hang together in a way of their own. Even in a farce as short and apparently simple as *Les Précieuses* the events are not simply strung out on a line. Repetitive patterns, parallelisms, and frame characters are unifying elements.

Recurrent themes are another unifying element in Molière farce. Nudity, which has a place in Molière's general repertory of themes (partly because it is the antithesis of costume) is a particularly expressive and felicitous theme in *Les Précieuses ridicules*. "Comment est-ce qu'on peut souffrir la pensée de coucher contre un homme vraiment nu?" asks Cathos when her uncle tells her that she and Madelon must accept the husbands he has found for them. The action of the play punishes them harshly for such squeamishness, and the undressing of Mascarille and Jodelet before their scandalized eyes is a sly reference back to it. Even before this ultimate humiliation they are threatened with embarrassment when Jodelet attempts to remove his britches in order to show the girls "une furieuse plaie." But it is Mascarille, imperturbable in disgrace as befits the true aristocrat, who delivers the final insult to Cathos and Madelon in his exit line: "Je vois bien qu'on n'aime ici que la vaine apparence, et qu'on n'y considère point la vertu toute nue." This hits the mark. Anything naked is abhorrent to the girls, and *la vaine apparence* is their only delight. They live in a fictional world which includes "les enlèvements, et ce qui s'ensuit," but the idea of "un homme vraiment nu" horrifies them. Mascarille's exit line which is completely in character and passably ridiculous under the circumstances comes closer to carrying the message of the play than does Gorgibus' final denunciation of *précieux* literature.

Les Précieuses has an engaging air of improvisation and spontaneity about it. The play no doubt catches some of its exuberance from its central character, Mascarille, who seems to be making it all up as he goes along. But unlike Molière's preceding play, *Le Dépit amoureux*, it shows no sign of fumbling or hesitancy. Its language is as fresh, vigorous, and expressive as that of any of the subsequent prose plays. It is put together with great skill. Nothing suggests that he could have written a better play of the same length on the same subject at a later stage of his artistic development. To enumerate techniques he uses in later plays which occur in *Les Précieuses* only in embryonic form should not imply that it is apprentice work. Within its limitations, *Les Précieuses* is quite perfect.

THE GEOPHYSICS OF RABELAIS' FROZEN WORDS

ABRAHAM C. KELLER
University of Washington

> "...*that French, which made his giants see*
> *Those uncouth islands, where words frozen be,*
> *Till by the thaw next year they're voice again.*"
> (J. Donne)

Readers of Rabelais, including this one, have always been intrigued by the episode of the frozen words (Bk. IV, chs. 55-56). There is a characteristically Rabelaisian pleasure about frozen sounds thawing before our eyes as they make themselves heard. Presented with a dash of color, with the familiar spectacle of Panurge overcome by fright, and some logical and historical discussion, the scene is pure Rabelais. I once asked a friend of mine who is an atmospheric scientist whether sounds could really freeze and thaw as Rabelais says, and to my surprise he answered that the phenomenon is very well known. This response immediately gave a new dimension to these favorite pages of mine, for discussions of them have ordinarily been confined to (1) Rabelais' literary sources and (2) possible hidden meanings which may have lurked in his mind. I think no one has ever asked what connection the episode might have with natural phenomena — an astonishing omission considering the fact that usually even the most fanciful yarns in Rabelais turn out, upon investigation, to have some connections with the real world. I think, indeed, that his steady contact with reality is one of the main things which give his fantasies their peculiar effectiveness as humor and as poetry; for Rabelais moved with rare freedom between the real and the imaginary. Whether, and to what extent, this is true here, we shall try to see, after a hasty glance at items (1) and (2), the more traditional points of interest in these chapters.

(1) Clues to the readings which lay behind Rabelais' account are provided by Rabelais himself. Either directly or by implication, the characters tell us that the idea of sound frozen in the air and subsequently thawing, or of the words of Homer coming alive, or of people seeing words, was treated by various writers in the past (e. g., Plutarch, Aristotle, and the Vulgate Bible). In addition, most scholars assume that Rabelais was acquainted with accounts by Caelius Calcagninus and Castiglione [1] in which frozen words melt and then become audible, though in the last case as a result of fire rather than of the arrival of spring or summer. It is possible that Rabelais took the idea from Castiglione and then proceeded, as he often did, to bring his classical erudition to bear as support and enrichment, and to subject the whole to his fertile imagination. The following quotation from Plutarch will make it clear, in any case, that the general idea of frozen words or frozen sounds was not invented by Rabelais.

> "This Antiphanes said merrily, that in a certain city the cold was so intense that words were congealed as soon as spoken, but that after some time they thawed and became audible, so that the words spoken in winter were articulated next summer. Even so, the many excellent precepts of Plato, which he instilled into the tender ears of his scholars, were scarce perceived and distinguished by many of them, till they grew men and attained the warm vigorous summer of their age." [2]

---

[1] A convenient listing of Rabelais' literary sources may be found in Jean Guiton, "Le mythe des paroles gelées," *Romanic Rev.*, XXXI, 1940, 3-15.

[2] Plutarch, "De Profectibus in Virtute," ch. 7, in *Plutarch's Essays* (in English), ed. by Andrew P. Peabody (Boston: Little, Brown, and Co.), 1881, p. 178. Rabelais' version of this is as follows: "D'adventaige Antiphanes disoit la doctrine de Platon es parolles estre semblable, lesquelles en quelque contrée, on temps du fort hyver, lors que sont proférées, gelent et glassent à la froydeur de l'air, et ne sont ouyes. Semblablement ce que Platon enseignoyt es jeunes enfans, à peine estre d'iceulx entendu lors que estoient vieulx devenuz." (Liv. IV, ch. 55, p. 227 in critical ed. by Marichal: *Le Quart Livre*, Lille et Genève, 1947.) Readers will also be aware of the use of frozen sounds, more recently, in the French-horn episode of Baron Mun-

(2) The question of possible hidden meanings is by its nature more controversial than that of literary sources. The idea that the episode is mere entertainment is excluded, in the thinking of some scholars, first by the fact that three times in Book IV Rabelais creates scenes in which there are unidentifiable sounds in the air, and second by the placement of our scene between two others which are of almost certain ideological importance. As for the first point, if Rabelais insisted so much on mysterious sounds, he must have had something in mind, runs this reasoning. As for the second, certain connections (rather too complicated to be detailed here) seem to indicate that the frozen words represent the Word of the Protestant Reformers, the frozen aspect representing the silence which many of the Protestant theologians urged true believers to practice. This interpretation, which makes Rabelais a champion, or at least in some measure a defender, of the new religious doctrines (a view for which there is some support in other parts of *Gargantua* and *Pantagruel*), leans in part on information not contained in Rabelais' text.[3] Guiton and Spitzer, on the other hand, limiting themselves to Rabelais' text, found in these chapters a poetic expression of the basic phenomenon of language: its objective, fixed character and its constant possibility of being actualized by man. By dealing with unintelligible sounds —which, nonetheless, have great impact— Rabelais placed himself at the frontiers of language, observing the relationship between language and words in some such way as Ferdinand de Saussure was to do in modern linguistics. The fact that Rabelais touched upon fundamental matters of human communication is what makes this episode a true myth.[4] It is also possible, as some scholars have said, that the whole episode exists

---

chausen's tales, ch. 6 (*The Adventures of Baron Munchausen*, New York, Parnassus, n. d., pp. 45-46), which is more like Castiglione than like Rabelais. Additional uses of the idea in modern literature may be found in Edward Bensly, "Frozen Sound," *Notes and Queries*, CLXXIV (Jan. 22, 1938), 65-66. It is to the latter that I owe the lines from Donne quoted as an epigraph to this paper.

[3] See V.-L. Saulnier, "Le silence de Rabelais et le mythe des paroles gelées," *Travaux d'Humanisme et Renaissance*, VII (1953), 233-47.

[4] Guiton, article cited in n. 1, above; Leo Spitzer, "Rabelais et les Rabelaisants," *Studi Francesi*, XII (1960), 401-23, esp. pp. 402-5.

as a simple reminder that the action of Book IV is laid in northern waters.

Paragraph (1), above, has reference only to literary sources, which have by now been well established. Less easy to pin down are the oral sources and recent travel accounts, whether oral or written, which Rabelais might have used. Given his interest in ocean travel and his detailed knowledge of ships, navigation, travel routes, and the talk of sailing men (errors and fanciful take-offs notwithstanding), it seems very possible to many students of Rabelais that he made it a point to become acquainted with sailors, perhaps in one or more French ports like Saint-Malo or Bordeaux;[5] besides, he may well have had an ocean trip on one of his returns from Italy. He would surely have consumed with great eagerness all available travel accounts and geographical treatises. In such readings, and in conversations with sailors, he could have heard about strange sounds hovering in the air overhead, far from any likely source, for we know that there were reports of such noises. Thus Thevet, whom Rabelais knew personally, reported these sounds in his *Cosmographie universelle* (1575),[6] and though the book itself was published too late to be a literary source of Rabelais' account, it is not unreasonable to think that Rabelais saw

---

[5] In a history of Saint-Malo by Jacques Doremet, published in 1628, the following sentence appears on p. 50: "Rabelais vint apprendre de ce Cartier les termes de la marine et du pilotage à Saint-Malo pour en chamarrer ses bouffonnesques lucianismes et impies épicureismes." (Quoted by A. Lefranc, "Pantagruel explorateur," *Rev. de Paris*, 1er fév. 1904, p. 532.) (Lefranc's article occupies pp. 514-44 of 1er fév. and pp. 827-50 of 15 fév. 1904.) On Bordeaux, see Ch.-A. Julien, *Les Voyages de découverte et les premiers établissements* (Paris, Presses universitaires, 1948), p. 353. Julien has some doubt as to the truth of Doremet's statement.

[6] "...Je vous diray chose très véritable, ... ce qui se voit en icelle Isle et lieux voisins de la mer, où aussi on tient qu'il y a des esprits tourmentans, tant de nuict que de jour, les hommes. Ce qui est vray, et me suis laissé dire, non à un, mais à infiniz pilotes et mariniers, avec lesquels j'ay longtemps voyagé, que lorsqu'ils passoient par ceste coste, comme ils fussent agitez d'une grande tempeste, ils oyaient en l'air comme sur la hune et mastz de leurs vaisseaux, ces voix d'hommes, faisans grand bruit, sans qu'ils entendissent rien formé de leur parolle, seulement un tel murmure, que vous oyez un jour de foire au meillieu des halles publiques. Ces voix leur causoient plus d'estonnemens cent fois, que la tempeste qui leur estoit voisine..." (A. Thevet, *Cosmographie universelle*, 1575, II, 1018, quoted by Lefranc, *op. cit.*, p. 840, and by many commentators since.)

this material in manuscript form or heard it from the lips of his friend Thevet. Besides, there are numerous other indications of interest in, and belief in, these unidentified sounds during the sixteenth century; [7] and Rabelais was just the man to give them a fanciful turn.

Rabelais' constant search for the bizarre in general, and more particularly his deep interest in geophysical phenomena —amply attested by the subterranean explorations, ocean voyages, earthquakes, and storms which appear in his books— must have made him suceptible to the appeal of the unidentified sounds in the air (which I call USA's). Indeed, his treatment of the frozen words must be taken as one of many facets of his concern with matters of earth and air, and my question as to what the frozen words represent in nature is a simple recognition of Rabelais' interests. On the other hand, Rabelais was no scientist: we know from various holes in the ground and geological formations which we meet here and there that neither his interest in the actual nor his respect for truth hampered his imagination very much. Yet myths like this one, coming from antiquity and reinforced by contemporary experience, are almost always based on phenomena observed but not understood by men, phenomena which, because of men's failure to understand them, are easily distorted, even beyond recognition.

What, now, are the phenomena involved here? What do scientific observers, with methods better than Plutarch's or Rabelais', have to tell us about USA's? Being more curious than knowledgeable in these matters, I consulted my colleague in Atmospheric Sciences, Professor Joost Businger, mentioned at the beginning of this paper. He answered my questions, guided me to readings, and let me consult him extensively; he really became a collaborator on this

---

[7] See articles by Saulnier, Guiton, and Spitzer. Lefranc wrote on this point: "Thevet n'a fait que fixer au passage une légende connue avant lui et populaire dans le monde des marins. S'il n'a pas publié sa grande *Cosmographie* du vivant de Rabelais, il est juste d'observer qu'il connut ce dernier de très près, dès 1536, et qu'il fut de ses intimes à Rome aussi bien qu'à Paris. Rabelais appartenant au même milieu scientifique, rien ne s'oppose à ce qu'il ait été au courant des données géographiques que Thevet vulgarisa par la suite" (p. 841). Julien (*op. cit.*, p. 363) points out that Thevet took Rabelais to task for his extravagant handling of his (Thevet's) Isle des démons episode.

article.[8] The first thing that struck me was the large number of rather reliable reports of USA's. Though surely not common, the phenomenon has obviously been witnessed often enough to be taken seriously, and sometimes the testimony is surprisingly similar to Rabelais' version — the following case, for example, reported from Shoshone Lake in Yellowstone National Park:

> "Here we first heard, while out on the lake in the bright still morning, the mysterious aerial sound for which this region is noted. It put me in mind of the vibrating clang of a harp, lightly and rapidly touched, high up above the tree-tops, or the sound of many telegraph wires swinging regularly and rapidly in the wind, or, more rarely, of faintly-heard voices answering each other overhead. It begins softly in the remote distance, draws rapidly near with louder and louder throbs of sound, and dies away in the opposite distance; or it may seem to wander irregularly about, the whole passage lasting from a few seconds to half a minute or more. We heard it repeatedly and very distinctly here and at Yellowstone Lake, most frequently at the latter place. It is usually noticed on still, bright mornings not long after sunrise, and it is always louder at this time of day; but I heard it clearly, though faintly, once at noon, when a stiff breeze was blowing. No scientific explanation of this really bewitching phenomenon has ever been published, although it has been several times referred to by travellers, who have ventured various crude guesses at its cause..."[9]

The second thing that struck me was the uncertainty surrounding the phenomenon. In this day of unprecedented scientific conquests, we might expect our modest question to be answered unequivocally, but instead we meet such a variety of explanations, and such a

---

[8] My colleague has been so taken with the frozen words of Rabelais that he is planning to write a paper on them for the edification of his scientific colleagues, thus providing one of those much desired links between the sciences and the humanities. I trust that our two articles together will serve to show in a small way that we can be of use to each other. His article will appear in an issue of *Weather*.

[9] I have appended at the end of this article, as an item of interest, several reports which appeared in *Weather*; they are but a sampling. See also S. A. Forbes "Aquatic Fauna of the Yellowstone National Park," *Bulletin of the U. S. Fish Commission* (Washington, 1893), p. 215.

real possibility of different factors at work in different cases, that it is easy to see how myths grew up around USA's. [10]

Atmospheric scientists recognize unidentified sounds in the air as brontides or mistpoeffers. Leaning to the first term, W. J. Humphreys wrote as follows:

> "From time immemorial, low, rumbling, thunder-like noises (brontides, mistpoeffers, 'Barisal guns,' etc.) of short duration, and that certainly are not thunder, for they often occur when the sky is clear, have been heard in many parts of the world, both singly and in irregular series. They appear to come from a distance, but are of uncertain direction, and are most frequent in actively seismic regions.
>
> Apparently, then, the true brontides (many other sounds have often been mistakenly reported as brontides) are only the rumblings of earthquakes too feeble for registration, or other than aural detection. And this inference is strengthened, if not indeed confirmed, by the fact that earthquake adjustments have been known to occur in a long irregular series of shocks that became feebler and feebler, until only the characteristic low rumbles (then properly called brontides) remained as presumable evidence of their passage." [11]

This description is not far from Rabelais' account; but the explanation on the basis of earthquakes does not fit, because water would not be able to conduct the sounds from the bottom of the sea to our travelers on shipboard.

Minnaert, discussing these sounds as "mistpoeffers" (=mist-explosions), concentrated his attention on the northern coast of Europe from Boulogne to the northernmost tip of Holland, and above all Flanders, thought he notes that they occur in many other parts of the world as well (Scotland, Italy, the Congo, Central America, the North Atlantic). In Flanders, USA's were noted one day in twenty during the summertime, the greatest occurence being in July, between 10 a.m. and 4 p.m., never at night, and almost always on fair, sunny days with high temperatures and calm, clear

---

[10] Bleeker (article cited in footnote 13, below, p. 16, n. 1) informs us that in India the USA's (or "barisal guns") are taken to be part of a festival of the gods celebrating the marriage of the Rivers Ganges and Brahmaputra.

[11] W. J. Humphreys, *Physics of the Air* (3rd ed., McGraw-Hill, New York and London, 1940), p. 442.

air, though occasionally with light fog. The sounds occur at irregular intervals, from zero to thirty minutes apart, in the former case producing a continuous rumbling. A typical observation of a few hours' duration showed an average of three booms per minute. Minnaert, after determining that the source was not gun-shots (naval exercises, carried on far offshore, have often been confused with USA's), suggested the following possible sources, in increasing order of probability: (1) the noise of the surf, (2) subterranean disturbances (unlikely, because uncommon in the Low Countries), and (3) distant thunder (which he accepted as the cause in over half of the cases). [12]

With Minnaert's conclusions in mind, we may profitably look at the close study of mistpoeffers made by Bleeker, based on data supplied by the Netherlands Weather Bureau. Systematically reporting mistpoeffers along with other phenomena, the Weather Bureau showed 200 instances of USA's from 1896 through 1903. Bleeker charted these occurrences by month, day, and hour, and did the same for thunderstorms, in order to see whether there was any correlation. He found that there was a significant correlation: on 130 of the mistpoeffer-days thunderstorms were observed. (For the remaining cases he found that gunfire was a significant source.) After charting the precise hours of both the thunderstorms and the mistpoeffers, Bleeker concluded that not all but surely some of the 130 mistpoeffers had thunder as their source. [13]

An interesting reference given by Bleeker, which may indeed be helpful to us, concerns a mistpoeffer case-study for one day, November 18, 1931. [14] Here the USA's were shown, on careful examination, to have come quite definitely from cruisers out at sea; but curiously the shots were not heard in the area between the point of origin and the point on land where they were reported. There was, in other words, a silent zone between the source and the place where the sound was again heard. In this phenomenon, which is termed "anomalous sound propagation," the sound ascends high into the air and comes back down to earth after traveling a con-

---

[12] M. Minnaert, *De Natuurkunde van't vrije veld*, 2nd ed., Zutphen, W. J. Thieme & Co., 1941, vol. II, pp. 45-46.

[13] W. Bleeker, "Mistpoeffers," *Hemel en Dampkring*, XXX (1932), 13-19, 43-51.

[14] E. van Everdingen, "De Trillingen op 18 November," *Ibid.*, p. 23.

siderable distance, even up to 100 miles, much farther than the sound would normally be expected to travel.

There seems no reason not to combine Bleeker's findings with the case-history of November 18, 1931. It would have been possible for Rabelais' USA's to come from distant thunder, transmitted by the process of anomalous sound propagation. What remains for us to examine is the likelihood of thunderstorms in the area where the frozen words are supposed to have occurred. Now, in spite of many fanciful touches in Book IV, almost all readers have agreed, especially since the studies of Abel Lefranc, that the voyage being depicted is across the North Atlantic, very possibly along a route suggested by the famous search for the northwest passage to India. There is good reason to believe, as Lefranc demonstrated, that Rabelais had knowledge of, and interest in, that search. (The fact that the fictional search is for the Dive Bouteille does not negate the possibility of the real-life basis of the route being the norhwest passage; such a transformation is normal Rabelaisian practice. An occasional Persian or Cuban touch does not bother the experienced reader.) French sailors in the 1530's and 40's were very much taken up with the search for the northwest passage through or above Canada, which had been discovered and claimed by the French, and it would have been difficult for Rabelais not to share some of their excitement and interest. A recent editor of Book IV has pointed out that Rabelais uses numerous devices to remind us that the voyage is in northern waters. [15] Let us then accept the fact that the isle and

---

[15] Marichal, *Le Quart Livre*, pp. xxi-xxii. Unlike most other scholars, Chinard, while granting that the voyage is over the North Atlantic and based on the travels of Cabot, Cartier, and Roberval, was more impressed by the non-realistic elements than the real. Thus the reference to Arismapéens "nous prouve une fois de plus que la géographie de Rabelais est plus conforme aux données de la légende qu'aux découvertes récentes des voyageurs." (G. Chinard, *L'Exotisme américain dans la littérature française au XVIe siècle d'après Rabelais, Ronsard, Montaigne, etc.*, Paris, Hachette 1911, p. 71.) Marichal (*op. cit.*, p. 322) thinks that Rabelais' Isle des Macréons was suggested by the Isle des Démons, north of Newfoundland, described by Thevet, an island abandoned by its inhabitants because of spirits whose voices were heard during storms. For us, this identification of Rabelais' Isle des Macréons with Thevet's Isle des Démons is useful in giving us a general location in the North Atlantic. The frozen words occur some three or four days after Rabelais' men leave the Isle des Macréons, therefore at a considerable distance from Thevet's sound-producing Isle des Démons, though surely in that part of the Atlantic.

the sounds referred to by Thevet, and afterward by Rabelais, were in the North Atlantic. Could thunder account for the USA's there? It seems possible, especially since the phenomenon is not pictured as occurring commonly or regularly. The fact is that thunderstorms are rare in the North Atlantic, diminishing to a frequency of approximately one day in ten years north of the Arctic Circle.[16] Around Newfoundland, which is well below the Arctic Circle, they are somewhat more frequent, and thus it is well within the range of possibility that French sailors in that area occasionally heard these baffling sounds which, in spite of calm seas and no perceptible turbulence, originated in distant thunderstorms and reached them by anomalous sound propagation.

The episode under consideration ought, thus, to be regarded as a case of the real and the legendary reacting upon each other in Rabelais' fertile imagination to emerge as a new and poetic synthesis of frozen words. The air, as we know from USA's, as well as from UFO's, contains more mystery than we are aware of. Rabelais said this of the earth [17] but could just as accurately have said it of the air. Though in recent years UFO's have received more attention, USA's have also been observed, and even recorded on tape for study by scientists, engineers, and folklorists. However, as far as I know, the conditions under which these observations and recordings have been made are not comparable to those pictured by Rabelais; therefore new sources of USA's which may be discovered will probably not apply to our case, and we are likely to be left with thunder, anomalous sound propagation, and a bit of legend as the basis of Rabelais' chapters.[18]

Readers who appreciate the episode of the frozen words must regret the gradual disappearance of zones of quiet. The modern

---

[16] B. F. J. Shonland, *The Flight of Thunderbolts*, Oxford, Clarendon Press, 1950, p. 59; P. E. Viemeister, *The Lightning Book*, Doubleday, 1961, p. 91.

[17] "Ce que du ciel vous apparoist, et appellez Phenomenes, ce que la terre vous exhibe, ce que la mer et autres fleuves contiennent, n'est comparable à ce qui est en terre caché." (Liv. V, ch. 47.)

[18] I append herewith the reports of USA's promised in note 9. In addition, the reader may be pleased to know that USA's also exist in the realm of radar, where they are called "angels"; but these are not detectable without instruments. (See Vernon G. Plank, "Atmospheric Angels Mimic Radar Echoes," *Electronics*, XXXI, 11 (Mar. 14, 1958), 140-44.)

atmosphere is so full of purrs, beeps, zooms, and booms that except for quieter places like the northwest coast of the United States (where in fact some good detection and recording has been done), USA's are largely lost. It is a boon to us all that Rabelais crossed the stage of history in a quieter age. Today, far from frightening anyone as they did Rabelais' Panurge and Thevet's sailors, the sounds of the frozen words would probably go utterly unnoticed.

APPENDIX

A) Richard Jefferson mentions the strange booming noises resembling distant thunder heard near large sheets of water in hot summers. I well remember my utter inability to locate the source of these sounds, while cycling for miles along the Cotswold escarpment from Bath to Cross Hands, on the main road to Stroud, parallel to the gleaming Severn (a few miles distant) on an intensely hot blue day, in the pitiless summer of 1911.

Years later, during the fine dry hot summer of 1933, they were heard in the vicinity of Lough Neagh, in Northern Ireland. Did Aldergrove experience anything of the like last year? On this last occasion, I discussed with a friend the possibility of thunder at a high altitude (consequent upon speeded evaporation effects). He suspected, on the contrary, a terrestrial cause in the shape of the sudden "emptying" of large quantities of water into deep-seated cavities, caused by the intense heat, in the first instance — with, I presume, violent expulsion of large quantities of air. Alternatively, would the rapid water-movement create a sound-wave in the bowels of the earth?

It occurs to me that some of our modern sound-wave detection apparatus might be profitably employed in tracking down this rare phenomenon.

(C. S. Bailey, "Subterranean Thunder," *Weather*, V, 3 (Feb., 1950), 68. Written at Belfast.)

B) Mr. C. S. Bailey's letter on Subterranean Thunder calls to my mind the subject of the Barisal guns. Barisal is in the delta of the Ganges, some 125 miles nearly due east of Calcutta. In its neighborhood sounds like gun fire used to be heard, and may be still. These sounds were never explained nor their source located. The captain of a river steamer reported that he had heard the sounds always ahead of him for three days, if I remember rightly. Various theories were propounded; earthquake, meteor, wave action, even spooks! But none of the explanations held water. Sir George Darwin, who was interested in many things besides astronomy, took the matter up and found that similar sounds were heard in many parts of the world. One place, I remember, was between the Shetlands and Iceland where they were known to fishermen as "mist puffers" from a belief that they betokened the clearing away of fog. Another place was in central Australia. A map was pubished in Nature showing the localities where the sounds had been reported, but no explanation was arrived at.

In this part of Hampshire the sound of firing is frequently heard from ships in the Channel doing target practice, or from forts in the Isle of Wight, but it was pointed out to me by neighbours that the sounds were sometimes heard on Sundays, and this I was able to confirm. My former Cambridge professor, Sir Alfred Ewing, was then at the Admiralty, and I wrote to ask him if he could find out whether firing was ever carried out by ships on Sundays. I still have the reply to Sir Alfred from the Director of Naval Ordnance, who said emphatically that none of our ships ever did any firing on Sundays. Then a neighbour asked me if I knew what Kipling meant by "the booming of the Downs"; emboldened by being at that time president of the Royal Meteorological Society I wrote to ask him what he did mean; I got quite a nice letter in reply, but he skirted round the subject, and I had a feeling that he had forgotten what he had meant.

And that is all I can tell about the Barisal Guns. It seems to me to be as great a mystery as ever, and it is time for the subject to be investigated again.

(C. J. P. Cave, "The Barisal Guns," *Ibid.*, V. 4, April, 1950, 149. Written at Storm Hill, Petersfield.)

C) I was very interested in Mr. C. J. P. Cave's letter about "The Barisal Guns." I have not heard of them for many years. As a shoolboy I used to wander in the woods and fields of Highgate in the late 1890's, and I remember on a few occasions, when the weather was hot and still and the sky cloudless, hearing distant booms or thuds which I thought might be thunder. An elder brother jokingly remarked on one occasion that someone was hitting a big drum in Alexandra Palace which we could see in the distance. Some years later, after I had joined the staff of the Meteorological Office, I heard the same sounds during the middle of a hot, still and cloudless day spent out in the country. On returning to the office I examined the charts for the day in question and there was no reason to expect thunder. Then it was that I first heard of "Barisal Guns." Others of the staff in the room gave similar testimony.

Such quiet in the open country as was experienced in those days has been impossible for many years. The noise of heavy road traffic, farm tractors and aeroplanes is seldom lacking, and I cannot say that I have heard the guns since the days of my youth.

(W. Hayes, *Ibid.*, V. 8, Aug., 1950, p. 293. Written at Wallington, Surrey.)

D) The letter from Mr. Cave on the Barisal Guns in your issue of April 1950, recalls an article which appeared in the June 1913 number of the *Australian Monthly Weather Report and Meteorological Abstract*. The writer of the article, S. H. Ebury, tells us that peculiar explosive sounds, known locally as "Hanley's guns," were heard from time to time in the districts lying between Daylesford and Maryborough in the Talbot county of Victoria. It was originally thought in Daylesford that the noises were merely those ordinarily caused by people shooting rabbits on an estate owned by Mr. Hanley, which lay eight miles to the north-west of the town;

but this explanation was shown to be wrong when it was discovered that people living far to the north-west of Hanley's property also heard the noises in a north-westerly direction. Neither were the noises due to blasting in the mines of Moolort, for they did not cease when the mines were eventually closed down.

During the years 1912-14 Mr. Ebury listened for the noises at Sandon South, recording the time of occurrence and the direction from which the sound appeared to come, and he collected similar observations from residents of the Kooroocheang district. The Weather Bureau of Melbourne also gathered information from various localities and placed it at Mr. Ebury's disposal. It appears that the noises could be heard at any hour of the day or night, but that they were most frequent in the forenoon, the average time of occurrence during 1913 and 1914 being about 11 a.m. The chart which accompanied Ebury's article shows the direction from which the explosive sounds appeared to come in various parts of the area. It is seen that the majority of the observations indicate an origin of the sounds in the district known as Stony Rises, lying two miles to the north-west of Mount Kooroocheang.

(J. Wadsworth, *Ibid.* From Meteorological Office, Kingsway, W.C.2). The original, too long to be quoted *in extenso* here, is in Vol. IV, June, 1913, pp. 307-9, of the *Australian Monthly Weather Report and Meteorological Abstract*: S. H. Ebury "On Peculiar Explosive Sounds heard near Central Northern Victoria."

E) I was much interested to read Mr. C. J. P. Cave's letter about the Barisal Guns appearing on p. 149 of the April 1950 issue of *Weather*. In this connection I wish to draw the attention of your readers to a paper of mine on the same subject entitled "Barisal Guns and the upper atmosphere" published a few years ago in the *Journal of the University of Bombay* (Vol. 16, Pt. 3, November 1947, pp. 56-61). The following short summary of that paper will, I hope, not only furnish an answer to the question raised by Mr. C. J. P. Cave about the origin of the mysterious natural sounds like the Barisal Guns, but also create a further interest in them as a novel means of upper-air investigation.

In this paper attention is drawn to an old publication (of 1888) entitled "Memorandum on the Barisal Guns" and other similar papers of that time which give a good deal of information on the nature and distribution in time and space of the loud sounds well known long since as "Barisal Guns." From the observed distribution of the alternate zones of audibility and inaudibility, the direction of approach of these sounds, etc., it was easily inferred that the place of origin of these sounds lies in the so-called "seash of no ground" in the Bay of Bengal. The sounds are thus definitely of subterranean origin.

(M. W. Chiplonkar, *Ibid.*, V. 12, (Dec., 1950), 425. Written at Poona, India.)

F) Recent correspondence recalls to mind the summer of 1915 when, in a lonely lane near Collingham, Notts (Newark Rural District), well removed from main roads, I sensed, on more than one occasion, a very distant booming. This could scarcely have been gunfire in France at that distance, a sound I became familiar with in mid-Kent a year later.

At the time I put it down to some trick of the nerve of the ear — or imagination.

I give the story for what it is worth.

(G. C. Wooldridge, *Ibid*. Written at Market Harborough.)

AN ASPECT OF OBSCENITY IN RABELAIS

RAYMOND C. LA CHARITÉ
University of North Carolina

Obscenities occur frequently in the works of Rabelais. They constitute much of the humor for which he is so famous and account, in some measure, for his lasting popularity, or notoriety as the case may be. In fact, Rabelais's orgiastic effusion of *esprit gaulois* has been severely criticized by every age. La Bruyère's reading of Rabelais has become classic: "Marot et Rabelais sont inexcusables d'avoir semé l'ordure dans leurs écrits... Rabelais surtout est incompréhensible: son livre est une énigme, quoi qu'on veuille dire, inexplicable; c'est une chimère, c'est le visage d'une belle femme avec des pieds et une queue de serpent, ou de quelque autre bête plus difforme; c'est un monstrueux assemblage d'une morale fine et ingénieuse, et d'une sale corruption." [1] Voltaire, the strait-laced and morally unimpeachable author of *Candide*, was no less vociferous in his condemnation of Rabelais:

> "dans son extravagant et inintelligible livre, [il] a répandu une extrême gaieté et une plus grande impertinence; il a prodigué l'érudition, les ordures, et l'ennui... on est fâché qu'un homme qui avait tant d'esprit en ait fait un si misérable usage." [2]

---

[1] *Les Caractères*, ed. Robert Garapon (Paris, 1962), p. 82.
[2] *Œuvres complètes*, ed. Louis Moland, XXII (Paris, 1879), p. 174. He later renounces this criticism expressed in 1734: see his letters "A Madame la Marquise du Deffant" (1759), *Correspondance*, XL, p. 192 and (1760), XL, pp. 350-51.

The astute but overly sensitive Sainte-Beuve felt ill at ease with the more ribald Rabelaisian passages:

> "Quand on veut lire tout haut du Rabelais, même devant des hommes (car devant les femmes cela ne se peut), on est toujours comme quelqu'un qui veut traverser une vaste place pleine de boues et d'ordures: il s'agit d'enjamber à chaque moment et de traverser sans trop se crotter; c'est difficile." [3]

Sainéan, in his monumental study of Rabelais's language, notes the lexical existence of certain "realistic" elements, particularly the *erotica verba*, but he does not analyze in detail their creation and significance: "Dans l'étude de cette partie scabreuse du vocabulaire rabelaisien, certaines réserves s'imposent." [4]

Nevertheless, it may be considered of some import to know how Rabelais creates this obscene, "realistic," humor and how much of it is due to his inventive imagination and to the written and oral sources available to him.

One facet of these obscenities is reflected in the numerous synonyms one encounters for the sexual act; there are thirty-six of them, and they recur throughout Rabelais's work. [5] An explication of their formation, a matter of linguistic and artistic interest, may also shed some light on Rabelais's linguistic resources and inventions, his attitude toward life, and his use of obscenity as a source of comedy.

BAUDOUINER

A ces motz les filles commencèrent ricasser entre elles. Frère Jan hannissoit du bout du nez comme prest à roussiner ou baudouiner pour le moins, et monter dessus comme Herbault sus paouvres

---

[3] *Causeries du lundi*, 3d ed. (Paris, 1851-62), III, 5-6.
[4] Lazare Sainéan, *La Langue de Rabelais* (Paris, 1923), II, 294.
[5] Cf. Pierre de La Juillière, *Les Images dans Rabelais* (Halle, 1912), p. 113: "Les héros de Rabelais, Panurge surtout, sont extrêmement friands du plaisir vénérien. Quand ils veulent désigner l'acte de chair, ils n'ont pas moins de trente synonymes à leur dispostion."

gens.[6] In the sixteenth century, the verb *baudouiner* is used primarily to mean *to copulate* with reference to donkies.[7] Rabelais and other authors of the sixteenth century gave it various connotations, but Rabelais may be the only one who extended its meaning to apply to human beings. The etymology of the word seems to be the proper name *Baldowin,* literally *bold friend*.[8] In fifteenth-century French, the term *baudouin* meant an ass, a donkey, but more importantly, the *membrum virile*.[9] Although Rabelais often makes use of the animal world, he was undoubtedly aware of the latter connotation in this example.

BELINER

Les compaignons joyeusement partirent….Mais quand ilz eurent long chemin parfaict, et estoient jà las comme pauvres diables, et n'y avoit plus d'olif en ly caleil, ilz ne belinoyent si souvent et se contentoyent bien (j'entends quand aux hommes) de quelque meschante et paillarde foys le jour (II, 23, 268). This word seems to appear for the first time in the works of Rabelais.[10] Its etymology is the Dutch word *belle,* which also gives the Modern French *bélier*.[11] Probably, Rabelais is thinking of the breeding of a ewe and a

---

[6] Rabelais, *Œuvres complètes,* ed. Jacques Boulenger (Paris, 1955), p. 681. Unless otherwise indicated, all references are to this edition and will appear within the text. The synonyms under study are listed alphabetically.

[7] Edmond Huguet, *Dictionnaire de la langue française du seizième siècle* (Paris, 1925 to date), I, 517-18. Sainéan, II, 302: "proprement saillir, en parlant des baudets. Dans le *Grand Testament* de Villon, le coït est désigné par 'jeu *d'asne,*' et le *Moyen de parvenir* donne *baster l'asne* comme synonyme de *baudouiner*." Randle Cotgrave, *A Dictionnary of the French and English Tongues,* facsimile editon by W. S. Woods (Columbia, 1950), s. v.: "To doe, leacher, or ingender, like an Asse."

[8] Oscar Bloch and Walther von Wartburg, *Dictionnaire étymologique de la langue française,* 3d ed. (Paris, 1960), p. 63.

[9] Walther von Wartburg, *Französisches Etymologisches Wörterbuch* (Bonn, 1928 to date), I, 214.

[10] Huguet, I, 539; Sainéan, II, 302.

[11] Wartburg, *FEW,* I, 318; Bloch and Wartburg, *Dictionnaire étymologique,* p. 66. Further references to these works appear within the text as *FEW* and *BW*.

ram.[12] Accordingly, the meaning of this word has remained unchanged; it is especially attested in Normandy, where it always means *saillir la brebis* in terms of the *bélier* (*FEW, loc. cit.*).

BELUTER

Guare diables qui vouldra, en cas que autant de foys je ne belute ma femme future la première nuyct de mes nopces (III, 11, 365)! The etymology of this word is the middle high German *biuteln* (*FEW*, I, 387). In the sixteenth century, it meant (1) to sift, to pass through a sieve; (2) to separate while sifting; (3) to agitate; (4) to examine attentively (Huguet, I, 546-47). Rabelais's use of the expression *beluter le temps* is undoubtedly a play on words on the meaning of *to pass* (*Ibid.*). As far as meaning *to copulate*, Rabelais seems to be the only one to use this verb in that sense.[13] It is apparent that Rabelais is referring to the to and fro movement of the strainer as flour is passed through it. It is interesting to note that there was a game at that time, also referred to by Rabelais with regard to Gargantua's games (I, 22, 67), the *belusteau*, in which two boys, placing themselves one in front of the other and interlocking their hands, would push one another back and forth as though they were sifting flour.[14]

BESOINGNER

Fin de compte, ilz besoingnoyent comme toutes bonnes âmes, sinon que à celles qui estoyent horriblement villaines et défaictes, je leur faisoys mettre un sac sur le visaige (II, 17, 245-46). This verb

---

[12] Cotgrave, s. v.: "To ramme." Cf. Iago's words to Brabantio in Shakespeare's *Othello* (The Yale Shakespeare), I, i, 13: "Even now, now, very now, an old black ram [Othello] / Is tupping your white ewe [Desdemona]."

[13] However, Wartburg, *FEW*, I, 387, finds that the Old French form *buleter*, i. e., *beluter*, also meant *to copulate*. Cf. Sainéan, II, 304: "Du Fail s'est servi de *beluteur*, au sens libre. Métaphore déjà usuelle dans la poésie galante du XVe siècle et dans les vieilles farces."

[14] Abel Lefranc, ed. *Œuvres de François Rabelais* (Paris, 1913), I, 209.

was easily adaptable and was actually in general use.[15] It is also found in Amyot and Saint-Gelais. The latter, for example, says: "Ils peuvent, en toute saison, / Besongner en vostre maison, / Par prix ou par douces prieres, / Vos filles et vos chambrieres" (Huguet, I, 562).

FAIRE LA BESTE A DEUX DOZ

En son eage virile espousa Gargamelle, fille du roy des Parpaillos, belle gouge et de bonne troigne, et faisoient eux deux souvent ensemble la beste à deux doz (I, 3, 13). The origin of this expression, whether French or English, has elicited much commentary.[16] However, it seems to have been quite common and, as is so often the case with Rabelais and his contemporaries, it is taken from animal life. One finds it in the *Cent nouvelles nouvelles,* in Cholières, in Coquillart's *Droits Nouveaux,* in Eustache Deschamps, in *Le Moyen de parvenir,* and in the *Mystère de saint Quentin.*[17] Of course, it appears in Shakespeare's *Othello*: "Your daughter and the Moor are now making the beast with two backs."[18]

BISCOTER

D'aultant qu'elles estoyent plus horribles et exécrables, d'autant il leur failloyt donner dadvantaige aultrement le diable ne les eust voulu biscoter.[19] The substantive *biscotte* seems to be a provincial

---

[15] Lefranc, IV, 203; Cotgrave, s. v.: "to doe, or leacher with."
[16] Sainéan, II, 302, n. 1, believes that Shakespeare borrowed it from Rabelais. See "Shakespeare et Rabelais," *Revue des études Rabelaisiennes,* IX (1911), 282-85.
[17] Lefranc, I, 39; Sainéan, II, 301-02.
[18] Tucker Brooke and Lawrence Mason, ed. (New Haven, 1947), I, i, 14.
[19] II, 17, 245. A Rabelaisian variant is the verb *brisgouter*: "Il ne te fauldra poinct de lunettes: tu la voyras en un mirouoir brisgoutant aussi apertement que si je te la monstrois en la fontaine du temple di Minerve" (III, 25, 419). Huguet, I, 719, lists it separately; La Juillière, p. 113, equates the two expressions. Cotgrave, s. v., indicates *to swine* for *biscoter* and *to leacher* for brisgouter. The latter form seems to appear only in Rabelais. Sainéan, II, 298, lists *brisgouter* as a dialect variant of *biscoter* whose primitive source may be *brisque,* a deer.

variant of *bicotte,* which is also a variant of the Modern French *bichette,* a small doe (Lefranc, IV, 202). Initially, the verb meant *to kid, to give birth,* with reference to goats and antelopes, It also meant *to hop* or *to jump about* like a small deer. *Biscoter,* meaning *to hop,* is still found in Poitou, [20] and Palsgrave gave it that meaning in his dictionary. [21] On the other hand, La Juillière (p. 106) believes, erroneously, that *biscoter,* an erotic term, is derived from *biscotte,* meaning a piece of rusk. Poirier's research (*loc. cit.,* n. 20) indicates that the original term may be *biscouette,* a dialect form of Poitou. The *biscouette,* that is a wagtail (often referred to in French as a *hochequeue*), moves its tail in an up-and-down fashion. As far as *to copulate* is concerned, Rabelais probably borrowed that connotation from a provincial dialect known to him, perhaps poitevin. In Hainaut and Normandy, the verb *biscoter* has the same meaning today that it had for Rabelais (Lefranc, IV, 202).

BOUTER

J'en aymerois mieulx (dist Panurge) une mouillée de quelque bon vin d'Anjou. Boutez doncq, boutez bas et roidde (IV, 49, 673)! Although this verb is often used in the *Cent nouvelles nouvelles* and, at times, in an equivocal way, it never seems to mean anything other than *to put, to place, to drive.* [22] Rabelais seems to be the first one to use it to mean *to fornicate.* [23] The dialect form *boutre,* from *bouter,* has the same meaning in many provinces. For a long time it was thought that *boutre,* with the meaning of *to put* or *to place,* had evolved through identification with the verb *mettre.* However, in the course of compiling the *Atlas linguistique de la*

---

[20] A.-D. Poirier, "La Langue de Rabelais dans ses rapports avec le Bas-Poitou, *Le Français moderne,* XII (1944), 140.

[21] Jean Palsgrave, *L'Éclaircissement de la langue française* (Paris, 1852), p. 589 (Collection de documents inédits sur l'histoire de la France): "*bistocquer* is but a fayned worde, for it betokeneth properly to stabbe or to foyne. Also in more coverte langage they use *je fays cela.*"

[22] *Cent nouvelles nouvelles,* ed. Thomas Wright (Paris, 1857-58), I, 9, and 43.

[23] Huguet, I, 670-71, does not note its erotic usage.

France, Gilliéron found that *bouter-boutre* had changed both in form and in meaning by association with the verb *foutre*. [24]

BRAGMARDER

Je (dist Panurge) entreprens de entrer en leur camp par le meillieu des guardes et du guet, et bancqueter avec eulx et bragmarder à leurs despens, sans estre congneu de nully (II, 24, 272-73). The *braquemart* was a short, stubby sword which was first used in the sixteenth century. Both the substantive and the verb appear frequently in Rabelais and are used for military and erotic purposes. *Jouer du braquemart* or *bragmarder* imply that *membrum virile* is replacing short, stubby sword. [25]

BRIMBALLER

Dedans un bassin plein d'eaue je te monstreray ta femme future brimballant avecques deux rustres (III, 25, 419). The etymology of this word is obscure. [26] In the sixteenth century, it meant (1) to swing, to dangle or (2) to agitate a question (Huguet, I, 716). In Modern French, only the primary meaning has remained. Strictly speaking, *brimballer* implies *sonner fortement les cloches,* and it is used in this manner in Chevallet's *Mystère de Saint Cristophle.* [27] Rabelais's imagination would have no trouble bridging the gap between *sonner fortement les cloches* and *sonner fortement les couilles*; Rabelais ascribes sonority, oscillation, and balancing to the latter. The metaphorical impact of the "cloches" in action is seen in their movement, both regular and erratic, and in their tonal qualities, rendered by onomatopeia and the alliterative *b* of *brimbal-*

---

[24] See *FEW*, I, 458-59.

[25] Cotgrave, s. v.: "to leacher."

[26] *FEW*, I, 217 gives *ballare*. Huguet, *Mots disparus ou vieillis depuis le XVIe siècle* (Paris, 1935), p. 82, notes the frequency of the verb *baller* as a synonym of *danser*. Bloch and Wartburg, pp. 88 and 642, note its affinity with *trimbaler*, also found in Rabelais, and itself of uncertain origin.

[27] Sainéan, II, 307. La Juillière, p. 106, lists the metaphorical origin of the verb under the rubric "cérémonies religieuses."

ler. On the other hand, it is possible that he was familiar with some dialect forms from Picardy, one of which was *brimbette,* meaning "jeune fille légère." [28] The verb *brimballer,* in its vulgar sense, is attested in Rabelais, Bretin, and D'Alcripe. The latter, for example, says: "Il y fit si bon guet qu'il descouvrit comment le Capitaine de la compagnie brimbaloit sa femme" (Huguet, *loc. cit.*).

BUBAJALLER

Dès lors les pauvres hayres bubajalloient comme vieulx mulletz (II, 17, 245). This verb is found only in Rabelais. It can be divided into *bube,* i. e., *bubon* or *bouton* and *jaller,* a variant of *galler,* i. e., *jouir* (Sainéan, II, 310). The idea would be *jouir du bouton,* the last word having the meaning of *clitoris.* Moreover, Rabelais's prolific imagination may be relying upon the unuttered aspects of the form *buba,* the outward thrust which the lips indicate in the formation of *bu* as opposed to the receding movement for *ba.* [29] On the other hand, the verb may consist of *jaller* and *bubaler,* for the latter form connotes the idea of copulating like buffalos (from the Greek *boubalos*; Modern French *bubale*). Both sources are plausible although the second possibility seems more apt when one considers Rabelais's predilection for comparisons with animal life.

CHEVAUCHER

Par Dieu, je vous feray chevaucher aux chiens (II, 21, 264). Although the literal meaning of this verb is *parcourir à cheval,* its use as a synonym for *to make love* was very widespread. [30] It is found not only in Rabelais, but also in the *Satire Ménippée,* the *Cent*

---

[28] Emile Littré, *Dictionnaire de la langue française* (Paris, 1956), I, 1258.

[29] Sainéan, II, 202: "Il ne recule même pas devant les sons inarticulés, les bruits sourds ou les vagues sonorités." The prefix *buba* recurs in the formation of a dish which was served to the "Dames Lanternes": "Des bubagotz" (V, 33 bis, 849).

[30] See Huguet, II, 254; *FEW*, II, pt. 1, 7; Lefranc, IV, 238; Sainéan, II, 302.

nouvelles nouvelles, the *Parnasse Satyrique,* Coquillart, Villon, and Marot. Its metaphorical intent derives from a sense of posture rather than a desire to assimilate animal characteristics.

COINGNER

O! mon doux amy (ce dict-elle),/Quel maillet vous voy-je empoingner?/C'est (dist-il) pour mieux vous coingner (IV, Prol., 532). This verb constitutes one of the more ingenious inventions or play on words of the fourteenth century (Lefranc, VI, 49), and Rabelais is only using what he undoubtedly heard from time to time. The verb means *to hit, to strike,* and that alone is ample reason for Rabelais to use it. Moreover, the verbal form, which emphasizes the action, is reinforced and enriched by its noun counterpart, a *cognée,* the instrument, a long-handled ax. Together, they connote etymologically *faire un coin,* and, from this expression, there is but a small step to having it imply what the *Cent nouvelles nouvelles* is so fond of calling "faire la chose que scavez" (II, 139). The erotic aspect of this expression is still in use (*FEW*, II, pt. 2, 1532-33).

FAIRE LA COMBRECELLE

Car rien n'y quiers, sinon qu'en vostre tour / Me faciez de hait la combrecelle / Pour ceste foys (II, 22, 265). This expression seems to appear for the first time in Rabelais. Its etymology is obscure. However, it may very well be the composite of the verb *cambrer,* "to bend" and of the noun *selle,* "saddle." Hence, it would mean *to bend one's back* (namely that of the woman) *in the form of a saddle.* In Languedoc, one finds today the expression *courco-sello,* literally *couche-selle* (Lefranc, IV, 240-41). The expression *faire la combreselle* still exists in some provincial dialects. In Berry, for instance, it implies the act of bending over so that one may jump on one's back. In the Blésois, *combreselle* designates a gymnastic movement, a complete flip of the body.[31] That may also be what Rabelais has in mind, i. e., *faire la culbute.*

---

[31] Cotgrave, s. v.: "*combrecelle*: A tumbling tricke, or Sommer-sault, wherein the heeles are cast over the head; also, reciprocation of venerie."

DECROTTER

Merde! merde! (dist Panurge). Ma seulle braguette espoussetera tous les hommes, et sainct Balletrou, qui dedans y repose, décrottera toutes les femmes (II, 26, 279). In the sixteenth century, this verb could be used to mean *to expedite, to do* or *say something rapidly* (Huguet, III, 59-60). Rabelais seems to be the only one to use it as a synonym for *to copulate*. In the preceding quotation, Panurge is in all likelihood implying that not only will he clean out the women, i. e., their sexual organs, but that he will also make short shrift of them. No doubt, the source lends itself to two distinct but equally plausible connotations; in the first place, *décrotter* may indicate posterior penetration; in the second place, *dé-crotte-er* may equate *crotte* with *membrum virile* and suggest the waning and loss of virile characteristics through intercourse.

DEPUCELLER

Frère Enguainnant ...juroit et se donnoit au plus viste diable d'enfer, en cas que mieulx n'aymast dépuceller cent filles que biscoter une vefve (III, 6, 350). This verb presents no difficulties, and it has long been in use. [32] One still finds it in the provincial dialects (*FEW*, 9, 525-26). Its metaphorical source is physiological and anatomical.

EMBOURRER

Je ne me vante d'en avoir embourré quatre cens dix et sept despuis que suis en ceste ville (II, 15, 236). This verb is a contamination of *rembourrer*, meaning *to stuff*, hence its Rabelaisian adaptation. Marot uses it equivocally as does Rabelais: "Mais n'embourre l'on plus le bas / A ces lingeres du Pallais" (Lefranc,

---

[32] *Ibid.*, s. v.: "to depucelate, or deflower a virgine; to take her maidenhead."

IV, 182). This play on words is based on *bât*, the packsaddle in which the flock is stuffed, and *bas*, that is, the lower parts of a woman. The metaphor is used even earlier by Coquillart (Sainéan, II, 306).

ESTOUPPER

Elle, ce croy-je, est toute trou, et il, de mesmes, tout cheville. Ores est à sçavoir si ce trou par ceste cheville peult entièrement estre estouppé (V, 9, 564). The verb *étouper*, of course, means *to stuff, to plug, to stop up* with tow or oakum, *étoupe*.[33] Like many other such terms in Rabelais, it is borrowed from the trades. Rabelais merely extends its meaning to include the sexual act.

FANFRELUCHER

Ainsi les compaignons joyeusement partirent, et, pource qu'ilz estoient frays et de séjour, ilz fanfreluchoient à chasque bout de champ, et voylà pourquoy les lieues de France sont tant petites (II, 23, 268). Its primary meaning is *orner de fanfreluches*, i. e., to garnish with baubles, trifles, or trinkets, in other words, small joyful tokens of love. *Fanfreluche* is an alteration of the Old French *fanfelue*, i. e., *bagatelle* (*BW*, p. 250), and Rabelais seems to be responsible for this change. Undoubtedly, the expression is to be equated with its modern equivalent *faire la bagatelle* (Lefranc, IV, 248).

FARBOULLER

On pouvoit après luy farbouller sans danger de chancre (V, 30, 839). This verb is not attested elsewhere; Huguet, La Juillière, and Marty-Laveaux [34] do not include it in their glossaries. It is possible

---

[33] Huguet, III, 724; Cotgrave, s. v.: "to stop, to close; to shut, or make-up." Also "*estoupe*: towe, heards; Ockam. *Clou d'estoupe*: A speeke, or sheathing nayle, used in shipping."

[34] Charles Marty-Laveaux, ed. *Les Œuvres de Maistre François Rabelais*, 6 vols. (Paris, 1870-1903).

that Rabelais may have coined the verb with the word *farbella* in mind. In Rabelais's time, *farbella* was a noun in use in the region of Lyons. Today, it still means a "personne dans l'inconduite" (*FEW*, 3, 397). However, a second possibility, admittedly remote, may be seen in the reunion of the verb *farcir* and the noun *boule* or the verb *bouler*. The verb *farfouiller*, first attested in Rabelais (1552; *BW*, p. 269), is probably composed of the prefix *far*, from *farcir*, and *fouiller*. In this case, the prefix reinforces the initial thought both alliteratively and connotatively. *Farbouler* may follow the same principle, hence *farcir la boule*, a metaphor which ideally retains the Rabelaisian turn of mind. However, *boule*, for the female sex, does not seem to have that metaphorical use in the popular literature of the sixteenth century.[35]

FRETINFRETAILLER

Compère, voicy qui est à toy si tu veulx fretinfretailler un bon coup (II, 17, 245). This expression is found only in Rabelais. Old French has three verbs: *freter* meaning *to rub*, *fertailler* meaning *to strike*, and *fresteler* meaning *to make noise*;[36] all three could be, both in meaning and formation, antecedents of *fretailler*. By relying upon initial denotations, the repetition of initial syllables for rhythmic purposes, and surely the onomatopeia "frt," Rabelais attempts to depict the sexual act in terms of both sound and the repeatedly short and rapid movement or agitation which creates it. In addition, a second metaphor may be culled from a separation of the terms *fretin* and *fretailler*. A *fretin* is a small fish in sixteenth-century French culinary terminology.[37] Since *fretailler* is also a variant of *frétiller*, Rabelais may have in mind the idea of "to wriggle like a fish."

---

[35] For a list of these metaphors in Rabelais as well as in many other authors of the period, see Sainéan, II, 300-09.

[36] Bloch and Wartburg p. 273; *FEW*, III, 754; Albert Dauzat, *Dictionnaire étymologique de la langue française* (Paris, 1938), p. 342.

[37] Cotgrave, s. v.: "Fretin: Cod, or Greene-fish"; *FEW*, III, 754.

FROTTER SON LARD

Que heureux sera celluy à qui ferez celle grâce de ceste-cy accoller, de la baiser et de frotter son lard avecques elle (II, 21, 261). Rabelais seems to be the first to use this expressive and colorful metaphor. Its meaning is unmistakable. Rabelais also uses it to denote hand to hand combat: "Allons nous battre guaillard et bien à poinct frotter nostre lard" (III, 42, 481).

GIMBRETILETOLLETER

Coingnée... .signifie aussi (au moins jadis signifioit la femelle bien à poinct et souvent gimbretiletolletée (IV, Prol., 531). The very length of this verb immediately indicates its Rabelaisian origin. The verb *gimberter,* and its variant form *gimbretiller,* means *to make love*; this verb is of Berry provenience, and it is still used there with no change in meaning.[38] In Blésois, *gimberter* is used in the sense of *to hop, to jump up and down* (Lefranc, *loc. cit.*). Sainéan (II, 311) believes that the latter part of the verb, *tolleter,* is either a reduplication of *tiller* or a separate form whose origin remains obscure. Yet, it is also likely that this form is one of Rabelais's original poetic formations whose purpose is the recreation of sound, movement, and rhythm. The explosive and staccato-like alliterative beat of the letter *t* (gimbre*t*ile*t*olle*t*er) hammers out a rhythm whose cadence is set by the distribution of the letters *i, o, e* and prolonged and enriched by the letter *l*, making the whole faintly reminiscent of the metaphoric bells in *brimballer*.[39]

---

[38] Lefranc, VI, 49; Cotgrave, s. v.: "*gimbreter*: to play the wanton, to doe lasciviously, to leacher it."

[39] Cf. Marcel Tetel, *Etude sur le comique de Rabelais* (Florence, 1964), p. 106:

> "Au lieu de créer de simples onomatopées, Rabelais se sert d'allitérations qui suggèrent ou traduisent l'action. Les allitérations, en devenant des onomatopées, conservent leur effet plaisant par le choc et la répétition des sons, mais elles créent un sens qui renchérit sur la signification ordinaire du vocable et qui vivifie l'action."

JOCQUETER

Venez veoir tous les chiens du pays qui sont assemblés à l'entour d'une dame, la plus belle de ceste ville, et la veullent jocqueter (II, 22, 266). The original expression used by Rabelais was *jocquer*, spelled *joquier* or *juquier* in Old French and *jucher*, "to go to roost, to perch," in Modern French. The verb indicates the hind tiptoe stance of dogs with relation to the recipient in the quoted passage and of man in general.[40] Rabelais substituted *jocqueter* for *jocquer* in the definitive edition of 1542. *Jocqueter* is a formation of Anjou, one which is still in use today (Sainéan, II, 298). The Angevins use the instransitive verb when they want to refer to the action of the handle of any tool which fits loosely in its socket and has too much play. Rabelais uses *jocqueter*, in preference to *jocquer*, because it phonetically retains the possible allusion to *jocquer* and its designation of posture, and, in addition, stresses the action of the participating parts.

LABOURER

Ma femme viendra au combat / Vénérien: Dieu, que d'esbat / Je y prévoy! Je laboureray / Tant et plus (V, 45, 884). The common verb *labourer* was easily adaptable. Its inherent reference to nature, the action of tilling the soil and its concomitant notion of fertility, the visual impact and implication of furrows, not to mention the notion of diligent, "laborious," work immediately designate it for transposition on an erotic level. This metaphor is also found in Coquillart, the *Cent nouvelles nouvelles,* Des Périers and Guillaume Bouchet (Sainéan, II, 303).

LANTERNER

Le vent de Galerne (dist Panurge) avoit doncques lanterné leur mère (IV, 9, 565)? This verb commonly meant *to say trifles* or more

---

[40] Cotgrave, s. v.: "to leacher; or, to line, as a dog doth a bitch."

importantly *to dilly-dally, to shilly-shally* (Huguet, IV, 767). Moreover, (Rabelais's use of *lanterne* in the quotation indicates that he was familiar with the legend about animals which are impregnated by the wind. The semantic field of *lanterne* is extensive. In Old French, and perhaps in Rabelais, *lanterne* euphemistically describes and stresses the phallus dimension of the clitoris. [41] Rabelais uses *lanterne* in order to depict the female sex; its masculine counterpart, a play on the word *phallus,* is *falot*: "Lors, les ménestriers plus que devant mélodieusement sonnantz, fut par la Royne commancé ung bransle double, auquel tous, et Falotz et Lanternes, ensemble dansèrent" (V, 33 bis, 851). Both Béroalde de Verville and Rabelais make use of the expression *va te faire lanterner*: "Va (respondit Panurge), fol enraigé, au diable et te faiz lanterner" (III, 25, 421).

JOUER DES MANEQUINS A BASSES MARCHES

Or (dist-il), ce me seroit bien tout un d'avoir bras et jambes couppéz, en condition que nous fissions, vous et moy, un transon de chère lie, jouans des manequins à basses marches (II, 21, 260). This phrase is used not only by Rabelais, but also by Des Périers, Du Fail, and Grévin (Huguet, V, 122). The term *mannequin* in this ribald expression and in others remains problematic. Amidst the jargon of the Baisecul-Humevesne episode, Baisecul perorates: "voulant obtempérer au plaisir du roy, je me estois armé de pied en cap d'une carrelure de ventre pour aller veoir comment mes vendangeurs avoyent déchicqueté leurs haulx bonnetz pour mieux jouer des manequins" (II, 11, 220). Although the language seems gratuitous, it may be that *mannequin* as an erotic metaphor is conspicuous by the noticeable absence of arms and legs, representative of a straight and stiff position.

Lefranc and Marty-Laveaux suggest that *mannequin* may refer to some sort of primitive musical instrument; [42] no doubt, this explanation relies upon the similarity of the following Rabelaisian

---

[41] See *FEW,* V, 166 and Bloch and Wartburg, p. 356.
[42] Lefranc, IV, 230; Marty-Laveaux, VI, 7; Cotgrave, s. v.: "*Manequin*: a rude instrument of Musicke; whence, Joüer des cymbales, & manequins. To leacher. Joüer des manequins à basses marches. The same."

metaphor: "Escargotz, Sarabouytes, Cauquemarres, Canibales seront fort molestéz des mouches bovines, et peu joueront des cymbales et manequins, si le Guaiac n'est de requeste."[43] In the erotic literature of the fifteenth and sixteenth centuries, the term *cimbales* represents testicles (Sainéan, II, 305); is it possible that *mannequin* is another synonym for *membrum virile*? At any rate, Sainéan rejects the possible instrumental origin of *mannequin*.

The last part of the expression, *à basses marches,* seems to have been borrowed from the weaving trade (Lefranc, *loc. cit.*). The *marches* were the pedals of the foot-looms which the operator activated in an up-and-down motion of the legs, so that the pulleys of the loom would raise and lower the heddles. Somehow, *mannequin* and *basses marches* clash; a musical instrument and a loom seem irreconcilable. *Mannequin* has never been used to describe a loom. Perhaps a musical instrument, of the organ type, is still at its origin. Certainly, the reconciliation of *basses marches* and *mannequin,* with the possible meaning of phallus, seems doubtful. However, the operator of the pedals, which depict the path of the action, might be said to be in the stiff position of a mannequin. Modern French still has the verb *mannequiner,* meaning *to pose in a stiff, unnatural, position.*

JOUEURS DE QUILLE

Tous bons beuveurs, bons compaignons et beaulx joueurs de quille-là (I, 4, 15). The expression *jouer aux quilles* or *planter la quille* (Huguet, VI, 292) is based upon the use of the word *quille* as a synonym for penis. One finds it in Marot, Rabelais, Jodelle, and Brantôme. The following lines are from Act I, scene 1 of Jodelle's comedy *Eugène*: "Si fussiez allé chacun jour / Cependant qu'Alix estoit fille, / Planter en son jardin la quille, / A l'envi chascun eust crié." The earliest appearance of the expression is probably found in the works of Eustache Deschamps: "Tu ne vois femme ou fille / A qui un tour ne joues de quille" (Lefranc, I, 50).

---

[43] *Pantagruéline Prognostication,* chapter VI, p. 903.

RATACONNICULER

Personne les blasme de soy faire rataconniculer (I, 3, 14). Rabelais seems to be the only writer to have used this expression. In the sixteenth century, the verb *rataconner* meant *to mend, to patch up*.[44] Lefranc (I, 45) suggests that it is the basis for Rabelais's *rataconniculer*, for the suffix *iculer* was in general use, as in the word *diabliculer*. This may be the case. However, Rabelais was undoubtedly aware of the word *connin*, which literally meant *rabbit*, from the Latin *cuniculus* (Sainéan, II, 311), when he coined this expression; it is unlikely that the metaphorical possibilities would have escaped him. Moreover, it seems obvious that his imagination would go beyond a mere extension of the meaning *to patch up*. His formation is probably based on *rataconner*, but quite possibly for reasons other than its primary meaning. If one divides the verb into what seem to be its component parts, one obtains *rata, con* and *cul*. *Ratati ratata*, like *rataplan* for the drum roll, is one of the onomatopeic expressions used to denote rapid, staccato-like sound, movements, and repeated blows. With this in mind, one can see that, for Rabelais, the last two parts of the formation but contribute the noise described by the first part.[45]

ROUSSINER

Frère Jan hannissoit du bout du nez comme prest à roussiner ou baudouiner pour le moins (V, 52, 681). This formation is also derived from animal life. A *roncin* or *roussin* is a war-horse, a charger, and *ronciner* or *roussiner* describes literally and metaphorically its horse-like, war-like, strong and sustained sexual activity (Godefroy, VII, 234). Quite naturally, the verb was applied to human beings. One finds it in the *Cent nouvelles nouvelles* and the *Moyen de parvenir*, and it is still actively used today (*FEW*, 10, 575).

---

[44] Frédéric Godefroy, *Dictionnaire de l'ancienne langue française* (Paris, 1937-38), VI, 615.
[45] Cotgrave, s. v.: "rataconniculer: to reiterate leacherie."

SABOULER

Les lacquais de court par les degréz, entre les huys, sabouloient sa femme à plaisir, laquelle estoit assez bellastre (III, 25, 416). The verb *sabouler* is probably a composite of *saboter* meaning *to knock, to shake carelessly* and *bouler* "to roll about" (*BW*, p. 559). In Modern French, *sabouler* means *to pull someone about, to take someone to task*. For Rabelais, it specifically means *to shake violently, to jostle* or *to jump on something*, and in this case, *on someone*.[46] Rabelais seems to be the only one to have used it as a synonym for *to fornicate*.

SABOURRER

Je voiray bas culz / De brief bien en poinct sabourréz / Par couilles (V, 45, 884). This verb is a navigational term of sixteenth-century formation and is based on the Latin *saburrare*; it means *to ballast* or *to weigh down a ship* (Sainéan, II, 305). On several occasions, Rabelais uses it to describe the action of copiously filling and feeding, that is weighing down, one's stomach: "J'ay bien saburré mon stomach" (I, 5, 18); "Nous estant bien à poinct sabourré l'estomach, eusmes vent en pouppe" (V, 9, 771). Erotically, Rabelais refers to the act of copulation as a weighing-down of the woman on the part of the man. Quite properly, the man acts as a ballast; specifically, the testicles operate as weights, anchoring the male in position. There is no evidence that this expression appears elsewhere in this sense.

SACCADER

Par Dieu, je les feray saccader encores une foys devant qu'elles meurent (II, 17, 245)! This verb, which is properly a term of equitation, means *to pull violently, to jerk repeatedly* a horse's rein.

---

[46] Cotgrave, s. v.: "To roll, tosse, or tumble with; to tread under, the feet; also, to tug, rumble, or scuffle with; and hence, to jumble a woman."

Rabelais attaches its meaning to the sexual act.[47] In the same way, he uses the expression *avoir la saccade*, "to receive the jerks and jolts": "elle aura, par Dieu, la saccade puisqu'il y a moynes autour" (I, 45, 132).

SACSACBEZEVEZINEMASSER

Je te demande (dist Panurge) si ...j'avoys sacsacbezevezinemassé ta tant belle, tant advenente, tant honeste, tant preude femme,...que feroys-tu (IV, 5, 553)? This is certainly one of Rabelais's most interesting, and not necessarily unintelligible,[48] gratuitous gigantic word formations. Its four component parts are *sacsac, beze, vezine,* and *masser* (Lefranc, VI, 110-11). In various combinations, these elements frequently reappear in Rabelais, particularly in chapter XV of Book IV: *morrambouzevezengouzequoquemorguatasacbacguevezinemaffressé, morcrocassebesassevezassegrigueliguoscopapopondrillé, enguoulevezinemasséz.* Sainéan (II, 311) suggests that the two interior elements of this erotic metaphor are *bouzine,* a trumpet, and *veze,* a bagpipe. It is difficult to find a relationship between the redoubling of *sac,* musical instruments, and the action of kneading dough, as he interprets *masser.* To be sure, *bouzine* and *veze* are musical instruments which one encounters in Rabelais: "Les vezes, bouzines et cornemuses sonnèrent harmonieusement et leurs furent les viandes apportées" (V, 33 bis, 848); however, it is unlikely that these same instruments are the source of Rabelais's copulative synonym.

Sacsac is probably the expressive reduplication of the verb *saccader,* itself a Rabelaisian synonym for the act of fornication; hence, one might translate it as *jerk-jerk.* Moreover, the onomatopeic sibilant recreates the frictional sound of a suction. The syllables *sacsac* also create an uncanny, almost incantatory, sense of rhythm and urgency: *sacsac* is perhaps an exhortation, not unlike the *à sac!* which encouraged soldiers to put everyone to the sword. *Beze* refers to the "bzz" sound of the fly and comes from the Old French

---

[47] Cotgrave, s. v.: "to throw, overthrow, cast down; also, to overturne a wench."

[48] Cf. Tetel, p. 87: "Tous ces mots démesurés vivent par le cliquetis des sons; il ne faut pas tenter d'y chercher une signification logique."

verb *beser* which was used to describe a cow or a horse which had been bitten by a horse-fly; for example, "elle a été besée." *Vezine* comes from the Norman *veser, vesonner,* meaning *to run about, to run hither and yon. Masser,* a variant of *massir,* means *to stuff.* Therefore, quite literally, one could translate it as *to stuff and to go back and forth in a noisy, jerky way.* Even today one finds *bezeux* used in Bas-Maine to mean *débauché, saint Bezet* is the patron saint of prostitutes, and in Limousin *vezon* means *prostitute.*

JOUER DU SERRECROPIERE

Ces bonnes femmes icy ont très bien employé leur temps en jeunesse, et ont joué du serrecropière à cul levé (II, 17, 245). This expression seems to appear only in Rabelais. It is composed of *serrer* "to squeeze" and *croupière / croupion* "rump, stern." One would have to translate it as *playing at squeezing one's rumps together.*

TABOURER

C'est (dist Panurge) comment je pourray avanger à braquemarder toutes les putains qui y sont en ceste après-disnée, qu'il n'en eschappe pas une que je ne taboure en forme commune (II, 26, 278). In Old French, *tabourer* meant (1) to beat the drums, (2) to make a loud noise, and (3) to strike (Godefroy, VII, 619). With these connotations, *tabourer* could easily be adapted to describe the sexual act. The *tambour,* of course, is the female sex upon which the male drums out the beat; the metaphor incorporates sound, nature of movement, and rhythm. One also finds it with the same meaning in *Le Moyen de parvenir* (Lefranc, IV, 270).

TALOCHER

Ilz auroient tant taloché leurs amours ...qu'ilz en restoient tous effiléz (III, 6, 350). This verb still means today *to cuff, to box someone's ears.* In Old French, it also meant *to strike with a stick*

(Godefroy, VII, 634), hence its adaptability for Rabelaisian purposes. Obviously, Rabelais relies upon the interrelationship of stick and thumping.

Both the quantity and the originality of these *erotica verba* are impressive and of significance. Even the *Cent nouvelles nouvelles*, a compendium of ribald tales whose characters for the most part are very much interested in the same activity, does not contain as many synonyms. Rabelais has thirty-six such terms; the late fifteenth-century work has but fourteen, of which only eight remain in the works of Rabelais.

The available vocabulary does not satisfy Rabelais's insatiable appetite for total expression; his inventive imagination bursts with linguistic and metaphorical creations. He devises approximately fifteen terms for the act of copulation and extends the metaphorical connotation to twenty-two others. Rabelais's lexical resources are plentiful; he draws upon contemporary French, Old French, and provincial dialects. His own fabrication of meaningful reproductions which attempt to capture sound, motion, and rhythm is perhaps the most fascinating part of this aspect of Rabelais's vocabulary.

Rabelais normally fashions these images by alluding to an almost limitless variety of sources. From the trades, in a general sense, and work habits, he culls *coingner, embourrer, estoupper, jocqueter, jouer des manequins à basses marches, décrotter, besoingner*. The military contributes *bragmarder* while agriculture is represented by *labourer*. Navigation provides *sabourrer*; equitation gives *chevaucher* and *saccader*. The general category of instruments and devices supplies *lanterner, tabourer, fanfrelucher,* and *brimballer*. Cuisine furnishes *beluter*, and gymnastics affords *bouter, faire la combrecelle, joueur de quille, sabouler, gimbretiletolleter*. *Sacsacbezevezinemasser* is based, in part, upon the adroit exploitation of epithets for lewd conduct. The two predominant resources are those of the animal world and of the human anatomy. The latter lends itself to *dépuceller, farbouler, talocher, frotter son lard, rataconniculer,* and *jouer du serrecropière*. Images from animal life abound: *baudouiner, beliner, faire la beste à deux doz, biscoter, fretinfretailler, bubajaller,* and *roussiner*.

Frequently, Rabelais's verbs belong to more than one category; hence, it is difficult and impractical to restrict their provenience.

The metaphorical impact of certain expressions frequently obliterates their original meaning; Rabelais jumbles and transforms denotations and accumulates connotations. The meaning of the image, particularly the more comic and lewd ones, is often extraneous to the initial source. *Brimballer* and *sabourrer*, for example, increase in meaningful and comic proportion when one glimpses the nature of the bells in the first expression and that of the weights in the second image.

His lewd allusions are often illusive. He shifts constantly the "realistic," sexual origin of the image. At times, Rabelais focuses on female sexual parts. However, he is usually more apt to emphasize the male, in terms of his sexual parts or the methodology of his activity; in this sense, Rabelais's obscene images are primarily phallic: sticks, lanterns, pins, swords, handles, etc. *Sacsacbezevezinemasser* and *sabouler* are good examples of this methodology. Some images stress reciprocity, *faire la beste à deux doz* and *rataconniculer*, to mention only a few. Again, others emphasize posture and appearance: *chevaucher* and *jocqueter*. Many images primarily depict upheaval and movement: *saccader* and *beluter*. Several expressions recreate the nature of the action in terms of sound, motion, and rhythm: *gimbretiletolleter*.

Rabelais's obscene expressions are living organisms; they have a reality of their own which constantly keeps the reader off balance. They repeatedly and instantaneously generate paroxysms of uproarious laughter; one need not have an immediate understanding of their structure. Context and, more importantly, Rabelais's persistent concern with sound automatically elucidate these verbs. They constitute but one of the many nuances through which Rabelais's sense of the comic unfolds. Those expressions which are new formations are, in and of themselves, extensions of the comic. Indeed, the linguistic, metaphorical, and philosophical humor which they embody is the product of a comic, loving, and beneficent vision of humanity.

Life for Rabelais has multiple facets, and all are to be explored, explained, experienced, and enjoyed. His boundless energy, wit, and imagination revel at being in the midst of humanity. Sex is a creative force; it gives pleasure and life. Man is a sentient being whose best and total means of expression is found in reproduction.

Rabelais's use of obscenities is not only humorous; it also represents his phenomenally irrepressible optimistic view of life.

Above all, Rabelais is a comic, polyphonic poet, a master observer and interpreter of the grotesque, the phantasmagoric, and the sublimely foolish which lie in the path of life's every step. Man is essentially comic; he is neither *ange* nor *bête*, but a potent blend of natural, but disparate elements —physical, intellectual, and spiritual— hopefully *un abysme de science* clothed in the garb of a *bon vivant*, giving free rein to natural impulses, gingerly aping the mores of lesser creatures in the knowledge that they are the embodiment of enlightened freedom. In a word, there is in Rabelais a poetry of obscenity.

CHAR'S SURREALIST EXPERIENCE: AN APPRAISAL OF *ARTINE*

VIRGINIA A. LA CHARITÉ
University of North Carolina

Le Marteau sans maître is a collective edition of poems which constitutes what is generally considered René Char's Surrealist period.[1] This collection of five volumes was originally published in 1934, and revised editions appeared in 1945 and 1963. As the Surrealist image of the title suggests, the underlying theme of the work is the notion of free creative activity.

Char was a formal member of the Surrealist group from 1930 to 1934;[2] but, although he owes much of his poetic growth to his affiliation with that movement, his adherence to Surrealism was never one of total commitment. On the contrary, Char spent these four years in independent exploration and evaluation of the theme of spontaneous creativity as proclaimed by Surrealism but not limited to it. In fact, it is the very theme which led him beyond Surrealism, for *Le Marteau sans maître* not only recognizes and affirms a Surrealist victory in the liberation of the poet and of the

---

[1] See in particular Anna Balakian, *Surrealism: The Road to the Absolute* (New York, 1959); Pierre Berger, "René Char," *Poètes d'aujourd'hui* (Paris, 1951); Pierre Guerre, "René Char," *Poètes d'aujourd'hui* (Paris, 1961); Georges Mounin, *Avez-vous lu Char?* (Paris, 1946) and "Situation présente de René Char," *Les Temps modernes*, 137-138 (juillet-août 1957), 272-288; Greta Rau, *René Char ou la poésie accrue* (Paris, 1957); Xavier Tilliette, "Poètes français contemporains II: Surréalistes," *Etudes* 266 (septembre, 1950), 241-245.

[2] Char signed the "Prière d'insérer" on the handbill of the second *Manifeste du surréalisme* (1929).

activity of poetry, but it also suggests the inability of surrealism to define poetry and to integrate man and reality into an absolute totality.

The pivotal point of Char's Surrealist journey is found in *Artine*, the second section of all editions of *Le Marteau sans maître*. Artine was initially composed and published in 1930. Significantly, it is Char's first work published by the Editions surréalistes.[3] Because it is the only section of *Le Marteau sans maître* which has remained textually intact since its original publication,[4] *Artine* offers the best available poetic document for the assessment of Char's Surrealist experience. Of even greater significance is the fact, never fully appraised and understood, that *Artine*, reputedly a Surrealist poem, announces Char's eventual rejection of Surrealism.

Artine is a prose poem which consists of 13 paragraphs. On the surface, it appears to be a Surrealist rendering of a dream, a series of dreamlike events related to the physical act of love. However, *Artine* is not a dream recital, but a single poem, unified by one theme: the value of surreality.

Artine is written in the form of a dramatic monologue in which the poet is a man in the "real" world, a dreamer in the dream world, and a poet of both worlds. The "rêveur-poète" describes his relation with Artine, "la modèle" who visits him in the world of sleep. According to Georges Mounin, "Artine ...c'est la surréalité."[5] Mounin is not entirely incorrect, but his explanation is too narrow. Artine is the surreal, but, in addition, she is the muse of inspiration and imagination, a muse who has existed throughout the history of poetic productivity. She represents the ageless poetical problem of divine fury, creative genius, and the Surrealist pure imagination in conflict with work, reflection, and engagement in a literary occupation. It is this conflict that Char treats in the poem

---

[3] *Ralentir travaux* was published by the Editions surréalistes six months earlier, but it is a work of collaboration by Breton, Eluard, and Char; *Artine* is Char's first individual volume published under the auspices of the Surrealist group.

[4] Only a footnote was deleted in the 1934 edition. Char considerably revised the texts of the other four sections of *Le Marteau sans maître* between their original publication and their appearance in the 1934, 1945, and 1963 editions.

[5] Georges Mounin, *Avez-vous lu Char?* (Paris, 1946), p. 73.

Artine; in his character of Artine, he concretizes the abstract notion of the poetic muse of inspiration, intuition, and imagination.

Artine may be divided into four parts: 1) the first paragraph prepares the evocation of the dream world; 2) paragraphs II-VI announce the dreamer's descent into the world of sleep; 3) paragraphs VII-XII present the actual experience which occurs in this dream world; and, 4) paragraph XIII contains the poet's assessment of his experience.

Paragraph I is printed in italics in order to set it apart from the rest of the poem; this paragraph is one of preparation and designates the setting of *Artine,* "un lit," the object from which one enters the world of sleep and dreams. In this bed, twenty objects are enumerated; all are related to the familiar everyday world of man. What is unfamiliar is the relationship of each to the other and the idea of placing them in a bed, an unusual setting for each one. This anti-realistic detachment of the familiar objects from their accepted position and application, a Surrealist dislocation of objects, disrupts logical sequence and establishes the dreamlike atmosphere of the poem. By the compilation of this specific series of images, the setting ceases to be limited to a bed in the concrete sense; rather, the "lit" represents a concretization of the universe; it is the universe which the first paragraph evokes, and it is from this enlarged setting that the poem gains its universal quality.

In the second part of *Artine,* the dreamer descends into the world of sleep in order to free his subconscious from all rational control. He hopes to find a knowledge different from that of the real world and reason; this "ordre des rêves" [6] is to free him from the constraints and limits of logic and renovate the knowledge of the mind. This experience is described in terms of physical love, for Artine comes of her own accord; she is neither invited nor sought; she is desired. The phrase "domaine de l'amour où l'activité dévorante" reinforces the concept of desire that Artine awakens. By its connotation, love is an exchange, a singleness formed from two opposites, and an effort at communication; above all, love carries with it a fusion of irreconcilables, for it is freedom and yet attachment, desire fulfilled and yet desire unfulfilled. This in-

---

[6] All quotations in this study are from the 1930 edition of *Artine.*

timate union of opposites is one of demanding activity, vitality, and energy. It is the idea of doing, not of mere existing; it is the freeing of one's inner self from all controls and inhibitions asserted by the logical real world. Moreover, this action is "en dehors du temps sexuel," that is, it refutes temporality; it is even beyond man's memory in its timelessness. The destruction of human temporal limits extends further the dreamer's desire to surmount his human condition. In this isolation from chaos, from limits, from logic, the dreamer completes the first stage of his journey to find the "ordre des rêves qui hanteraient dorénavant son cerveau"; he falls asleep; he is now closed off from his known order of reality.

"Artine traverse sans difficulté le nom d'une ville" concretizes the movement into sleep and denotes the *a priori* existence of the real world. Even imagination has some contact with the real. The real world has an *a priori* existence to the dream world; the isolation of the dreamer or the absence of the concrete presence of the experience is a prerequisite for such a Surrealist experience. Although the world of dreams distorts the real, it does not abandon spatiality and temporality. On the contrary, it disrupts and alters the appearance of the real. The roots of the dream world and of the Surrealist experience are in the real world and complete elimination of this real world would result in a total loss of value in the Surrealist experience.

The sixth paragraph is a Surrealist effort to submerge the conscious in order to reach the depths of the subconscious where imagination and inspiration function freely and purely. "L'état de léthargie qui précédait Artine" confirms the Surrealist notion that one must attempt to render one's self into a passive physical and mental state, liberate one's self from all control, and enter a realm of sensory receptivity; this preparation is the preliminary requisite for the liberation of the creative thought processes of the imagination; it is necessary if one wishes the experience to occur properly within the subconscious where the logical sequence of the known is disrupted and the new vision attained: "Artine apportait les éléments indispensables à la projection d'impressions saisissantes sur l'écran de ruines flottantes..." This passive condition is analogous to the "édredon" which recalls "lit," the concretized setting of the poem; but this state, passive externally, will be one of activity within the innermost depths of the wealth of the subconscious: "en perpétuel mouvement." The importance of paragraph six is to set aside rational control in order to reach the dream world, and it is an explicit announcement of the consuming activity in which the dreamer is to participate.

The third section of the poem describes the dream experience. Even though Artine enters through the real world, she maintains the ability to renew and revitalize with each visit the dreamer's experience. The reference to "la transparence absolue" signifies the Surreal divination of the hidden meaning of the objects of the real world; Artine permits this new perspective of the real to be projected on the mind's screen; in crossing through the real, she frees the intuition and the imagination and permits the Surreal to come into existence.

Artine's visits must precipitate the dreamer beyond mere sleep, for in that state the real and the dream conflict, each distorting the other in turn. In order that the imagination, freed within the dream world, may gain its proper ascendency over the real, there must be a more active destruction on the part of the dream: "Les apparitions d'Artine dépassaient le cadre de ces contrées du sommeil, où le *pour* et le *pour* sont animés d'une égale et meurtrière violence." These visits accomplish this necessary transformation through an all-consuming act; still in contact with the real, it distorts the real by giving it an unusual perspective. Although Artine effects an animated and new evolution, the real world continues to assert its presence; "il s'agissait d'accueillir ...la multitude des ennemis mortels d'Artine." As saltpeter attempts to subdue the sexual drive, the objects of the real world insist on resuming their usual position in their habitual setting. The odious appearance of the "visage de bois mort" implies a rupture in the action; a footnote to this phrase in the 1930 edition explains this image as referring to Jesus Christ, that is, to a crucifix made of wood, indicating the intrusion of the real world in one of its more restrictive aspects, organized religion. Omission of this footnote in subsequent editions reveals that no footnote is necessary to qualify the image; in fact, the deletion of the footnote widens the possibilities of interpretation.

In the eleventh paragraph the real world disrupts this journey for the second time; it returns the dreamer into contact with the concrete. "Une tête qui n'était pas la mienne" not only asserts an interruption of the experience or an intrusion from the outside, but it is also the dreamer's realization that it is his real physical condition and his reason, unlike his subconscious existence, that has threatened to dispell Artine. The appearance of this unknown head is the manifestation of the conscious self previously set aside. This second interruption is not overcome as quickly; it has a lingering quality as does the effect of sulphur on the olfactory senses. Moreover, in this second contact with the outside world, the real seems to have some significance in and of itself: "présence en soi et immobilité vibrante." The real world has become more difficult to escape.

The return to the dream world in paragraph twelve completes the quest for the knowledge or truth that the dream world offers. It seems that this truth can only be understood within the dream world; the absence of light indicates the absence of a cipher to this truth in the real world and, consequently, implies the lack of practical application of this knowledge in man's daily existence.

The twelfth paragraph is a parody of filmed epic with a repetitious traditional portrayal of the human condition in a tragic world and emphasizes the shortcomings of dream knowledge. The truth gained from this experience is no more practical than the cinematic world and no more original than the classical concept of man. This lack of a new and profound truth to enlighten man's perspective of his reality and totality is further qualified by the notation that each truth offered by Artine has correlation with a previously accepted concept. Because the imagination is unable to liberate itself from the *a priori* existence of the real world, it perpetuates unknowingly the prior imaginative creations of man. The dream world, in its attempt to transform the real through the liberation of the imagination and stimulation of the subconscious, is never able to break with the real world, and yet it loses contact with the real condition of man's everyday problems.

The last part of the poem announces the rupture with the dream world and the return to the real world; it is the triumph of the real world as the basis of a potential aesthetics; it is a choice in favor of a poetics that maintains definite and positive contact with reality against a poetics of pure imagination and intuition based within the subconscious. The "modèle" is Artine, the incarnation of the Surreal who glides from the real into the subconscious dream world; she is eliminated ("tué") as the only possible source of poetic activity. The "rêveur" is now the "poète"; these terms are not synonymous; a dreamer can be a poet in the sense that a poet must have imagination, but this dreamer without a specified occupation will produce the same shallow "épopée," "héros," "livre." The poet is related to the dreamer, but unlike the dreamer, he must not abandon the real world. The term "poète" is a vocational term; the poet has an occupation, a need to work, to use his reason in order that he may judge which experience or insights revealed by the imagination are to be communicated within the poem. There must be imagination before the poem comes into being, but there must also be work to realize and present the poem. There is no elimination of the role of imagination and inspiration; rather, it is an option to fuse imagination with reality, inspiration with control, emotion with conceptual thought. It is the addition of a conceptual value to the Surrealist notion of poetry as activity that *Artine* presents. It is what Char later formulates: "Le poème émerge d'une imposition subjective et d'un choix objectif." [7]

There is, therefore, only one theme in *Artine,* that of poetry, its activity, its domain, and the position of imagination, intuition, and inspiration within that domain. Artine impresses the poet by her singularity, but her visits satisfy only the dreamer, not the poet. It is important to note that at no time within the poem is Surrealism rejected; although its scope is expanded, Surrealism is affirmed as having value in poetic activity.

Artine is a tightly knit prose poem. The dominant characteristic of the vocabulary is the juxtaposition of concrete and abstract terms; the concrete terms refer to the real world, while the abstract ones reflect the dream world; they are constantly placed in juxtaposition in order to concretize the abstract dream world. Because of this juxtaposition, the vocabulary seems to be erudite, but

---

[7] Char, *Partage formel,* XXIX, in *Seuls demeurent, Fureur et mystère* (Paris, 1948).

all of the terms are familiar ones: there are no rare or unusual words. The concrete terms are commonplace, everyday words, but they are placed in unusual and unfamiliar combinations in order to attract attention, to express the impossible, and to materialize the abstract world of dreams. Combinations such as "Offrir ...un verre d'eau à un cavalier lancé" and "édredon en flammes" create new meanings out of familiar associations. The juxtaposition of terms also gives the vocabulary an emotional, rather than an intellectual, appeal.

Many of the terms are words expressing motion and activity; the persistence of a vocabulary of movement to describe a somewhat passive state is not contradictory, for there is much activity within this passivity. The terms of motion enhance this notion of activity and increase the emotional intensity of the poem. Above all, the vocabulary is condensed; there is much effort to express the maximum by the minimum in order to necessitate participation by the reader.

The syntax is highly controlled and rigorous. There are a few syntactical difficulties which arise through the suppression of transition words and connectives; this effort to suppress linking terms creates an effect of non-control and forces the reader to take part in the creation of the poem.

The main part of speech which carries the weight of the action are nouns; this is a Surrealist technique to enhance the visual quality of the poem. Nouns not only abound in their familiar subject-object usage, but they are also the basis for adjectival and adverbial clauses which are placed where a simple adjective or adverb would have sufficed. This method of qualification and clarification results in an effect of extension and accumulation; it dramatically reinforces the emotional intensity of the poem, and it permits greater freedom in the juxtaposition of concrete and abstract terms to create new images.

The verb tenses used in *Artine* are of particular interest; proportionately, the imperfect tense dominates, and it is used to denote description and repetition in the past of these escapes into the dream world and the encounters with pure imagination. Through the imperfect tense, the past is completely separated from the present, for these escapes no longer occur; they belong solely to the past. The present tense is used to express factual knowledge, and it describes the properties of the objects and attributes of the personnages of the poem. It must be noted that the real world is associated with the present tenses and the dream world with the imperfect. The conflict between the two is thus reflected in the syntax.

The last line of the poem contains a "passé composé"; this is the only use made of this tense throughout the poem. The fact that the single appearance of the "passé composé" is in the final line separates this action from the rest of the poem; this separation, which indicates the completion of one single act in the past, completes the destruction of the time of the poem. The last line becomes the poem; the preceding twelve paragraphs cease to denote a narrative of a past event and become an explanatory extension of the only event that actually does occur in the poem: "Le poète a tué son modèle." Poetry gains its authenticity from the real world.

The vocabulary, syntax, and rhythm support the content of the poem and are in unity with it. The tone alone presents a contrast; the tone is pensive, reflective, cogitative in contrast with the poem which appeals to the imagination through its visual imagery and which emphasizes activity in its theme. However, this pensive tone does not break with the content and form; there is an inherent conceptual dimension to the poem, and it is this conceptual quality that the tone expresses.

In *Artine,* Char affirms what may be considered the Surrealist notion of poetry as activity. As a concretization of the dream world which distorts the real world, *Artine* is a Surrealist setting; there is expressed the idea of a new order of knowledge that might be gained from this dream level of existence and experience. The attempt to escape from the real world and man's reason in order to penetrate the domain of man's thought processes and find pure imagination is also a Surrealist trait. The emphasis placed on the participation of the subconscious, inspiration, intuition, imagination, and liberty within poetic action and the evocation of the involuntariness of the poetic state are directly related to orthodox Surrealism. Similarly, the personification of Artine as a woman, the allusions to the love act, and the subsequent importance of woman within the construction of the poem are Surrealist. The presence of the real world is Surrealist in its relation to the dream world, for the surreal has its cornerstone in the concrete.

However, the presence of numerous Surrealist qualities in the form and content does not restrict *Artine* to being representative of Surrealism, for *Artine* goes beyond Surrealism. The last line of *Artine* is, without question, an affirmation of reality; it is such a strong affirmation that it nearly succeeds in negating the abundant Surrealist traits. With the disposal of Artine, the muse of inspiration and imagination, the poet negates the unique value of the dream world; this is not a refutation of Surrealism, but an implicit rejection of it as the ultimate solution for poetry. It is an option on Char's part to return to reality and to integrate imagination into the world of the concrete and to exercise rational choice in what is of value in inspiration. It is this decision which is foreshadowed in *Artine*.

Additional early evidence that Char's rejection of Surrealism is first announced in *Artine* is found in the 1931 and 1934 text of "L'Esprit poétique." [8] The last part of "L'Esprit poétique" is the prose poem "Chère Artine." This poem in the form of a letter addressed to Artine is concerned with the growing importance of the real, and it questions the values of inspiration and the dream world: "J'ai l'impression que vos rêves majeurs ne m'atteignent plus comme par le passé... Notre rencontre remonte à Octobre 1929. Depuis cette date les hippodromes ont cessé de m'être favorables." The date, October 1929, is most likely a reference to Char's first trip to Paris and his introduction to the Surrealist group. In *Artine*, Char affirms the importance of the real; in "L'Esprit poétique," he rejects pure inspiration as being ineffectual in the real world; Artine has outlived her usefulness as a guide, for she stops short of the true source of poetic truth: "à la proximité de la Beauté." Inspiration is only of value if it begins in the real world, not in the sleep or dream world of Artine: "...une jeune fille... égorge un coq, puis tombe dans le sommeil léthargique, tandis qu'à quelques mètres de son lit coule tout un fleuve et ses périls. Ambassade déportée." The phrase "Ambassade déportée" added in 1934 rein-

---

[8] Char. *L'Action de la justice est éteinte* in *Le Marteau sans maître* (Paris, 1934).

forces the idea that the muse of pure inspiration and imagination, Artine, has been sent back to her own realm by the poet; she fulfilled her post as the highest ranking agent of the dream world sent to represent this other possible state of knowledge, but her services are no longer required by the poet who has opted for the real world. The dismissal of Artine foreshadows Char's rejection of Surrealism.

Although *Artine* is representative of Char's Surrealist experience, it contains evidence that he never fully adhered to Surrealism. As early as 1930, Char recognizes Surrealism's failure to fuse imagination and reality, inspiration and work, poetic activity and exaltation of language and poetry. In the 1930 text of *Artine* and the 1931 text of "L'Esprit poétique," Char indicates that he will mature into a poet whose task is to be the conscious instrument, "le marteau," of objective reality which can be discovered through creative activity. Moreover, he must be free from all limitations, "sans maître," in order to explore, discover, and reveal all means (Surrealist and non-Surrealist) of attaining this reality in which alienation and contradiction are replaced by integration and fulfillment. It is Char's addition of a non-Surrealist conceptual quality to the notion of poetry as activity which is affirmed in *Artine* and which leads him beyond Surrealism at the very height of his participation in that movement and persists throughout his poetry.

THE SCUDÉRYS REVISITED: GEORGES DE SCUDÉRY (1601-1667) [1]

JEROME W. SCHWEITZER
University of Alabama

> "Un grotesque? Un fantoche? Un matamore? Sans doute... Mais, dans son outrance même, un type bien latin. Moustache de chat, feutre emplumé, fou comme don Quichotte, fier comme Bragance et vantard comme Tartarin, ce bohème de lettres d'autrefois a des titres à notre indulgence. On l'oublie, on l'ignore, on ne le comprend plus. Après tout, c'est peut-être dommage..." [2]

May 14, 1967, marked the tercentenary of the death of Georges de Scudéry. As some critics have remarked and Rathéry and Boutron intimate, [3] this so-called *matamore des lettres* had less merit than he thought but more than his adversaries attributed to him.

It is fitting, I think, that some notice be taken at this time of the life and works of this man who, despite all his foibles, his vanity, his conceit, his jealousy and pettiness at times, had in truth no little merit as a writer; he was a warm and faithful friend in

---

[1] Bibliographical note: Since the cut-off date in 1959 of the Cabeen and Brody critical bibliography, very little has been published on Georges de Scudéry, in fact only one article according to the *PMLA International Bibliography*. Stedman Kitchen, Jr., of North Carolina State University has in progress a dissertation which studies *Ibrahim* in detail. Other articles mentioned by *PMLA* deal with specialized subjects in the work of Madeleine.

[2] G. Lenôtre in his preface to Charles Clerc, *la Vie tragicomique de Georges de Scudéry*, Paris, 1929, p. 247.

[3] *Mlle de Scudéry, sa vie et sa correspondance*, Paris, 1873, pp. 49-50.

the adversity of those who befriended him or had his admiration, and he was a kind and considerate husband to the lady who became his wife in 1654, just seven years prior to his death.

Born of an old family of Apt in Provence, the Scudérys claimed Italian origin. Their grandfather, Elzéar Escuyer, was a soldier of distinction and governor of La Coste under Charles IX. Georges Scudéry, père, left Apt near the end of the Sixteenth Century, adopted the spelling "Scudéry" and followed Brancas-Villars to Lyons, Rouen, and finally to Le Havre, where he served as captain of ports. In 1599 he married Madeleine de Goustimesnil, a demoiselle of good family by whom he fathered five children. Only Georges born in 1601 and Madeleine in 1607 survived infancy. Scudéry, père, was imprisoned shortly for sinking a Dutch vessel off the coast of Brazil. He died in 1613 to be followed soon after in death by his wife. Georges entered the army at age fifteen while Madeleine entered the household of an uncle who reared and educated her. In 1620 Georges was back in Apt where he encountered his first love and first poetic inspiration, Catherine de Rouyère who jilted him for another.

It should be noted here that Scudéry in *Almahide* (IV, p. 471 ff.) introduced himself as Abindarrays Abencerrage. The latter is somewhat like the Hylas of d'Urfé's *Astrée*, constant in his inconstancy, dabbling in love with a large variety of women, rich and poor, young and old, comely and homely, until he finally wed Aldoradine (Mlle de Martin-Vast, his future wife). Now Georges was a confirmed bachelor until his marriage in 1654 to a girl in her early twenties and all of the biographical material I have read indicates there were only three women in his life: Catherine de Rouyère; Angélique-Céleste de Harville-Palaiseau, seduced and abandoned by Scarron and later taken into his house as housekeeper when the convent in which she resided went bankrupt; and Mlle de Martin-Vast whom he married. The affair with la Sœur Céleste went no further than Georges for a time standing in the street watching her window as he munched on a crust of bread. Thus the only serious love affair he had appears to have been with his future wife. He may have been willing but evidently the ladies were not attracted to him.

Before picking up anew the threads of this brief biographical sketch, perhaps I should include here the portrait which he draws of himself which is a sort of parallel with that of Madeleine (Sapho) in *le Grand Cyrus*. He states that Abindarrays possessed a prodigious memory and all of his inclinations were noble and elevated (*Almahide*, IV, 465). He was generous, magnificent, liberal, and never was a friend more true and faithful than he. The last part of this self-estimate is more fact than fiction as attested to by his loyalty to the Condés in their disgrace and by his defense of Théophile de Viau, thus risking violent royal displeasure and imprisonment at the least. The tone of his voice was "doux," his temperament "un peu mélancholique" and "le feu lumineux" of his "esprit" made him quick to anger "mais ce Tonnerre ne dure point" (IV, 468). He describes his bravery of which there is no doubt and his modesty (?); his musical, poetic, and artistic accomplishments, and his amorous inclinations (IV, 468 ff.) which, as I have pointed out above, were probably highly exaggerated.

He was already 59 years old when the first volume of *Almahide* appeared in 1660; thus we may assume that the following portrait of himself is highly exaggerated also:

> sa taille ... mediocre, & iustement entre la trop grande & la trop petite: mais si belle, si noble ... Il a l'air haut, le port maiestueux, le marcher graue, & l'action vn peu fiere ... Ses cheueux ... ni fort noirs ni fort blonds ... d'vne couleur fort agreable; son visage ... ouale ... ses yeux ... noirs, grands, & bien fendus ... ses sourcils bruns & fort espais; son teint vif; le nez bien fait, quoy qu'vn peu grand pour vn Grenadin (which Georges was not): & la bouche si extraordinairement belle ... qu'il n'est point de si belle Dame qui n'en fust contente, si elle l'avoit ainsi ... Il a encore les plus belles mains du monde pour vn homme (IV, 471 ff.).

This is the *miles gloriosus* speaking and bears little resemblance to the description given of him by Lenôtre or to reproductions of portraits published in various biographies.

Now that we have met Georges as he saw himself, let us return to his biography. Little is known of his life for the next ten years after the adventure with Catherine de Rouyère but it appears that during this period he was in the service of his king on land and sea. He speaks of his military experience in his foreword to *Ligdamon et Lidias* although some would have us believe that he commanded nothing more than the troops of the Hôtel de Bourgogne and of the Marais. In 1629 he served under Louis XIII during the Piedmontese expedition and seems to have distinguished himself in the retreat from the Pass of Suse. Substituting the pen for the sword, he began a career of letters, editing the works of his friend Théophile in 1632, and as a result of his sixteen theatrical productions won a position as one of the better second-rate dramatists. In 1637 he gained prominence as author of *Observations sur le Cid* and his *Lettre à l'Académie*. During these years he maintained with Madeleine a household on la Rue Beauce but, as we shall see, life with her does not appear to have been particularly happy and when he departed for Normandy in 1654 it was for Madeleine a relief and a liberation. Never again did he share the same roof with her: once when he appeared at her home asking for hospitality, he was told that all beds were taken.

In 1644 through the influence of his sister he was appointed governor of Notre-Dame-de-la-Garde in Marseille whence he returned in 1647. Relationships between Georges and Madeleine did not improve and her platonic friendship for Pellison did not improve matters. With the outbreak of the Wars of the Fronde he fled to Normandy where he met and married Françoise de Martin-Vast and with her encouragement and aid wrote *Almahide*. Their marriage was blessed with a gifted son who later entered the Church. When Condé and his friends were granted political amnesty in 1660, Scudéry returned to Paris with his wife, was granted a pension by the king, and spent his remaining years translating the Italian Marini's *Calloandro fedele* published posthumously in three volumes in 1668.

In 1638 or 1639 Madeleine came to Paris to establish a literary partnership that was to be broken permanently by his flight to Normandy and his marriage. Tallemant de Réaux did not have a high opinion of Madame de Scudéry but she seems to have been a beauteous and gifted young woman who was flattered by the attentions of the novelist, poet, and dramatist. Bussy-Rabutin, however, held her in the highest esteem and corresponded with her.

Her correspondence shows that she had the gift of writing well and there is no doubt in my mind concerning her collaboration in composing *Almahide*. When she was widowed, she mourned Georges' passing as a true and loving wife and she wrote to friends that he was a good husband, a friend, a good man who always praised and esteemed her and treated her well. What more could a wife ask?

As for Scudéry and his sister, aside from their literary collaboration, their life together was at times stormy as has been indicated. Already seemingly headed for bachelorhood when she joined him, he was set in his ways and apparently was determined to be the master of the household. G. Lenôtre states in his preface to Clerc's biography that Georges was "si sincère dans sa suffisance, si plein d'admiration pour son propre talent, si parfaittement dédaigneux de celui des autres, si amusant —non point dans ses œuvres, mais dans sa personnalité..."[4] Moreover, he claimed all the credit for his sister's success despite the fact they had been separated for years during the period of her intellectual formation. "Je l'ai faite ... ce qu'elle est", he wrote to Eléanore de Rohan-Montabazon, abbesse de Caen.

At the same time as a man of exquisite tastes who took pride in his status as an *amateur des arts,* extravagantly collecting paintings or engravings or tulips, he was at the same time disdainful of her financial assistance which he so desperately needed. He is charged with having dominated Madeleine for fifteen years and is held responsible for breaking up a possible marriage with Pellisson with whom she shared a tender friendship for about forty years. Pellisson arrived at court in 1650 and without doubt drove a wedge between brother and sister. Pellisson was noted for his homeliness and Madeleine was no raving beauty. They in our day and time would have been called the "gruesome twosome"! Georges is also accused of keeping Madeleine locked up while she completed some literary chore assigned to her by himself. His dislike for Pellisson stemmed from the fact that he had allotted Georges little space in his *Histoire de l'Académie française.* As rebuttal of the charge of breaking up the romance it is more likely that Madeleine as a *précieuse* prized

---

[4] Clerc, *op. cit.,* pp. 10-11.

amitié far more than marriage and there is no evidence to disprove that she could not have married Pellisson had she so willed. To the charge of keeping Madeleine a prisoner it is more likely that she needed and demanded privacy and quiet to work on her literary productions (and to be free of Georges so she could relax). As for Pellisson's *Histoire* I can find nothing to justify Scudéry's reaction to his treatment therein. As Dorothy McDougall points out [5] Pellisson allotted twice as much space to Georges as to Pierre Corneille and the author stated categorically that he could not deal as freely with living academicians as with the dead. For that reason he did not give Scudéry the eulogy the latter felt he merited.

As for the Scudéry *modus operandi*, it is so well-known that there is no need to do more than summarize. In the preface of his long heroic poem *Alaric* he took credit for the authorship of both *Ibrahim* and *le Grand Cyrus*. Tallemant wrote that for the latter novel Georges prepared only the prefaces and the *épîtres dédicatoires*. According to La Calprenède Georges touched up portraits appearing in the Scudéry novels. Victor Cousin states:

> "ils faisaient ensemble le plan. Georges, qui avait de l'invention et de la fécondité, fournissait les aventures et toute la partie romanesque, et il laissait à Madeleine le soin de jeter sur ce fond assez médiocre son élégante broderie de portraits, d'analyses sentimentales, de lettres, de conversations." [6]

But Rathery and Boutron reply:

> Peut-être ne faut-il voir là qu'une exagération en sens contraire de l'opinion primitivement reçue. Car il y eut réaction dans les jugements de littérateurs et des bibliographes, quant aux ouvrages d'imagination portant le nom Scudéry. Après avoir tout attribué au frère, on veut maintenant donner tout à la sœur. La vérité ne serait-elle pas entre ces deux extrêmes? Ainsi, lorque'on se rappelle que Scudéry avait servi, et qu'on le voit, en toute circonstance, se piquer de ses connaissances dans l'art militaire, il est

---

[5] *Madeleine de Scudéry, Her Romantic Life and Death,* London, 1938, p. 142.

[6] *La société française au dix-septième siècle d'après "Le Grand Cyrus",* Delbos edit., Oxford University Press, London, 1909, p. 169.

difficile de croire que les épisodes de guerre, où se complaît l'auteur du *Cyrus* ... ne soient l'ouvrage du soldat romancier dont le nom figure partout, sur le titre et dans les dédicaces de l'ouvrage." [7]

I am inclined to agree with this judgement that Georges contributed a great deal more to the common effort than contemporaries credit him. I attempted to prove in my study of *Almahide* [8] that not only did Georges have the ability and the know-how to write a long-winded novel without his sister's assistance but that he and his wife actually wrote the unfinished eight-volume effort (1660-1663). This work was in the making at a time when he and Madeleine were physically and mentally separated. His effort also became the dumping ground of several of his own works which had met with some success, including two tragi-comedies *Axiane* and *le Prince déguisé*, as well as the didactic poem *Solomon instruissant le Roy*.

What then is the place merited by this much maligned author? Lenotre wrote that "Scudéry méritait de trouver son historien, car il est une de ces figures qui résument une époque et caractérisent toute une société..." [9]

Le Cabinet de M. Georges de Scudéry is such in the plasticity of description of paintings (the same plasticity of description is found in *Almahide*) that these descriptions are reminiscent of Diderot's *Salons*. Two centuries later, Clerc states, the Parnassian poets would have recognized him as one of themselves because he had a sense of the plastic in what he described: he did so as a connaisseur, as an expert, and with the practiced eye of an art critic. [10]

The author of more than sixteen tragicomedies he was certainly one of the most applauded tragic poets of his time notwithstanding the fact that Théophile Gautier includes him among his *Grotesques*. Chapelain, perhaps overly enthusiastic, termed him "L'Apollon du Marais". Guez de Balzac, after referring to some emendations he

---

[7] See *supra*, note 3.
[8] *Georges de Scudéry's 'Alhamide'*, Baltimore, 1939.
[9] Clerc, *op. cit.*, p. 12.
[10] Idem., p. 121.

would suggest in *l'Amour tyrannique,* continues "Mais le reste, à mon gré, est incomparable".

As a man of the theater he was a recognized purveyor of the Hôtel de Bourgogne and of the Marais, and his plays were staged at the royal court.[11] In his theater he was attracted by the melodramatic. He falls short of a Racine because his plays lacked simplicity and true emotion and his *préciosité* went to the extremes which Molière took to task. His best work is to be found in his comedies noted in spots for their verve. But generally he used the tone habitual to the *Précieux,* thus becoming the victim of his own facile pen.

Yet his theater won the praise of Alexandre Hardy and of Pierre Corneille in his early years and Scudéry was idolized by apprentices in letters as a master of his craft. Rotrou, who helped to lend prestige and dignity to the stage before Corneille, received Scudéry's early plays with acclaim which may prove that Scudéry was no mean dramatist, at least no worse than those outside the great Triumvirate. Nevertheless, he is forgotten today. Like many a dramatic hero of his day he possibly has been punished more than he deserved as a dramatist.

H. Carrington Lancaster in his monumental history of French dramatic literature in the seventeenth century has studied the complete theater of Scudéry and it is to that work and to Alfred Batereau's *Georges de Scudéry als Dramatiker* that the reader is referred for details.

Lancaster points to *le Prince déguisé,* first acted in 1634 and used as an intercalated episode in Scudéry's *Almahide,* as a play with greater unity, more exciting intrigue, and a more spectacular setting than earlier plays such as *Ligdamon et Lidias, le Trompeur puny* and *Orante.* This play was designated along with Du Ryer's *Cléomédon* as a typical example of a play with a "belle intrigue". Lancaster wrote:

"Nobody seems to have noticed that the situation is here remarkably like that of Chimène in the Cid." (I, p. 483). He points out that a few years later Scudéry was to criticize Corneille because Chimène did not decline to wed Rodrigue, her father's slayer. Cléarque in Scudéry's play is innocent but there was no way for

---

[11] McDougall, *op. cit.,* p. 16.

others to know it. So he criticizes Corneille for a situation for which he had himself furnished the model!

La Comédie des comédiens (1632) consists of two acts in prose followed by an insipid pastoral play in verse which is in reality the rehearsal for the actors of the first two acts. This play is interesting as a study of manners and of the criticism to which plays and actors were subjected in the seventeenth century. It includes a defense of actors against charges of moral turpitude and is a forerunner of Molière's *Critique de l'Ecole des femmes*.

La mort de César (1635) was classed by Lancaster with Tristan l'Hermite's *Mariane* and Jean Mairet's *Sophonisbe*. In this play Scudéry showed his characteristic predilection for spectacle and physical action, his dislike for hampering rules, and his inability to make careful character study. Professor Lancaster wrote of this play that for the modern reader the most interesting thing about it is that Scudéry produced something of a critical edition of his own play providing elaborate marginal notes including interpretations of his own allusions. Some contemporary critics including Guérin de Bouscal termed it among the leading tragedies of 1634-1635, and Lancaster points out that some of its details were imitated by Corneille in *Cinna, Polyeucte*, and *Pompée*.

Eudoxe (1639), Lancaster shows, has details resembling Racine's *Andromaque* and *Phèdre*. The play won the praise of Richelieu.

L'Amour tyrannique (1639) was apparently written to give Corneille a lesson in the art of dramaturgy but it falls short of the mark. It was composed in accord with the unities of time and place and the *bienséances* but is melodramatic in style. However, some spectacular, animated and dramatic scenes won success for the play and it led Balzac to insist that Scudéry was a great poet, not sufficiently admired. Chapelain, while refusing to state that it surpassed the *Cid*, termed it one of Scudéry's best and it was admired by Richelieu and Sarazin. It was translated to Dutch four times between 1647 and 1746.

Andromire (1641) is an example of Scudéry's ingenuity in plot construction; it is lacking in some of the bombast and absurdities of other Scudéry plays and was in the repertory of the Hôtel de Bourgogne in 1646-1647. *Ibrahim* (1643) was also popular. It was better written than earlier plays of the author and it was republished several times. Although *Arminius* (1643), the last of his plays that have survived, was weak in motivation and structure, it was successful enough to have had a run of several years and was in the repertory of the Bourgogne in 1646-1647.

As a poet he wrote much that is worthless but in certain passages are to be found a lyrical note, a feeling for nature in all her moods which preclude treating Scudéry as negligible as a versifier. McDougall, citing Scudéry's series of sonnets *La fameuse fontaine de Vaucluse* said that when Scudéry was inspired by nature, he forgot his heroics. His second sonnet, she writes, opens in a mood in which on these real occasions he shows himself to have been a lyrical poet of no mean order.[12]

Indeed, Charles Livet in his *Précieux et Précieuses* (pp. 257-258) writes:

> Il semble que tout ait été dit sur le poème d'*Alaric*, le jour où Despréaux [Boileau] en a raillé le premier vers:
>
> Je chante le vainqueur des vainqueurs de la terre.
>
> ....Que si l'on ne se laisse pas arrêter, dès le début, par une opinion preconçue, j'ose penser que l'on trouvera dans l'*Alaric*, comme dans les sonnets que nous avons loués plus haut (p. 247), des passages parfaitement beaux et d'une ampleur vraiment cornélienne. Je ne dis pas qu'on puisse citer partout au hasard, mais j'affirme qu'on trouve dans l'*Alaric* plus d'un morceau digne d'être conservé: tel est cet admirable tableau de Rome dans la décadence (1er livre, vers 45 et suiv.)
>
> ....le poème d'*Alaric* fut accueilli avec faveur, reçut les honneurs de plusieurs éditions fort rapprochées, et fut publié dans tous les formats.

The influence of Scudéry and his sister as novelists is evident on Samuel Richardson, father of the modern English novel. He and they were noted for the character drawing of real people though changes in taste later in the Seventeenth Century relegated the Scudéry works to the limbo of the half-forgotten. But Madeleine and Georges de Scudéry cannot be totally forgotten.

---

[12] *Op. cit.*, p. 51.

Thomas P. Haviland has studied the vogue of the French *roman de longue haleine* in England [13] and notes that they were read in England until the second quarter of the Eighteenth Century. John Dryden used *Almahide* as source material for his own theater.

Ibrahim was translated by Henry Cogan in 1652 and another edition was published in 1674 and possibly still others in 1665 and 1723. *Le Grand Cyrus* was translated by F. G. Gent (1653-55) followed by another edition in 1691 and the first two parts of *Clélie* were published in translation in 1655 and 1656 followed by a complete edition (1656-1661), while other editions appeared in 1659 and 1678. *Almahide* was translated in 1677 by J. Phillips who also added an ending to the unfinished novel to satisfy English readers.

In conclusion, Scudéry cannot be dismissed on the grounds of his foibles. He was vain, he was bombastic, he wrote too facilely to be a careful workman: of these weaknesses he was guilty and of a lot more along with many writers of his epoch. However, his virtues must be placed in the other balance of the scales: he was a good husband; he was a faithful friend when discretion might have been the better part of valor. He was a man of integrity: witness his refusal to make certain deletions from *Alaric* in exchange for a valuable gold chain offered him by Christina of Sweden. He was a good soldier even though he boasted of his deeds like a Captain Fracasse. But he was not wholly lacking in humility as is shown in the opening remarks of his *Discours* before the French Academy on the occasion of his admission in 1650:

> Je ne sçay comment j'ai l'audace de venir mêler les défauts qui sont en moy avec les perfections qui sont en vous, et d'oser me mettre au rang des Dieux, moy qui suis parmy le commun des hommes. Il est vray que je suis d'une profession à qui la témérité est sinon permise, au moins tolérée; en un mot, je suis soldat, et par conséquent obligé d'être hardy. Et puis, Messieurs, je ne me présente pas à votre illustre corps avec la croyance d'en être digne, mais avec l'intention de tâcher de me le rendre, et de vous témoigner par mes services, à tous en général et à chacun en particulier, combien je me sens votre redevable de l'honneur que vous me faites. [14]

---

[13] *The "Roman de longue haleine" on English Soil*, Philadelphia, 1931.
[14] Quoted by Charles Livet, *Précieux et Précieuses*, Paris, 1897, p. 248.

His plays were no masterpieces despite his exalted opinion of his own work but they were no worse than most and if his purpose was to entertain and please, then he succeeded, regardless of the opinions of more discriminating critics. As a poet he was admittedly mediocre except on those rare occasions when inspired by nature or by a sense of history. The Scudéry novels have their settings in exotic climes but they portray life in the France of their day and time and their characters are for the most part men and women who were no figments of the authors' imagination but real flesh and blood men and women who lived, loved, suffered, and died, representing both the nobility (*le grand Cyrus*) and the bourgeoisie (*Clélie*).

Charles Livet writes:

> "Qui sait? Un temps viendra peut-être où des gens de goût trouveront trop timide un éloge que nous croyons presque téméraire."

The laudatory comment was applied to Scudéry's volume of poetry, one-third of which Livet says "est très remarquable". [15]

Perhaps in the not too remote future his work will find a literary historian and critic who, without being biased by Tallemant or Boileau, will make a thoroughly objective study of Georges de Scudéry's total work and demonstrate by use of internal evidence his true worth as a writer. His role in the Quarrel of the *Cid* has assured his immortality in letters if nothing else.

---

[15] *Ibid.*, p. 247.

CREATIVE IMITATION, ORIGINALITY, AND LITERARY TRADITION IN RONSARD

Isidore Silver
Washington University

I. "J'allai voir les étrangers"

"La doctrine du larcin légitime en matière de poésie s'appuyait sur les imitations des anciens par les anciens," said Pierre de Nolhac,[1] quoting Latin verses of Jean Dorat to the effect that the poets of antiquity —Orpheus, Musaeus, Homer, Hesiod, Ennius, Virgil— had to some degree engaged in literary larceny.[2] The last thought to have crossed the mind of Dorat would have been the notion that there was anything reprehensible in such plagiarism. "Le siècle n'avait pas, sur l'originalité, nos idées ni nos exigences."[3] He started from the position that had dictated the famous verses of Horace:

> ....vos exemplaria graeca
> Nocturna versate manu, versate diurna.[4]

---

[1] *Ronsard et l'Humanisme* (Paris, 1921), p. 21, n. 2. — See Grahame Castor's *Pléiade Poetics* (Cambridge, England, 1964), pp. 51-76, for an excellent discussion of some of the matters presented in this chapter.

[2] Aristotle, *Poetics*, 1448b25-29, seems to imply that Homer had many precursors who represented noble actions and those of noble personages. Homer himself repeatedly refers in *Od.* VIII to the bard Demodocus and in both epics to the κλέα ἀνδρῶν (*Iliad*, IX, 189, 524; *Od.*, VIII, 73) which preceded his poems.

[3] V. L. Saulnier, *Du Bellay, l'homme et l'œuvre* (Paris, 1951), p. 37.

[4] *A. P.*, 268-269; cf. 323-324.

This became one of the fundamental premises of the *Deffence* which naturally went beyond Horace's recommendation by including the Roman authors as objects of assiduous study: "Ly donques et rely premierement (ô Poëte futur) fueillete de main nocturne et journelle les exemplaires grecz et latins. ..."[5]

Du Bellay had no superficial view of the nature of imitation as practiced by the writers of Rome. How, he asks, had they succeeded in so enriching their language as to make it almost equal to Greek? And he answers:

> "Immitant les meilleurs aucteurs grecz, se transformant en eux, les devorant, et, apres les avoir bien digerez, les convertissant en sang et nouriture, se proposant, chacun selon son naturel et l'argument qu'il vouloit elire, le meilleur aucteur, dont ilz observoint diligemment toutes les plus rares et exquises vertuz, et icelles comme grephes ... entoint et apliquoint à leur langue."[6]

His reading of Quintilian confirmed him in his conviction that the imitation of excellent authors was a discipline not to be undertaken lightly:

> "Mais entende celuy qui voudra immiter, que ce n'est chose facile de bien suyvre les vertuz d'un bon aucteur, et quasi comme se transformer en luy ... Je dy cecy, pour ce qu'il y en a beaucoup en toutes langues, qui sans penetrer aux plus cachées et interieures parties de l'aucteur qu'ilz se sont proposé, s'adaptent seulement au premier regard, et s'amusant à la beauté des motz, perdent la force des choses."[7]

The doctrine of the imitation of the ancients, which was extended to embrace chiefly the Italians among the moderns, became at once the central principle of the new poetry, for it combined the *deffence* and the *illustration* into a single concept:

> "Toutes personnes de bon esprit entendront assez que cela que j'ay dict pour la deffence de notre langue, n'est pour

---

[5] *Def.*, II, IV, p. 201; [pp. 107-108].

[6] *Def.*, I, VII, p. 99; [pp. 42-43]; cf. I, III, pp. 70-71; [p. 25]. Cf. V. L. Saulnier, *Du Bellay*, p. 45.

[7] *Def.*, I, VIII, pp. 104-105; [p. 46].

> decouraiger aucun de la greque et latine: car tant s'en fault que je soye de cete opinion, que je confesse et soutiens celuy ne pouvoir faire œuvre excellent en son vulgaire, qui soit ignorant de ces deux langues, ou qui n'entende la latine pour le moins." [8]

The enunciation of the principle is perhaps even clearer in the second book of the *Deffence*. Chapter I, "L'intention de l'aucteur," contains the following declaration:

> "Mettons donques pour le commencement... [9] que sans l'immitation des Grecz et Romains nous ne pouvons donner à notre langue l'excellence et lumiere des autres plus fameuses." [10]

Du Bellay leaves no doubt as to the radical interpretation he places upon this principle when he adds in the third chapter of this book:

> "... d'autant que l'amplification de nostre langue ... ne se peut faire sans doctrine et sans erudition, je veux bien avertir ceux qui aspirent à ceste gloire, d'immiter les bons aucteurs grecz et romains, voyre bien italiens, hespagnolz et autres, *ou du tout n'écrire point,* si non à soy ... et à ses Muses." [11]

The vibrant "Conclusion de tout l'œuvre," with its exhortation to French poets to plunder ("piller") the treasures of antiquity for the greater glory of the national literature, is the eloquent culmination toward which Du Bellay's argument had moved from the outset.

In the preface *Au lecteur* of the *Odes*, published soon after the *Deffence*, Ronsard describes the pursuit of letters as the very felicity of life without which one must despair of perfect happiness (I, 44-45). "J'allai voir les étrangers," [12] he says, because the poets of France offered him no models worthy of imitation.

---

[8] *Def.* I, XI, p. 147; [pp. 74-75].
[9] "Posons donc en principe." Note by Chamard.
[10] *Def.*, II, I, p. 171; [p. 90].
[11] *Def.*, II, III, pp. 194-196; [p. 104]. My emphasis.
[12] "Je me mis à étudier les poètes Grecs, Latins et Italiens." Note by Laumonier, I, 44.

The treasures that Du Bellay urged his fellow-poets to pillage had long been the objects of Ronsard's covetous desire — witness the final verses of the ode *A Madame Marguerite* [13] which summarize the arduous studies of the years immediately preceding:

> Et comme imprimant ma trace
> Au champ Attiq' & Romain,
> Callimaq', Pindare, Horace,
> Je deterrai de ma main
> (I, 78).

In the extraordinay poem *A sa lire* [14] which closes the first book of odes, he uses language that conveys a clear idea of the degree to which his thought and that of Du Bellay coincided on the question of the imitation of the ancients:

> Je pillai Thebe', & saccagai la Pouille, [15]
> T'enrichissant de leur belle dépouille
> (I, 164).

The imagery of the *Deffence* is still present in the 1567 edition of Ronsard's *Art poëtique* almost a score of years later when, after urging poets to write in French, he adds: "Non qu'il faille ignorer les langues estrangeres, je te conseille de les scavoir perfaictement, & d'elles comme d'un vieil tresor trouvé soubz terre, enrichir ta propre nation..." (XIV, 14-15, var.). In the final preface to the *Franciade* Ronsard reiterated the thought of Dorat that even among the authors who stood upon the threshold of the western literary tradition the writing of poetry was not an act of completely spontaneous and unmediated creation. He says of Virgil that Homer "estoit son maistre, & son patron" (XVI, 342), and of Homer himself that having found the matter of his epic in "quelque vieil conte de son temps de la belle Heleine & de l'armée des Grecs à Troye ... fonda là dessus son *Iliade*" (XVI, 339).

---

[13] Laumonier, *RPL*, p. 63, dated the composition of this ode in the second half of 1549, a few moths after the publication of the *Deffence*.

[14] Written toward the end of 1549, according to *RPL*, p. 56.

[15] Pindar was born in Thebes, Horace in Apulia.

Convinced that the French language would receive its maximum *illustration* if they and their fellow-poets sought their models in literatures other than their own, especially in those of classical antiquity, Ronsard and Du Bellay advanced two additional and complementary theses: the first against the imitation of the French writers of the preceding generation; the second against the use of any language other than French. The most momentous renewal that the poetry of France has ever known followed from the enunciation and adoption of these postulates. They explain Ronsard's claim in the preface of the *Odes* of 1550, proud to the point of arrogance and yet essentially true, that he was inaugurating a glorious new era in the literature of his country (I, 44). They explain the tone and substance of the poem to the lyre with which he closed the first book of odes, and of the one to the Muse that eventually came to occupy the most significant place of all at the end of the fifth and last book:

> Je voleray Cygne par l'Univers,
> Eternizant les champs où je demeure
> De mes Lauriers honorez & couvers:
> Pour avoir joint les deux Harpeurs divers [16]
> Au doux babil de ma Lyre d'yvoire,
> Que j'ay rendus Vandomois par mes vers
> (Ed. of 1587, II, 372).

They are the armature upon which his life's work is constructed, making possible the many successes and causing the occasional failures which he recognized with the humility of a sincere artist:

> ...à genous Franciade
> Adore l'Æneide, adore l'Iliade
> (XVI, 354).

The same postulates account ultimately for one of the most valuable characteristics of the critical edition of Ronsard by Paul Laumonier:

> "Ce qui domine dans notre commentaire, c'est l'indication des sources où l'auteur a puisé son inspiration, et des ré-

---

[16] Pindar and Horace.

> miniscences qui ont excité sa verve ou nourri ses développements. Nous y attachons une grande importance, parce que leur connaissance permet seule de mesurer le degré de son originalité et d'en apprécier la valeur."

After describing Ronsard's assiduous studies of the Greek, Latin, neo-Latin, Italian, and even French poets whom he exceptionally admitted as having some merit, Laumonier continues:

> "Tous ces auteurs, Ronsard ne s'est pas contenté de les lire, de les approfondir, d'en faire des extraits; il les a imités, souvent 'pillés', le mot est de lui. Loin de dissimuler ses emprunts, il s'en glorifiait; car le principal but qu'il poursuivait avec ses amis littéraires, c'était de transposer dans sa langue, en essayant de les égaler, et même de les surpasser, ce que les poètes anciens et modernes avaient si bien dit dans la leur" (I, pp. xxxiii-xxxiv). [17]

In the *Caprice au Seigneur Simon Nicolas,* written in the year before Ronsard's death, he looked back with pride at the result of his labors, in which the imitation of the poets of antiquity had played so large a part:

> Bien que l'envie en tous lieux animée
> Se mutinast contre ma renommée
> De toutes pars, & que mille rimeurs
> Fussent aux champs en despit des neuf Sœurs,
> Je passay outre, amenant de la Grece
> Leur troupeau sainct, dont la voix charmeresse
> Par mon labeur en la faveur des Rois,
> Donna le prix au langage François...
>
> (*LL.,* VI, 62).

II. Tradition, Priority, and Originality

This very claim to priority as an innovator that Ronsard never grew tired of asserting, but which is not necessarily identical with poetic originality, was itself a part of the literary tradition that

---

[17] See *RPL,* p. 294, for an excellent general summary of Ronsard's imitative procedures.

he sought to revitalize. For he had read Horace to some purpose. The new path to immortality that Ronsard's feet had first trodden in his generation was well known to the Roman poet, who had, indeed, anticipated the Pléiade by many centuries in formulating their fundamental positions:

> O imitatores, servum pecus, ut mihi saepe
> Bilem, saepe jocum, vestri movere tumultus!
> Libera per vacuum posui vestigia princeps.
> Non aliena meo pressi pede. [18] Qui sibi fidet,
> Dux regit examen. Parios ego primus iambos
> Ostendi Latio, numeros animosque secutus
> Archilochi...   (*Ep.*, I, xix, 19-25).

This was Horace's "J'allai voir les étrangers," strangers who for him could only have been the poets of Greece. Horace, too, had toyed with the idea of imitating the Greeks in their own language, but had seen the vanity of this effort (*Sat.*, I, x, 31-35).

Although Ronsard and his fellow-poets believed that their contribution consisted in great measure in having rejected the national in favor of the classical literary tradition, none of them would have wished to sacrifice any values that were genuinely French. They felt, however, that the introduction of the substance of the literatures of antiquity not only did not entail such a sacrifice, but would, on the contrary, bring immense advantages. They were carried away by their infatuation with their own program, which blinded them to the real merits of many of their French predecessors.

But a national tradition in literature cannot be rejected by a simple act of will. "Il en est d'un individu comme d'un parti, d'une école, d'un peuple, de tout organisme; pas d'arrêt brusque, mais continuité, transformation lente de ses énergies." [19] Laumonier devotes a good part of the Introduction of his thesis to establishing the proposition that the ode, a genre in which Ronsard claimed personal priority with the utmost insistence, was in reality the final step in a rather long evolution. In a note found among his papers, the same scholar asserts that the renovation of French poetry that

---

[18] Verses 21-22 were quoted by Ronsard in the preface to the *Odes*, I, 45.
[19] *RPL,* p. 203.

Du Bellay and Ronsard sought to bring about had been foreshadowed for half a century:

> "Lorsque Ronsard et Du Bellay entreprirent une *réforme* poétique, la tâche leur était préparée; ils ont profité de tout un mouvement d'art et de pensée. La date de 1549-1550, celle de leurs *manifestes,* doit rester une date fameuse, [elle] est utile et commode à retenir; mais elle ne marque ni une découverte, proprement dite, ni un brusque changement de direction, ni une rupture réelle avec le passé, quoiqu'ils aient pensé. Elle indique un point de maturité, et l'apparition d'une jeune école ardente, décidée à faire aboutir hâtivement ce qui s'élaborait lentement en France depuis un demi-siècle. Mais de là à dire qu'ils n'ont rien innové, il y a un abîme. ..." [20]

It is useful to distinguish the two seemingly rival traditions between which the leaders of the Pléiade appeared to be choosing: the national tradition from which they turned away, and the classical European tradition to which they wished to give all their loyalty. But this distinction must undergo a further refinement if it is to correspond adequately with the literary reality. To Clément Marot, who, if not precisely rejected, was merely tolerated by Ronsard among a small number of precursors, the Pléiade was indebted for the introduction into French literature of an important group of classical genres: the epigram, elegy, epistle, satire, and eclogue. [21] The Pléiade could not, therefore, indiscriminately disparage all of Marot's work without denying a significant part of the classicizing program which had already begun to make a place for itself in the national tradition.

When Ronsard wrote in 1545 or 1546 to celebrate, after Marot, a military victory of François de Bourbon-Enghien:

> L'hinne [22] que Marot te fit
> Apres l'heur de ta victoire,

---

[20] *Ronsard continuateur*, in *Paul Laumonier Manuscripts,* 22 (undated — 11 × 17-1/2 cm.); emphasis in text.

[21] Henri Chamard, *Histoire de la Pléïade* (Paris, 1939-1940), I, 193-194.

[22] The poem in question is the *Epistre envoyée par Clement Marot à Monsieur Danguyen* (éd. Jannet, I, 71-73). In his copy of this edition, loc. cit., Laumonier wrote: "C'est cette pièce, à n'en pas douter, que Ronsard appelle hymne, et qu'il refit dans une Ode pindarique."

> Prince vainqueur, ne sufit
> Pour eternizer ta gloire.
> Je confesse bien qu'à l'heure
> Sa plume étoit la meilleure
> A desseiner simplement
> Les premiers trais seulement,
> Attendant la main parfaite
> D'un ouvrier ingenieus,
> Par qui elle seroit faite
> Jusque au comble de son mieus...
> (I, 82-83).

he was reluctantly conceding a certain degree of priority to Marot. "Ronsard a été, lorsqu'il travaillait à ses premies ouvrages, un disciple de Marot," said Henry Guy in an article that analyzed in addition the multiplicity of the Vendômois' debts to the French writers of the Middle Ages and the early Renaissance.[23]

It remains true, however, that the theoretical orientation and practice of Ronsard and his colleagues overwhelmingly emphasized the need for giving a new direction to French literature that would bring it into the mainstream of the European tradition. This was the central achievement of the Pléiade, their originality as a literary movement as distinct from their individual poetic originality. So true is this that Laumonier was able to say of Ronsard: "A ses yeux, être original, c'était beaucoup plus arriver le premier à faire ces transcriptions [of Greek, Latin, neo-Latin and Italian authors] et s'y montrer habile écrivain, qu'exprimer des idées personnelles ou développer des thèmes nouveaux" (I, p. xxxv). This was especially true with respect to Ronsard's imitations of the Greek poets:

> "La preuve, c'est qu'il n'a jamais indiqué ses sources néolatines ... et qu'il a rarement indiqué ses sources latines, mais qu'en revanche, il a fait connaître très volontiers ses sources grecques, d'Homère à Lycophron"[24] (VI, p. xvi).

---

[23] "Les sources françaises de Ronsard," *Revue d'Hist. litt. de la France*, IX (1902), 219.

[24] Thus, for example, most of the Greek epigrams that Ronsard translated in 1553 are preceded by the name of the author, and all are introduced by a verse or two of the original Greek (V, 77-91).

Imitation was with Ronsard a procedure so deeply ingrained that he sometimes followed Greek and Latin authors in the very act of affirming his independence of them, just as he did in asserting his priority:

> Belleau, s'il est loisible aus nouveaus d'inventer
> Cela que les plus vieus n'ont pas osé chanter,
> Je dirois voluntiers que l'amour n'a point d'aisles,
> Las! car s'il en avoit, s'ebranlant dessus elles
> De mon cœur quelquesfois se pourroit absenter
> (VIII, 196-197).

This wingless Eros is an image taken from the elegy of Propertius, *De Amore:*

> In me tela manent, manet et puerilis imago:
>   Sed certe pennas perdidit ille suas;
> Evolat heu! nostro quoniam de pectore nusquam...
> (II, xii, 13-15).

Even more striking is the beginning of the *Hymne de la Mort:*

> On ne scauroit, PASCHAL, desormais inventer
> Un argument nouveau qui fust bon à chanter,
> Soit haut sur la trompette, ou bas dessus la lyre:
> Aux Ancians la Muse a tout permis de dire,
> Si bien, que plus ne reste à nous autres derniers
> Que le vain desespoir d'ensuyvre les premiers...
> Je m'en vois decouvrir quelque source sacrée
> D'un ruisseau non touché, qui murmurant s'enfuit
> Dedans un beau vergier, loing de gens & de bruit...
> Je boiray tout mon saoul de ceste onde pucelle,
> Et puis je chanteray quelque chanson nouvelle...
> Et suivant ce conseil, à nul des vieux antiques,
> Larron, je ne devray mes chansons poëtiques,
> Car, il me plaist pour toy de faire icy ramer
> Mes propres avirons de sur ma propre mer,
> Et de voler au Ciel par une voye estrange,
> Te chantant de la MORT la non-ditte loüange.
> (VIII, 161-164).

As Laumonier indicates in a note on the last verse of this passage, the poet, "Quoi qu'il en ait dit ... s'est amplement inspiré des anciens ... notamment de Plutarque et de Lucrèce ... de Stobée ...

Enfin l'éloge de la Mort [la non-ditte loüange] avait déjà été fait par Cl. Marot, dans la *Deploration sur la mort de Florimond Robertet.*" What is perhaps most curious of all is the fact that the nautical image in which Ronsard, proud of his literary independence, assures Paschal that he is determined to row with his own oars upon his own sea, is itself of Pindaric origin, as Ronsard well knew, for he had already employed that image a number of times in his own poetry.[25]

But it would be a singular error to supose that in the presence of authors whom Ronsard profoundly admired, his own role, in theory or in practice, was reduced to that of a servile plagiarist. In fact, something like the contrary was probably true. He would have given his complete assent to Peletier's wish that the aspiring epic poet be thoroughly practiced in the works of Homer and Virgil and yet never descend to the level of an "imitateur juré ni perpetuel."[26] For Ronsard the encounter with another great poetic mind could only be a profoundly stimulating experience. He enumerates a number of moving passages in the *Aeneid* and adds,

> "...mille autres telles ecstatiques descriptions, que tu liras en un si divin aucteur, lesquelles te feront Poëte, encores que tu fusses un rocher, t'imprimeront des verves,[27] et t'irriteront les naifves et naturelles scintilles de l'ame que des la naissance tu as receues, t'inclinans plus tost à ce mestier que à cestuy-la: car tout homme dés le naistre reçoit en l'ame je ne sçay quelles fatales impressions, qui le contraignent suivre plustost son Destin que sa volonté" (XVI, 333).

The dialogue between tradition and originality was a phase of the incessant debate in Ronsard's mind between art and nature, a debate whose origins must go back to the time when meditation on the essence of artistic creativity in general first arose among men. We must leave to the palaeoanthropologists all speculation

---

[25] I, 119, vv. 193-196 and 209-215; III, 22, vv. 287-291 and 398-400; see the notes on these passages for the sources in Pindar; cf. my *Pindaric Odes of Ronsard* (Paris, 1937), pp. 36 and 133.

[26] André Boulanger, ed., *L'Art Poëtique de Jacques Peletier du Mans (1555)* (Paris, 1930), pp. 95-96.

[27] "Imagination." Note by Laumonier.

as to what the absolutely spontaneous poetic act may have been, but it seems fairly certain that in periods that follow a recorded or even orally transmitted literary history of any scope, the creation of poetry does not proceed by a series of abrupt acts of totally unmediated inventiveness. A certain degree of literary-historical sophistication, of attained and secure civilization, is implied in the conception of poetic invention that Ronsard adopted from Horace: "Car le principal poinct est l'invention, laquelle vient tant de la bonne nature, que par la leçon des bons & anciens autheurs" (XIV, pp. 5-6) [28] The tendencies toward the natural and the traditional complement each other and make possible a literary perfection. How keenly alive Ronsard was to this inescapable conflict-in-resolution that lies at the heart of poetic creation is clear fom the opening sentence of his *Art poëtique:*

> "Combien que l'art de poësie ne se puisse par preceptes comprendre ny enseigner, pour estre plus mental que traditif: toutesfois, d'autant que l'artifice humain, experience & labeur le peuvent permettre, j'ay bien voulu t'en donner quelques reigles icy, afin qu'un jour tu puisses estre des premiers en la congnoissance d'un si aggreable mestier..." (XIV, 3).

It is probable that Ronsard went to the grave convinced that poetry was "plus mental que traditif." But the activity of his entire life was a permanent affirmation of the great dependence upon tradition of any serious involvement in poetic creation. Though he might not have formulated his thought in these terms, he would have found no difficulty in the reflection that just as law is the indispensable condition of individual liberty (VIII, 69-70), so tradition in poetry, as he and his colleagues conceived of it, was an indispensable condition of creative originality. He came to see that inevitably he had taken his place in the succession of generations in which men, though themselves ephemeral, are able to affirm their personal vision of a common destiny, and to transmit to future ages, somewhat deepened, perhaps, by their own experience of life,

---

[28] Cf. Horace, *Ars poetica*, 408-411.

the human values they have received from near and remote periods in the past.[29] For he had also read Lucretius to some purpose:

Inque brevi spatio mutantur saecla animantum
Et quasi cursores vitai lampada tradunt.[30]

---

[29] See *LL.*, I, 344, "J'ay couru mon flambeau..."
[30] *De Rerum Natura*, II, 78-79.

N. B.: References unaccompanied by any letters, e. g. XVI, 339, are to Paul Laumonier's critical edition of Ronsard in course of publication by the Société des Textes Français Modernes (Paris, 1914-   ).—ABBREVIATIONS: *Def.*, Henri Chamard, ed., *La Deffence et Illustration de la Langue Francoyse* (Paris, 1904 [1], 1948 [2]); notes give first the pagination of the 1904 edition followed in square brackets by that of 1948; the text reproduced is that of 1904. — *LL.*, Paul Laumonier, ed., *Œuvres complètes de P. de Ronsard*, 8 vols. (Paris, Lemerre, 1914-1919). Text of 1584. — *RPL*, Paul Laumonier, *Ronsard poète lyrique* (Paris, 1923 [2]). — The *Paul Laumonier Manuscripts* mentioned in note 20 are among the papers of the late scholar which were made available to the present writer by Mme A. Laumonier when he assumed responsibility, in collaboration with Professor Raymond Lebègue, emeritus, of the Institut and the Sorbonne, for the completion of the critical edition of Ronsard. — It is regrettable that severe limitations of space made it impossible to cite the excellent studies of Hermann Gmelin, Alfred Noyer-Weidner, Wilhelm Blechmann, Margaret L. M. Young, Sir C. M. Bowra, and A. Severyns which are related to our subject. The omissions will be corrected in the chapter of a work in progress on "The Intellectual Evolution of Ronsard" of which the present study is a fragment.

PASCAL AND FRANÇOIS MAURIAC

MAXWELL A. SMITH
Florida State University

One of the most striking examples of the influence of French Classicism on French writers of the present century is that of Pascal. It would not be difficult to point out the influence of Pascal on Saint-Exupéry —the only one of contemporary authors who like Pascal was equally gifted for mathematics and scientific inventions— or on Malraux. In the latter's *Les Noyers de l'Altenburg,* we find the famous quotation from the Pensées:

> Qu'on s'imagine un nombre d'hommes dans les chaînes, et tous condamnés à la mort, dont les uns étant chaque jour égorgés à la vue des autres, ceux qui restent voient leur propre condition dans celle de leurs semblables, et, se regardant les uns et les autres avec douleur et sans espérance, attendent à leur tour. C'est l'image de la condition des hommes.

Is this not only a leitmotiv in all of Malraux' novels, but also the origin of the title for his greatest work, *La Condition humaine?* Even Giono, so close to the pagan Greeks, has found in Pascal the title for one of his novels, *Un Roi sans divertissement.* Yet in no case, perhaps, has the affiliation between Pascal and a contemporary author been more conclusive and far-reaching than in the lifelong devotion of François Mauriac for Pascal.

In his autobiographical *Commencements d'une vie,* Mauriac pays homage to his professor of rhetoric at the Collège Grand Lebrun, l'abbé Péquignot, to whom he owed the privilege, at the age of 16, "d'avoir goûté Montaigne, entrevu ce qu'est l'apport de Descartes, et surtout chéri Pascal. L'exemplaire du *Pascal* de Brunschwiecg, qui ne me quitte pas, est le même dont je me servais en rhétorique."[1] In his essay on Pascal in *Mes Grands Hommes,* Mauriac recalls again lovingly this "bouquin traîné partout avec moi depuis l'année de ma seconde, déchiré, jauni, chargé de notes, de coups d'ongles, de photographies, de dates, de pétales séchées"[2] which was opened certain evenings as an effervescent spring to quench the thirst of his soul. For the young François and his comrades, fledglings just out of the nest about to discover the double universe of knowledge and of passions, this encounter with Pascal was decisive:

> C'est l'instant que Blaise Pascal peut les sauver, surtout s'ils le voient tel qu'il fut réellement, avant sa conversion définitive; différent d'eux infiniment par le génie et par les connaissances, mais leur frère par l'orgueil intellectuel et par un certain attrait qu'il trouve aux passions.[3]

In one of his most recent books, *Ce que je crois,* in the chapter entitled "La Dette Envers Pascal," Mauriac states that Pascal is the writer to whom he owes the most, who has affected him the most, who has been his master from his sixteenth year and remains so today (more than sixty years later). To Pascal Mauriac gives full credit for having been able to resist in large measure the religious doubts and temptations of the senses in his youth and maturity. "Pour moi qui eus dans ces jours où l'Eglise de France payait les frais de l'Affaire Dreyfus, ... où l'Encyclique 'Pascendi' paraissait interdire à l'étudiant que j'étais tout contact avec la pensée moderne, je l'atteste aujourd'hui, ce fut le Christ de Pascal qui me dit en ces heures-là: 'Reste avec moi.' "[4] If this sincere homage were not enough to attest the hold which Pascal has always exerted over Mauriac, one might enumerate the number of his writings devoted to his beloved master: two books, *Blaise Pascal et sa sœur*

---

[1] Fr. Mauriac, *Commencements d'une vie,* (Paris: Bernard Grasset, 1932), pp. 55-56.

[2] Fr. Mauriac, *Mes Grands Hommes,* (Monaco: Éditions du Rocher, 1944), pp. 1-3.

[3] *Ibid.,* pp. 4-5.

[4] Fr. Mauriac, *Ce que je crois,* (Paris: Grasset, 1962), p. 144.

Jacqueline and *Les Pages immortelles de Pascal*, the first article in his volume *Mes Grands Hommes*, (and a second one, entitled "Voltaire contre Pascal"), a ten page article on *Les Provinciales* in Mauriac's *Mémoires Intérieurs* and the chapter "La Dette Envers Pascal" in *Ce que je crois* from which we have just quoted. In addition to all this should be mentioned innumerable references to and quotations from Pascal throughout the personal and critical writings of Mauriac; I do not suggest substituting a computer for the literary critic, but it requires only a hasty glance at the index to reveal thirty-one references to Pascal in the two volumes of *Mémoires Intérieurs* and thirty-four in the two of *Bloc-Notes*.

An analysis of these publications will show us I think what was the image of Pascal in the mind of Mauriac, to what extent Mauriac found himself in agreement with Pascal and hence influenced by him, and also the few points of view on which Mauriac took issue (or at least thought he was taking issue) with the great Jansenist. First of all, it should be mentioned that Mauriac himself gives us the right to deduce from his works on Pascal an intimate awareness of Mauriac's own attitudes and principles. In his article, "Voltaire contre Pascal," for instance, Mauriac writes: "s'il est vrai qu'un auteur n'admire que soi-même dans les autres, n'y-a-t-il pas déjà du Voltaire dans la verve des *Provinciales?*"[5] And again, in the opening paragraph of Mauriac's *Vie de Racine* we find this striking admission:

> Chaque destinée est singulière, unique; mais un auteur ne se décide à écrire une biographie entre mille autres, que parce que avec ce maître choisi il se sent accordé; pour tenter l'approche d'un homme disparu depuis des siècles, la route la meilleure passe par nous-même.[6]

How strongly Mauriac felt about this necessity for identification of the critic with his subject is shown by a third example in his *Journal:*

> Les meilleures biographies sont dues, presque toujours, à une certaine ressemblance entre le narrateur et l'homme

---

[5] Fr. Mauriac, *Mes Grands Hommes*, p. 149.
[6] Fr. Mauriac, *La Vie de Racine*, (Paris: Plon, 1928).

> dont il raconte l'histoire. Ce sont des réussites, si l'on peut dire, par analogie. Nous ne connaissons les autres que par nous-mêmes et *notre propre secret nous livre celui des cœurs les mieux défendus* [7] (Italics mine).

To fully understand Mauriac's devotion to Pascal, it is necessary, I think, to recall the religious crisis which Mauriac underwent in 1928, caused in part by the hostility of many Catholic critics who attacked the burning intensity of passion depicted in his novels up to this time, in part doubtless because of tragic inner conflict within Mauriac himself, inherent in his effort to reconcile amorous passion with the demands of sanctity. Thus in *Souffrances du chrétien* of that autumn we find the complaint: "Le Christianisme ne fait pas sa part à la chair, il la supprime. 'Dieu veut tout' écrit Bossuet. Et Pascal: 'Seigneur je vous donne tout.' "[8] Then Mauriac speaks of the anguish experienced by so many excellent priests and persons consecrated to God: "cette terreur qu'ils surmontent mais qui souvent les étreint, d'avoir renoncé en vain à 'l'usage délicieux et criminel du monde' dont parle Pascal." [9] Their comfort can only be the famous word which Pascal attributes to Christ: "Tu ne me chercherais pas si tu ne m'avais déjà trouvé." Do we not feel in the following words of Mauriac a desperate groping out for a sign that his suffering is not in vain? "Il y a chez le concupiscent que Dieu harcèle la honteuse crainte de renoncer à la proie pour l'ombre. Cette misère dont il se délecte demeure une certitude à quoi on n'oppose qu'une promesse et qu'une menace." [10] This is why "le concupiscent réclame un signe," such as the healing of his little niece Mlle Périer by the Sainte Épine which confirmed Pascal in his faith, and also

> Ce feu qu'il vit ou dont son cœur ressentit la blessure, le lundi 23 novembre, 1654, depuis environ dix heures et demie du soir jusqu'à environ minuit et demie. Aussi, sur ce papier qu'il portait cousu dans son habit en souvenir

---

[7] Fr. Mauriac, *Journal I*, (Paris: Grasset, 1942), p. 211.

[8] Fr. Mauriac, *Souffrances du chrétien*, in volume entitled *Dieu et Mammon*, (Paris, Grasset, 1931), p. 97.

[9] *Ibid.*, p. 107.

[10] *Ibid.*, p. 122.

de cette nuit bienheureuse, à peine a-t-il fait mention de ce feu qu'il écrit par deux fois le mot *Certitude*.[11]

What a contrast between the restless anxiety and despair evident in *Souffrances* and the radiant serenity apparent a few months later in its sequel *Bonheur du chrétien!* Whether the intervening period marks a sort of second conversion (similar to that of Pascal) has been a matter of debate among critics, but at any rate, Mauriac wrote on the flyleaf of my copy of the combined essays "Ceci marque toute l'histoire de ma vie." Indeed the second volume shows the change in tone at the very beginning by Mauriac's quotation of Pascal's comment, in a letter to Mlle de Roannes, of Tertullian's remark: "Quel plaisir plus grand que le dégoût même du plaisir." Reminding her that the life of Christians need not be a life of sadness, Pascal adds: "On ne quitte les plaisirs que pour d'autres plus grands."[12] Yet, prefiguring a theme which we shall find in all his biographical writings on Pascal, namely his certainty that Pascal did not escape the temptations of human passion, Mauriac writes: "sa méfiance démesurée, cette horreur de la moindre caresse et des paroles les plus innocentes telles que: 'Cette femme est jolie', tout cela témoigne d'une vie longtemps impure."[13]

It was at this period that Mauriac, provoked by a letter from Gide who at the same time praised Mauriac's literary excellence (*Destins*) and questioned his religious sincerity, wrote his treatise *Dieu et Mammon* in an effort to justify himself not only to Gide but also to his Catholic adversaries. A certain *pensée* of Pascal, to which Mauriac will refer many times in his later work, seems to him to clarify the entire debate.

> On a beau dire. Il faut avouer que la religion chrétienne a quelque chose d'étonnant. 'C'est parce que vous y êtes né' dira-t-on. Tant s'en faut; je me roidis contre, pour cette raison-là même, de peur que cette prévention ne me suborne; mais quoi que j'y sois né, je ne laisse pas de le trouver ainsi.

---

[11] *Ibid.*, p. 122.
[12] Fr. Mauriac, *Bonheur du chrétien*, in volume entitled *Dieu et Mammon*, p. 128.
[13] *Ibid.*, pp. 157-158.

Like Pascal, Mauriac was born and brought up in the Catholic religion. "Voilà mon drame." He had tried to criticize it, like Pascal to stiffen himself against it, he envied believers like Psichari and Maritain for whom Catholicism had been a *choice*. Sometimes he had felt himself prisoner of a little Mediterranean sect. But impossible to escape from it,

> avec quelle passion je m'efforçais, à seize ans, de me prouver à moi-même la vérité de cette religion à laquelle je me savais attaché pour l'éternité. L'édition des *Pensées* de Brunschwiecg, déchirée, annotée, qui est toujours sur ma table, rend témoignage de ce partipris passionné.[14]

Mentioning the temptations he experienced in his youth — intellectual objections to the faith, passions of the flesh, how many times he was precipitated into the ditch, almost stifled by mud, until he submitted himself at last

> à cette loi de la vie spirituelle, la plus méconnue du monde et qui lui répugne le plus, mais sans laquelle la grâce de persévérance demeure inaccessible: le renoncement à son autonomie, c'est cela qui est exigé — ce qu'exprime parfaitement le mot de Pascal: 'Renonciation totale et douce. Soumission totale à Jésus-Christ et à mon directeur'."[15]

In Mauriac's *Blaise Pascal et sa sœur Jacqueline* as well as in his biographical introduction to *Les Pages immortelles de Pascal*, it is a thoroughly human figure of Pascal that we see emerging from these pages. Before his conversion Pascal showed himself capable of bitterness in attacking the heresy of Père Saint Ange, not adverse to financial considerations in his discussions over his sister's dowry on her entrance into Port Royal, delighted with the admiration shown him for his scientific achievements and inventions such as the arithmetic machine (precursor of all calculating machines) so highly praised by Queen Christina's doctor. But the two aspects of Pascal's nature which seem to have fascinated Mauriac most, no doubt because of their particular relationship to his own work as a novelist, were his capacity for understanding the

---

[14] Fr. Mauriac, *Dieu et Mammon*, pp. 19-20.
[15] *Ibid.*, pp. 71-72.

innermost nature of man and his first-hand acquaintance with human love, revealed by Pascal's *Discours sur les passions de l'amour*.

As a psychologist, Pascal is a true descendant of Montaigne in his delight in the study of man. Even after his conversion Pascal shows a strange indulgence towards Montaigne: "On peut excuser ses sentiments un peu libres et voluptueux en quelques rencontres de la vie." [16] One is certain that Mauriac must have had his own novels in mind when he praises Pascal for having recognized that evil in man demands sometimes "une grandeur extraordinaire de l'âme," a certain genius usurping the place of God in a man's heart to set in motion virtues of strength and rashness. [17] It is because of this ability to understand his fellow man that Mauriac calls Pascal

> le seul humaniste digne de ce beau nom; le seul qui ne renie rien de l'homme; il traverse tout l'homme pour atteindre Dieu... Parce qu'il est passionné pour la connaissance des singularités, des contradictions de l'homme réel... il est le moins isolé des maîtres, il demeure, au sens le plus profond, notre *semblable,* accordé à la part de nous-même la plus particulière, la plus individuelle. [18]

Whether Pascal himself experienced the joys and tortures of love is a subject which fascinates Mauriac, for he returns to it on several occasions. Some critics doubt that Pascal was the author of the *Discours sur les passions de l'amour,* but Mauriac finds in it the unmistakable accent of *Les Pensées*. After reading this *Discours,* Mauriac feels that an open-minded critic cannot fail to find in it "l'aveu involontaire, le mot qui ne s'invente pas, le cri d'une joie ou d'une douleur dont le cœur saigne encore." [19] How well Pascal has portrayed the embarrassment of a lover who, after preparing his plan of battle, finds himself tongue-tied when faced by the presence of his beloved. "Quand on est loin de ce que l'on aime, l'on prend la résolution de faire et de dire beaucoup de

---

[16] Quoted in Fr. Mauriac, *Blaise Pascal et sa sœur Jacqueline* in *Œuvres Complètes,* Vol. VIII, (Paris: Hachette), p. 258.

[17] *Ibid.,* p. 258.

[18] *Ibid.,* pp. 298-299.

[19] Fr. Mauriac, *Les Pages immortelles de Pascal,* (Paris: Editions Corrêa, 1947), p. 15.

choses." Mauriac contends that Pascal has summarized the entire Proustian conception of love, when he writes that the presence of one you love is only a "cessation d'inquiétude." [20] Likewise Pascal knew what Proust was later to call in his famous phrase "les intermittences du cœur" when he wrote:

> L'attachement à une grande pensée fatigue et ruine l'esprit de l'homme. C'est pourquoi, pour la solidité du plaisir de l'amour, il faut quelquefois ne pas savoir que l'on aime; et ce n'est pas commettre une infidélité, car l'on n'aime pas d'autre; c'est reprendre des forces pour mieux aimer. Ça se fait tant que l'on y pense.

From this discussion it is but a step to consider whether Pascal had actually been tempted by vice. Pascal has Christ say: "Je t'aime plus ardemment que tu n'as aimé tes souillures." How shall we interpret this word? His sister, Gilberte Périer, refuted this by her remark: "Mais quoi que par la miséricorde de Dieu, il se soit toujours exempté des vices." Yet his beloved Jacqueline wrote to him after his conversion:

> "Je ne m'étonne pas que Dieu vous ait fait cette Grâce car il me semble que vous aviez mérité, en bien des manières, d'être encore importuné de la senteur du bourbier que vous aviez embrassé avec tant d'empressement." [21]

And Mauriac concludes that if purity had been natural to Pascal he would not have experienced so powerfully a feeling of délivrance. "Sans Jésus-Christ," Pascal says in one of the *Pensées*, "il faut que l'homme soit dans le vice et dans la misère," and again: "Hors de Jésus-Christ il n'y a que vice, misère, erreur, ténèbres, mort, désespoir." While conceding that this dark pessimism is colored by Pascal's Jansenism, Mauriac nevertheless suggests: to adhere to this judgment of despair "ne faut-il avoir l'expérience secrète de plaies invisibles aux yeux du monde?" [22]

---

[20] Fr. Mauriac, *Blaise Pascal et sa sœur Jacqueline* (*Œuvres Complètes*, VIII), p. 204.
[21] Fr. Mauriac, *Les Pages immortelles de Pascal*, p. 20.
[22] Fr. Mauriac, *Blaise Pascal et sa sœur Jacqueline*, p. 215.

We now come to the two matters, both of them related to Jansenism, in which Mauriac takes issue with his beloved master. In the first place, Mauriac reproaches Pascal for this same Jansenistic pessimism, which led him to believe that, soiled from birth, we are invincibly drawn into evil, for which we are punished by eternal chastisement. Against this doctrine Mauriac protests —it is ironic to see that he himself was accused of the same tendency by his Catholic colleagues—:

> "Ici il entrait de pleine voie dans l'hérésie; il professait que nous sommes réprouvés à jamais pour suivre un penchant invincible, comme si, dans le monde matériel, c'eût été un crime pour l'homme d'être pesant." [23]

The second aspect of Pascal's thought that distresses Mauriac is Pascal's conviction that he belongs to the small number of the elect who have been chosen by Divine Grace in preference to all others. Mauriac feels that such heresy, shared by Jansenists and Presbyterians, can only be explained by the law announced by l'abbé Brémond: the more terrible the doctrine, the more ingenious is the believer in reassuring himself. [24]

If we proceed now to a brief consideration of Pascal's influence on the fiction and theater of Mauriac, the first matter which we must discuss is the extent of Mauriac's Jansenistic tinge. When I asked M. Mauriac a few years ago, bluntly and perhaps indiscreetly, whether or not he considered himself a Jansenist, he replied without any hesitation "Oui et non." He then went on to explain very logically this apparently equivocal statement by asserting that he is not a Jansenist with his head, but is one with his heart. Thus he feels that a victory for Pascal and Port Royal would have been a disaster for the Church and he is glad that their cause did not prevail. Yet he reminded me that he had been brought up by a mother who, without ever having read a Jansenist work, was, however, one at heart. To this day he feels great respect and admiration for the Jansenist way of life.

---

[23] Fr. Mauriac, *Les Pages immortelles de Pascal*, p. 10.
[24] Fr. Mauriac, *Blaise Pascal et sa sœur Jacqueline*, p. 175.

There is no doubt that the most frequent attack on Mauriac's novels by Catholic readers, particularly in the twenties, has been against the atmosphere of evil passions and human turpitude found therein. Mauriac, quoting with approval Pascal's affirmation: "une passion ne peut pas être sans excès," feels that any novelist, obliged to paint the realities of love, ought to place this at the base of his work. But there is another statement of Pascal which seems to have influenced Mauriac even more deeply. When Pascal defines marriage, even Christian marriage, he terms it: "La plus périlleuse et la plus basse des conditions du christianisme, vile et préjudiciable devant Dieu." The reader of Mauriac's fiction will recall many examples of this attitude, in such novels as *La Chair et le sang, Le Baiser au lépreux* and many more. In fact, Robert North, on the whole a rather fair and discerning critic of Mauriac, can find only one example in all his novels of a truly happy marriage —that of the Puybaraud couple in *La Pharisienne*— a marriage which comes to a speedy conclusion through death. Yet even in this novel North notes this significant passage: "Je crois que tout le malheur des hommes vient de ne pouvoir demeurer chastes, et qu'une humanité chaste ignorerait la plupart des maux dont nous sommes accablés." [25]

As a foreword to his novel *Le Fleuve de feu,* Mauriac places, along with similar quotations from Saint John and Bossuet, the following sombre outcry of Pascal: "Malheureuse la terre de malédiction que ces trois fleuves de feu embrassent plutôt qu'ils n'arrosent." As a natural corollary to the novelist's dark view of human misery, vice, cruelty and egotism, we find as solutions in so many volumes a sudden intervention of Divine Grace, as in *Le Nœud de vipères, Les Anges noirs* and others. In the opinion of North these are too much like "coups de théâtre," insufficiently prepared, in which the rôle of human will power seems almost absent. We are reminded of Mauriac's own words in regard to Pascal when we read North's criticism: "Mauriac représente la Grâce comme arbitraire, créant ainsi l'impression que l'homme impuissant ne peut être sauvé que par une élection divine. C'est méconnaître la doctrine

---

[25] Robert North, *Le Catholicisme dans l'œuvre de François Mauriac,* (Paris: Editions du Conquistador, 1950), pp. 102-122.

de la Grâce suffisante et friser de près l'hérésie janséniste."[26] Mauriac himself has acknowledged that the criticism in regard to "calumniating and soiling carnal love" is the reproach which troubles him the most, yet he adds in the same book:

> "Les enfants, et ceux qui n'ont jamais perdu la grâce de l'enfance ont le droit de Vous aimer dans la joie de leur chair intacte. Mais chez les autres, la source de la joie physique est corrompue à jamais."[27]

Mauriac's four dramas, unlike his novels, lack almost completely any religious element, probably, as Gabrial Marcel suggests, because he feared unconsciously to degrade what in his eyes is the highest and most holy verity by making it a theatrical tool.[28] In his theater also, Mauriac was attacked for giving only "pièces noires," yet Pol Gaillard quotes with approval Mauriac's assertion that only a Christian could have written *Les Mal-Aimés* and adds:

> The apologetic value of the plays and novels of M. Mauriac, whose blackness scandalizes so many devout souls, is in our opinion exactly the same as that of Pascal's *Pensées:* to show us man in an odious light in order to strike down in us the pride of our self-assurance and prepare our humiliated souls for the coming of Divine Grace or at least of the Wager.[29]

Whether or not we share the criticism of Mauriac's novels and dramas for their excessive pessimism, we may see perhaps in his remarkable gift for rendering his characters vivid and palpable a reflection to some extent of his familiarity with Montaigne and Pascal. And in regard to Mauriac's felicity of style and phrasing, there can be no doubt that he looked upon Pascal as his master. For Mauriac, Pascal "apparaît comme le point de perfection atteint chez nous par l'écriture et par la pensée. L'extrême à la fois de la profondeur et de la limpidité."[30] In a letter sent out to a subscriber of the *Table Ronde* of which he was editor, Mauriac emphasized

---

[26] *Ibid.*
[27] Fr. Mauriac, *Le Bonheur du chrétien*, pp. 159-161.
[28] Gabriel Marcel, *La Table Ronde*, janv., 1953, pp. 125-130.
[29] Pol Gaillard, *La Pensée*, nouv. série, janv.-mars, 1945, pp. 110-114.
[30] Fr. Mauriac, *Ce que je crois*, p. 38.

his rule of clarity and simplicity: "Montaigne and Pascal ... have shown us that one can go very far in the knowledge of man by using the language of simple people." [31] In discussing the danger of literary "ronron" and romantic exaggeration Mauriac writes: "Qui de nous peut se dire sans péché, même ceux (dont je crois être) que le contrepoison de Pascal et de Racine avait immunisés dès le départ." [32] When Mauriac in the decade of the fifties entered the career of journalism, it was to Pascal's *Lettres Provinciales* that he turned to seek the secret "de cette verve qui, d'un débat éphémère, a fait un débat éternel." [33]

The most succinct and poetic summary of this lifelong association between Mauriac and his master Pascal is to be found in the closing paragaph of *Ce que je crois:*

> "Le feu d'une seule nuit de Pascal aura suffi à nous éclairer durant toute notre vie et comme l'enfant que la veilleuse rassurait dans la chambre peuplée d'ombres, à cause de ce feu nous n'aurons pas peur de nous endormir."

---

[31] Fr. Mauriac, *Lettres ouvertes*, (Monaco: Éditions du Rocher, 1952), p. 70.

[32] Fr. Mauriac, *Nouveaux Mémoires intérieurs*, (Paris: Flammarion, 1965), p. 218.

[33] Fr. Mauriac, *Ce que je crois*, p. 144.

THE CULT OF TASTE IN BOUHOURS' *PENSÉES INGÉ-NIEUSES DES ANCIENS ET DES MODERNES* (1689)

Frederick W. Vogler
University of North Carolina

Time and post-Classical literary criticism have not been kind to the memory of Dominique Bouhours, that urbane, gracious Jesuit *littérateur*, polemicist, and conversationalist of the second half of the Seventeenth Century. His posthumous reputation has undergone much the same course as that of his great friend and literary colleague, Boileau, although with even greater discredit befalling it in the Nineteenth Century and with seldom-relieved general obscurity its present condition. In the last hundred years, Bouhours' active life and numerous works of criticism, biography, and religious controversy have attracted the attention of only one biographer, George Doncieux, whose now ninety-year-old monograph [1] remains the basic study as the only extensive treatment of the subject. Nearly thirty years ago, Professor Hamm published an interesting, favorably disposed essay on Bouhours' career and influence in a Jesuit-sponsored *Festschrift*. [2] Apart from these two studies, however, Bouhours' *état présent* is a matter of some dozen widely spaced articles and chapters (or sections of chapters) in more general studies

---

[1] *Un jésuite homme de lettres au XVIIe siècle: le Père Bouhours* (Paris: Hachette, 1887).

[2] V. M. Hamm, "Father Dominique Bouhours and Neo-Classical Criticism," in *Jesuit Thinkers of the Renaissance: Essays Presented to John F. McCormick, S.J.* (ed. Gerard Smith, S.J.; Milwaukee: Marquette University Press, 1939), pp. 63-74.

of French Classicism and its international influence.³ Other mention has usually appeared as brief, passing comment in connection with contemporaries of better-preserved fame. What has probably been the most widely disseminated judgment on him in recent times was made by Antoine Adam, who dismissed him as "l'un des plus médiocres prosateurs de l'époque."⁴ But even Adam does not fail to acknowledge Bouhours' remarkable, enduring influence—for better or worse—on French writers of the following generation, particularly among younger Jesuits who proved to be far more articulate and effective than any of Pascal's outclassed adversaries had been when the *Provinciales* overwhelmed them half a century before.⁵

The literary prominence enjoyed by Bouhours during his lifetime, the genuine deference paid him by a large number of the "Grands Classiques," the influence he exerted within his own order, all can probably be attributed to an exceptional talent possessed by him: a consciousness of the prevailing literary taste of his immediate generation, for which the ultimate aesthetic standard was no longer primarily objective and easily demonstrable but instead largely a matter of intuitive perception, of the supremacy of *goût*, defined by Bouhours as "une harmonie, un accord de l'esprit et de la raison."⁶ Pascal had already written of the heart and its reasons; Bouhours in turn defended intuitive understanding and appreciation as being exempt from rational analysis in a once-famous chapter on "le je ne sais quoi."⁷ With such an outlook, he was

---

³ As a matter of fact, four such articles have been devoted exclusively to Bouhours' outspoken disapproval of most of Italian literature up to his own time.

⁴ *Histoire de la littérature française au XVIIᵉ siècle* (Paris: Domat, 1948-56), IV, 206.

⁵ *Ibid.*, V, 78.

⁶ Bouhours, *La Manière de bien penser dans les ouvrages d'esprit* (Paris: Delaulne, 1715), p. 516.

⁷ Bouhours, *Les Entretiens d'Ariste et d'Eugène* (4e éd.; Paris: Mabre-Cramoisy, 1673). (Three of the six dialogues were re-edited and published by R. Radouant in the series "Collection des chefs-d'œuvre méconnus" [Paris: 1920].)

The best modern discussion of Bouhours' position in this respect (seen as demonstrating the inadequacy of the usual modern notion of "Classical standards") is to be found in Professor E.B.O. Borgerhoff's admirable book,

well equipped to achieve prominence as a literary critic attuned to an age which paid official homage its own great writers but still savored the works of Madeleine de Scudéry and Voiture. For the same reason, Bouhours was elusive rather than partisan in the Quarrel of the Ancients and Moderns while at the same time playing a significant rôle in the evolution of modern aesthetic theory.[8] He seems to have been curiously representative of the cultivated men of his age, which may well explain his enduring vogue as a valued conversationalist and esteemed author, an authority earnestly consulted by Racine, Boileau, and many others. His principal works continued to be read long after his death in 1702, as proved by the frequent appearance of new editions of them throughout the Eighteenth Century.

One such solid publishing success was his *Pensées ingénieuses des anciens et des modernes,* which first appeared in 1689 [9] and enjoyed a dozen reprintings by various publishers during the next seventy-five years.[10] How one edition could ever have been sold —much less a dozen well-spaced ones— might well puzzle a modern reader unaware of the vogue of pearl-stringing anthologies throughout the Renaissance and Classical periods. Bouhours' work is a 400-duodecimo-page compilation of quotations from some thirty Greek and Roman authors alternating with quotations from more than twice as many modern French, Italian, Spanish, and English authors. Since he is seeking to demonstrate unusual and effective literary expression, he includes numerous examples of exaggerated and unsuitable writing by way of contrast, with his Italian and Spanish sources providing most of them. This is no mere collection of epigrams, for many of his selections run to several pages each.

The Freedom of French Classicism (Princeton: Princeton University Press, 1950), pp. 186-200.

[8] Bouhour's contribution is sympathetically discussed by Ernst Cassirer in *Die Philosophie der Aufklärung* (Tübingen: Mohr, 1932), pp. 400-404.

[9] Paris: Mabre-Cramoisy. Subsequent page references are to Paris: Mabre-Cramoisy, 1693.

[10] Among this book's late-18th-Century readers (or at least owners) were two prominent Diluvian victims; the Bibliothèque Nationale lists a copy of the 1758 edition bound in Marie-Antoinette's arms and one of the 1761 edition done in those of Louis XVI's equally ill-fated sister, Madame Élisabeth.

The title chosen by Bouhours probably reflects a desire on his part to share some of the interest aroused by Fontenelle's *Digression sur les anciens et les modernes* and Perrault's first *Parallèles des anciens et des modernes,* both published the preceding year. As for the contents of his work, Bouhours made a candid admission in his "Avertissement":

> Ces pensées ne sont la plûpart que les restes de celles que j'ai mises en œuvre dans *la Manière de bien penser*. Elles avoient été destinées les unes et les autres au même Ouvrage; mais le tour que les Dialogues ont pris, et les sujets auxquels Eudoxe et Philante se sont attachés, ont fait que certaines pensées n'y ont pas eu place. Comme je les avois recueillies avec soin, et que la dépense en étoit faite, pour parler ainsi, je n'ai pas voulu les perdre, et j'ai cru que le Public ne seroit pas fâché de les voir dans leur simplicité naturelle, c'est-à-dire, sans les ornemens du Dialogue, et même sans les liaisons du discours.

The "simplicité naturelle" of his quotations is modified only by brief comments on them and on their authors, and the effect created is that of a random flow from topic to topic.

The improvised nature of the work is further accentuated by Bouhours' providing a rostrum for his longtime friend Bussy-Rabutin, whose *Histoire amoureuse des Gaules* had earned him permanent banishment to his estates in Burgundy twenty-three years earlier. The disconcerting result in the *Pensées ingénieuses* is that the letters of Bussy-Rabutin constitute by far the most extensively quoted modern material, with the letters of Ovid, Bussy-Rabutin's Roman counterpart in disgrace, figuring as the most frequently cited Ancient authority. The prominence of this ax-grinding theme of the chastened, loyal exile addressing his sovereign becomes tiresome, then absurd; one of Bouhours' enemies was quick to pounce upon his misplaced emphasis:

> L'antipode d'un janséniste,
> De divers bons auteurs assez mauvais copiste,
> Fait voir, par le recueil qu'il vient de mettre au jour,
> Qu'il lit et prose et vers de folie et d'amour:

> C'est un plaisir plus doux que de prendre la peine
> De débrouiller saint Augustin,
> Le dur Tertullien et l'obscur Origène,
> Le bon Père sans doute y perdrait son latin.
> Il vaut mieux commenter Ovide et La Fontaine,
> Et les plus beaux endroits de Bussy-Rabutin. [11]

Another anonymous epigrammatist ironically noted Bouhours' omission of Pascal, "Qui pourtant ne pensait pas mal," [12] and a third praised his good judgment in avoiding any selection from his own works. [13]

Yet despite the apocryphal incident of Boileau's dismay at having to share a place of honor with such "méchante compagnie," [14] it must be recognized that the *Pensées ingénieuses* were warmly received by most of Bouhours' cultivated contemporaries. Even La Buyère saw fit to repay a debt of gratitude for his own honorable inclusion by inserting a remark intended as praise in the fifth edition of the *Caractères* (1690), "écrire comme Bouhours" ("Des Ouvrages de l'esprit," no. 32). [15]

In his discussion of the *Pensées ingénieuses,* Doncieux is without indulgence toward Bouhours for having given his critical approval just as freely to the works of obscure or even notoriously unclassical writers as to those of the truly meritorious "Grands Classiques." After noting several examples of justified and misplaced enthusiasm in Bouhours' judgments, Doncieux observes,

> Supposé qu'un étranger n'eût pour s'éclairer sur la littérature du siècle de Louis XIV que ces deux volumes du jésuite: *la Manière de bien penser* et les *Pensées ingénieuses,* comment se reconnaîtrait-il en ce pêle-mêle de noms illustres et de réputations éphémères? Et quelles gloires à ses yeux brilleraient davantage? Racine avec ses

---

[11] Quoted in Doncieux, p. 295.
[12] *Ibid.,* p. 294f.
[13] *Ibid.,* p. 295.
[14] *Ibid.,* p. 248f.
[15] Another surprise for modern readers follows immediately: "écrire comme Bouhours *et Rabutin*" (*Œuvres* [ed. G. Servois; Paris: Hachette, 1865], I, 126). More bizarre still, as Servois observes in a footnote, this passage is actually an amplification of the original text of the fourth edition (1689), in which Bussy-Rabutin's name stood alone.

> tragédies, ou le Chevalier de Cailly avec ses épigrammes? Madeleine de Scudéry, ou Pierre Corneille? Pascal, ou bien M. de Méré? [16]

Although the names of Madeleine de Scudéry and Méré have regained a certain lustre in literary criticism since Doncieux wrote sneeringly of them in 1887, his point would seem to be well taken; Bouhours does appear to show an unjustified impartiality in citing all sorts and conditions of contemporary authors. Admittedly, he displays an irksome predilection for the oratory of fellow Jesuits and other clergymen of the day in citing so many as models of distinguished expression, giving in this case an impression of uncritical partisan solidarity rather than of thoughtful literary judgment.

Yet Doncieux's criticism in this regard should not be accepted without an important modification: Bouhours was not so undiscriminating as Doncieux represents him, for in applying a subjective standard of literary merit the Jesuit did note flaws and deficiencies of taste in the authors quoted when these served to demonstrate the superiority of another's *délicatesse*. The obscure Cailly does indeed figure twice in the *Pensées ingénieuses,* but one of Bouhours' comments could not be called ingenuous, unqualified praise:

> Les pensées qui ne roulent que sur de pures équivoques sont bien fades, et déplaisent fort aux gens de bon goût, quelque ingénieuses qu'elles paroissent. Le Chevalier d'Aceilly [anagram of "de Cailly], qui excelle en naïvetés, tombe quelquefois dans ce défaut, et l'affecte même comme quelque chose de joli: témoins les deux Madrigaux suivants.... [17]

On the other hand, Racine draws no such reproof for any of the five selections taken from his tragedies. Another eminent contemporary, Thomas Corneille, cited three times, is shown to be capable of missing the mark of true eloquence:

> Un fameux Académicien dit, dans la Harangue qu'il fit pour l'Académie Françoise, au retour de Sa Majesté après

---

[16] Doncieux, p. 249.
[17] Bouhours, *Pensées ingénieuses*, p. 139.

> les conquêtes de l'année 1676, que c'est le propre de la grande admiration, et de toutes les passions violentes, de donner de la voix aux muets, et de rendre l'éloquence muette; que le peuple, jusqu'au plus bas, jusqu'à celui qu'on prendroit pour insensible, parle en ces occasions d'une manière si naturelle et si vive, que nulle étude ne la sçauroit imiter: mais que l'Académie, après avoir cultivé avec tant de peine l'art de bien parler, n'a point de paroles en un sujet si ample: presque réduite à honorer par sa confusion et par son silence ce qu'elle ne peut ni relever, ni égaler par ses discours.
> C'est beaucoup dire en ne disant rien. [18]

Fontenelle is blandly praised as a "Lucien moderne" [19] and as a writer "qui pense toujours délicatement," [20] yet is gently reproached for the unnecessary intransigence of his theory of the equality of all generations. [21] Voiture is clearly one of Bouhours' favorite modern authors, with a score of citations figuring in this collection. Doncieux attributes this to a great affinity between the two and considers it proof of Bouhours' latent preciosity. [22] Yet Bouhours does devote several pages specifically to examples of exaggerated, unnatural expression to be found in Voiture's works, applying a standard of taste which had not yet been conceived in Voiture's day. One of the most striking examples of Bouhours' literary judgment is to be found in his comparison of poems by Malherbe and Boileau:

> La peinture de Malherbe fait du siècle heureux qu'il prédit lui-même, sous le nom d'un Berger Devin, est charmante. [...] La description du Règne de LOUIS LE GRAND, faite par un excellent Poëte [Boileau], est encore plus belle, *quoiqu'elle ne soit pas si poëtique...* [23]

---

[18] *Ibid.*, p. 143.
[19] *Ibid.*, p. 250.
[20] Although not included in the earliest editions, this observation appears as an "augmentation" in the 1698 Lyon edition (p. 252).
[21] *Ibid.*, p. 67.
[22] Doncieux, p. 249f. This judgment is seen by Borgerhoff (p. 192) as evidence of Doncieux's own limited understanding of the complex nature of French Classicism.
[23] Bouhours, *Pensées ingénieuses*, p. 65.

In view of the long, close friendship between Boileau and Bouhours, such a reservation is remarkable indeed on the part of a man famous for his gentle complaisance toward his friends and admirers.

At the very least, the fact of the publishing success of the *Pensées ingénieuses* constitutes further proof that our own judgments on French Classical literature were not necessarily those of that age itself, that many of the admirers of the Generation of 1660 did not conceive of an absolute divorce between the preceding age and their own. Viewed more positively, Bouhours' long hodgepodge of literary celebrities and nonentities may be appreciated for a quality not apparent to his 19th-Century biographer: a conscious application of the standard of *raison-goût* in literary criticism, representative of the most widely shared literary outlook of that moment in the evolution of French Classicism.

MONTAIGNE'S CONCLUSION TO BOOK II OF HIS *ESSAIS*

Philip A. Wadsworth
Rice University

The attentive reader of the *Essais,* watching their themes come to life or branch out in new directions, must necessarily pause at the end of Book II to look back at the ground he has covered. This was the author's stopping place, when he published his first two books in 1580, then set out on his travels, and later came home to take up his duties as mayor of Bordeaux, almost completely abandoning his literary activities for a period of five years. The work of 1580, without Book III and without the accretions identified as "texts B and C," was already a monumental accomplishment. Here are some of the great early chapters —on education, friendship, cannibals, cruelty, presumption— and also the strangely sprawling edifice erected in defense of Raymond Sebond. The very pleasant final essay in Book II, "De la ressemblance des enfants aux pères," may seem surprisingly inconclusive or digressive. Here Montaigne speaks briefly of his habits as a writer, indulges in some family reminiscences, and describes the "inherited" kidney disease which has recently assailed him. He then embarks on a forceful but humorous denunciation of medical arts and practitioners, interrupts himself to address some chatting remarks to Madame de Duras, returns for a moment to the theme of illness and health, and ends with a mild comment on differences of opinion: let others feel free to disagree with him.

"La Ressemblance" is a personal essay, far advanced beyond most of the material in Book I, but can it be considered a conclusion to Book II? In approaching this question we must exclude any search for a logical development, since the essay clearly does not resolve an argument or stand out as a climax in some system of ideas. And, in spite of Villey, chronology is not very helpful either. If the composition of the essay (or of some pages in it) took place in the winter of 1579-80, just prior to the work's publication, the same date can be given to various other essays (or lines or pages in them). The problem is primarily artistic: does "La Ressemblance" form a conclusion —or ending or even afterthought— which is intimately related to themes presented elsewhere in Book II and which somehow illuminates them? Given the loose and open structure of individual essays and their rather haphazard arrangement within each book, it is still possible to see some elements of a finale in the closing chapter of Book II.[1]

Of course this essay was in ways the direct result of Montaigne's kidney stone affliction which made its first onslaught in the spring or summer of 1578. This loss of health and experience of great recurring pain turned his thought in oddly happier directions as he practiced the art of survival and learned to appreciate the sheer joy of existence in periods of respite. He was beginning to achieve his triumph over suffering as he wrote "La Ressemblance": "J'entre des-jà en composition de ce vivre coliqueux; j'y trouve de quoy me consoler et dequoy esperer."[2] In earlier years he had shown his dread of the stone while he still enjoyed perfect health. His father had succumbed to this painful ailment, a fact which may have contributed to Montaigne's discussion of suicide (II, 3) or to his pointed allusion to a passage in Pliny on certain maladies which may justify taking one's life; "la plus aspre de toutes, c'est la pierre à la vessie quand l'urine en est retenuë" (p. 336). He in fact confessed in "La Ressemblance" that he had played with the idea of killing himself as a way to avoid the ravages of old age and disease (p. 737).

---

[1] On the arrangement of essays in the three books see, with great caution, the prefaces by Michel Butor for an edition in the collection "Le Monde en 10/18": Montaigne, *Essais*, Paris, Union Générale d'Éditions, 1964-65 (4 volumes). Butor goes much too far in his numerology but he makes penetrating remarks on the role of La Boétie in Book I and on the "Apologie" as the center of gravity of Book II. He says nothing helpful on "La Ressemblance."

[2] II, 37; p. 737. Page references are in the Thibaudet-Rat edition of Montaigne's *Œuvres complètes:* Paris, Gallimard, 1962 (Bibliothèque de la Pléiade).

It is sometimes difficult to determine the timing of Montaigne's references to his physical condition. A page in the "Apologie" which is usually said to date from 1573 makes use of the well-known anecdote of Pyrrho's pig (which remained perfectly calm when threatened by a storm at sea) to show the power of our imagination to make us feel sick or afraid (p. 470). One may suffer from "la pierre en l'âme" before the real disease attacks the kidneys. A few sentences later the essayist pays tribut to the pleasures of good health, which he enjoys only rarely now that he is subjected to "l'amertume d'une nouvelle et contrainte forme de vivre" (p. 471). He makes a similar statement in his essay on solitude, speaking of his need for bodily comfort or what he calls "les commoditez corporelles": "l'aage m'ayant tantost desrobé celles qui estoyent plus à ma fantasie, j'instruis et aiguise mon appetit à celles qui restent plus sortables à cette autre saison" (p. 241). We may conjecture that Montaigne added these passages to his text in the period 1578 to 1580, after the outbreak of his illness. They seem to show the author in the same frame of mind as in "La Ressemblance." He was naturally much concerned with the prospect of invalidism and he was determined to take full advantage of whatever pleasures remained.

In 1580 Montaigne was eager to have his work published and he could not foresee that he would take up writing again. He announced to Madame de Duras, with much exaggeration, that he was "prest d'abandonner le commerce des hommes" (p. 764). His immediate activities were to visit Paris, where he presented a copy of his book to the King, to take some small part in a military campaign, and to make a pilgrimage to Rome, stopping at various spas to try the possible curative effects of mineral springs. One senses a holiday spirit in "La Ressemblance," as though the author were already making plans for a long vacation. He speaks with relish of two trips he has already made to watering places, which he enjoyed but which had inconsistent effects, if any, on the progress of his illness (p. 1616). A theme which becomes very prominent in a later essay, "De la vanité," —his need to escape from domestic life and his insistence that his health will not suffer when he is away from home— is already sketched here in a few lines: "Tout lieu m'est bon à m'arrester, car il ne me faut autres commoditez, estant malade, que celles qu'il me faut estant sain. Je ne me passionne point d'estre sans medecin, sans apotiquaire et sans secours" (p. 745). He and his family probably debated the point, after the onset of his disease, whenever he contemplated extensive travel. Surely there is a private joke, near the end of the essay, when he says that doctors as a last resort send their patients "les uns au secours des vœuz et miracles, les autres aux eaux chaudes." He adds that they have one other desperate trick to get rid of us, "c'est de nous envoier cercher la bonté de l'air en quelque autre contrée" (p. 765). Perhaps a warm water cure and a change of climate had been recommended to Montaigne by his physicians. In any event, since they were under attack in his essay, he might as well include such a treatment (to which he looked forward eagerly) as an example of their ignorance and incompetence!

* * *

For Montaigne the body's health was always associated with that of the soul, a word which he wisely refused to define, giving it the many meanings and connotations of everyday speech. There is no need to point out his many statements concerning these two "principales parties de notre être" — their inseparability and their interaction in the life of the whole man. Sometimes he stressed the influence of thought or emotion on the functions of the body and sometimes he dwelled on the help which the body could provide for a wavering soul, but he invariably saw two forces that needed to work in staunch alliance. At the same time he had grave doubts as to our knowledge, or even the possibility of attaining knowledge, of how body and soul operate. His denunciation of medicine and physicians is closely related to the skeptical attitudes in the "Apologie de Raymond Sebond," in particular to what he called our "peu de clarté en la cognoissance des choses humaines et naturelles" (p. 517).

These words in the "Apologie" appear in the middle of the section where his Pyrrhonism is strongest (pp. 480-540, usually dated 1576), at the point where the author embarks on a discussion of human ignorance concerning body and soul. He makes extensive comments, running to about twenty pages, on the views of philosophers who have attempted to describe the nature of man's soul, or its location, or its immortality. But his treatment of physiological knowledge is surprisingly brief and evasive. He does introduce the subject: "Il n'y a point moins de temerité en ce qu'elle [la science humaine] nous apprend des parties corporelles. Choisissons en un ou deux exemples, car autrement nous nous perdrions dans cette mer trouble et vaste des erreurs medecinales" (p. 538). There follows a paragraph, one page or less, on the mysterious nature and functioning of human semen. Then, suddenly turning in a new direction, he dismisses this theme: "En voylà assez pour verifier que l'homme n'est non plus instruit de la connoissance de soy en la partie corporelle qu'en la spirituelle" (p. 539). The page stands out as one of the seams of the "Apologie," the result of sewing and patching as the author put together pieces of his lengthy work. Why did he avoid, or drop so briefly, what he calls the errors of medicine? He had more than enough material available, or seems to say so, and was perhaps setting it aside or using it elsewhere, i.e. in "La Ressemblance."

There may be more than mere coincidence in the fact that the example of "notre semence," which Montaigne uses in the "Apologie," is also the point of departure for his attack on medicine in "La Ressemblance." In the latter essay he shifts the emphasis from the mysteries of procreation to those of genetics and he proceeds to speak of his illness as an inheritance from his father. But the lines evoking "cette goute d'eau" (p. 741), which are accompanied by reflections on human ignorance and presumption, could take their place easily in the essay on Raymond Sebond. Without attempting to explain how Montaigne revised and edited his manuscript for publication —what pages he may have added here and there, or transferred from one place to another— we can feel fairly sure that the "Apologie" and "La Ressemblance" had brushed together in some sort of textual contact.

Just as the soul and the body were closely linked in Montaigne's thought, so were their professional guardians, philosophers or theologians on one hand, physicians on the other.[3] He often brought

---

[3] It was a habitual pattern of thought for the French to associate doctors of divinity and doctors of medicine, perhaps because of the organization of university studies. For learned advice on his marriage problem Panurge went to the experts on body and soul, a physician and a theologian (and also to a *juriscosulte* for legal information); *Le Tiers Livre*, chapter 29.

together and showed his scorn for "nos medecins spirituels et corporels" and their inability to provide any cure for the "maladies du corps et de l'ame" (I, 30, p. 198). Our whole being is endangered by the broken promises of "les arts qui promettent de nous tenir le corps en santé et l'âme en santé" (III, 13, p. 1057). As one of his first arguments against medicine in "La Ressemblance" Montaigne develops the parallel between these two "arts": two kinds of dogmatism, of learned jargon, of imposture and mystification in interpreting things unknown. He takes pleasure in satirizing ancient doctors as performers of rituals and hoaxes. They invented gods and demons to deceive their patients and for a long time people had faith in them: "C'estoit une bonne regle en leur art, et qui accompaigne toutes les arts fantastiques, vaines et supernaturelles, qu'il faut que la foy du patient preoccupe par bonne esperance leur effect et operation" (p. 749). There was something "mysterieux et divin" in the way they chose strange drugs and subjected their victims to "un enchantement magicien." One is likely to recall, in the "Apologie," a similar comparison of medicine to superstition (p. 542) or the many passages on man's acceptance of pagan rituals and beliefs. [4]

According to Montaigne, doctors eventually lost their spellbinding power because they exposed their secrets through wrangling.

> "Car il advient de cette faute que leur irresolution, la foiblesse de leurs argumens, ...l'âpreté de leurs contestations, ...venant à estre descouverts à un chacun, il faut estre merveilleusement aveugle si on ne se sent bien hazardé entre leurs mains."

The author pursues at some length the conflicting and changing views which physicians have held, such as their ridiculous theories on the causes of disease (p. 750). He gives a colorful history of the rise and fall of various medical authorities in ancient and modern times, comparing them to governments where one regime

---

In his preface to *Tartuffe* Molière rather curiously invoked the prestige of philosophy and medicine in defense of comedy, saying that all three arts have risen from a state of corruption to one of wholesome moral influence.

[4] In a very early essay (I, 32, p. 214) Montaigne had already protested against the impostures of physicians, alchemists, sorcerers, and the "interpretes et contrerolleurs ordinaires des desseins de Dieu."

soon replaces another (pp. 750-751). This line of attack runs parallel to numerous pages in the "Apologie" where he points out the manifold disagreement, and thus the ignorance, of philosophers who have endeavored to describe the nature of the soul, or of God, or of the universe.

Such widespread differences of opinion are partly the result of chance or fortune, and this thought leads Montaigne into a characteristic digression. Man's physical condition is a matter of such complexity, so changeable, and so much affected by outside influences that the doctor's diagnosis has no possible validity: "...comment trouvera il le signe propre de la maladie, chacune estant capable d'un infiny nombre de signes?" (p. 753). Drugs are complicated too and any "mixtion de breuvage" adds one confusion to another and increases the likelihood of error. The author comes back to this idea later in his essay (pp. 761-763) with an eloquent denunciation of medical discoveries said to have been made through chance or experimentation; he sees an infinite number of variable diseases and circumstances which preclude all hope for scientific progress. This vision of flux and instability, of changing man unable to grasp his changing environment, seems to penetrate much of Montaigne's thinking on medicine. As he says of Paracelsus in the "Apologie" (p. 554), here is a new and famous physician but why should the common man turn like a weathervane to each new theory that comes along? One's life is too important to entrust it to some random "profession de nouvelletez et de reformations physiques." For Montaigne it is manifestly more reasonable and less risky to avoid drugs and doctors, letting nature take its course. His skeptical viewpoint raises doubts about advances in knowledge and also, on a practical level, urges the acceptance of one's natural condition as the best rule of health. [5]

---

[5] The best and fullest treatment of Montaigne's skepticism is the recent study by Philip P. Hallie, *The Scar of Montaigne: An Essay in Personal Philosophy*, Middletown, Wesleyan University Press, 1966. For early skeptical tendencies see Maturin Dréano, "La Crise sceptique de Montaigne?" in *Bibliothèque d'Humanisme et Renaissance*, 23: 252-264 (1961). The contributions of Donald Frame are also invaluable; many of them are summed up in *Montaigne: A Biography*, New York, Harcourt, Brace and World, 1965.

The essayist returns to the theme of contradictory doctrines —and comes closest to Pyrrhonism— as he tries his hand at a method of argumentation which he had found in Sextus Empiricus. It will be recalled that in the "Apologie" he attempted to give an explanation of Pyrrho's philosophical doubt (pp. 482-487). One point he emphasized was the way skeptics carried on debate, maintaining an antithesis for every proposition of their adversary. To combat a dogmatic opinion they would defend an opposite one which was equally plausible: "Si vous establissez que la nege soit noire, ils argumentent au rebours qu'elle est blanche. Si vous dites qu'elle n'est ny l'un, ny l'autre, c'est à eux à maintenir qu'elle est tous les deux" (p. 483). In this form of disputation Montaigne saw an analogy with the disagreements among doctors and also a literary device for ridiculing the medical profession. One of the most amusing pages in "La Ressemblance" consists of absurdly contradictory pieces of advice for the treatment of kidney stones:

> Les choses aperitives son utiles à un homme coliqueus, d'autant qu'ouvrant les passages et les dilatant, elles acheminent cette matière gluante de laquelle se bastit la grave et la pierre... Les choses aperitives sont dangereuses à un homme coliqueux... Il est bon de tomber souvent de l'eau, car nous voyons par experience qu'en la faisant croupir nous lui donnons loisir de se descharger de ses excremens et de sa lye... —il est bon de ne tomber point souvent de l'eau, car les poisans excremens qu'elle traine quant et elle, ne s'emporteront poinct s'il n'y a de la violence... Il est bon d'avoir souvent affaire aux femmes, car cela ouvre les passages et achemine la grave et le sable; —il est bien aussi mauvais, car cela eschaufe les reins, les lasse et affoiblit. Il est bon de se baigner aux eaux chaudes... —mauvais aussi est-il... (pp. 754-755).

At the end of this lively satire of medical pronouncements Montaigne added a sentence of commentary which shows that he was conscious of employing a Pyrrhonistic form of presentation: "Voilà comment ils vont bastelant et baguenaudant à nos despens en tous leurs discours; (*b*) et ne me sçauroient fournir proposition à laquelle je n'en rebatisse une contraire de pareille force."

Near the end of "La Ressemblance" the essayist introduces two "contes," or reports from his own experience, which touch upon the dangers of medicine. One is merely an example of superstitious remedies: the story of a goat which was given a special diet so that its blood would have curative effects, and which turned out when slaughtered to be itself a victim of the stone. The other has broader applications to Montaigne's ways of thought. He tells what has recently happened to the peasants of Lahontan, a remote and uncivilized corner of Gascony. They lived peacefully and healthfully for many centuries until one of them became a notary, introducing them to law suits, and a doctor came along who taught them the names of diseases and the use of various medicines. Now they worry about their health, suffer fancied pains or really become sick from taking drugs, and hasten their own death: "...ils apperçoivent un general deschet en leur ancienne vigueur, et leurs vies de moitié raccourcies" (p. 759). Montaigne's admiration for the natural life of primitive people is of course a recurrent idea in his essays and is developed at length in the chapter "Des cannibales," which he apparently wrote around the same time as "La Ressemblance." The uneducated natives of Lahontan also bring us on a roundabout course to one of our points of departure: the passage in the "Apologie" (pp. 470-471) where the author evokes Pyrrho's ignorant but fearless pig, speaks of "la pierre en l'âme" as an example of mental suffering, and mentions the recent decline in his own health.

Perhaps illness fortified Montaigne's skepticism, adding to his doubts about man's knowledge of man. Or perhaps these doubts already weighed on his mind a few years earlier when his readings in Sextus Empiricus supposedly led to the choice of inscriptions for his library, to the famous motto inscribed on a medal, and to the most outspokenly skeptical pages in his defense of Raymond Sebond. Recent scholars have gone far in countering Villey's view of a dramatic "crise sceptique" in the evolution of Montaigne's thought. His discovery of Pyrrhonist texts was important but it was not a source of aberration or a flash of blinding light. He claimed to be a Platonist long before he heard of Plato, and he could have made the same comment on his Pyrrhonism. His skeptical questioning of medical theories is apparent in many small passages throughout the early essays. It comes back in full force in "De l'expérience" (III, 13) where, after ten years of sickness, he gives his final expression to a philosophy of healthy enjoyment of life.

Here we are concerned primarily with "La Ressemblance" and its many points of contact with the skeptical themes in the "Apologie." It seems clear that the final essay of Book II must be considered a kind of companion piece to the "Apologie," which it echoes, in a sense completes, and recalls to the attention of the reader. As he struggled to defend Sebond, assembling so many materials to undermine the presumptuous claims of human reason, Montaigne also had in mind this other essay which would deal scornfully and amusingly with the claims of medicine. At the same time it would add details to the personal portrait which he was sketching and would serve as an appropriate ending for his book.

* * *

Montaigne's desire to provide a portrait of himself, which he seemed to recognize as the best justification and the only usefulness of his essays, forms the framework of "La Ressemblance." The first lines refer to his work as "ce fagotage de tant de diverses pieces" which he has composed intermittently, when he found himself at home with leisure time to fill. He has not corrected or rewritten his manuscript from year to year because he has tried to show the changes in his thinking. Some pages have been stolen, he adds, but this loss doesn't matter much in a book of so little consequence.

These remarks are developed at greater length toward the end of the essay in a sort of farewell speech to Madame de Duras. She has seen him during a recent visit and, when he is dead, she can find the same personality in this work which may outlast him by "quelques années ou quelques jours." He has not painted a flattering picture but has simply given a projection of his ordinary self. He does not try to press this point, having often explained already his conception of the essays as a "livre consubstantiel à son autheur" (II, 18, p. 648).

There follows one of those passages, so characteristic of Montaigne, where he speaks disparagingly of himself but incidentally reveals his feeling of pride or satisfaction. He insists that he has no talent and no ambitions as a "faiseur de livres." He has been too busy to become a writer: "Mon art et mon industrie ont esté employez à me faire valoir moy-mesme; mes estudes, à m'apprendre à faire, non pas à escrire. J'ay mis tous mes efforts à former ma vie" (p. 764). He says that he cannot expect any honor or glory from his essays, "ces sottises," but he points to their value as the faithful record of a life well lived.

As he reaches the end Montaigne weaves together two major themes of this chapter, medicine and self-study. He expresses the fear that this final portrait may seem dark and sickly, because he has lost his former vigor. He teases Madame de Duras because she has more respect for the mysteries of medicine than he does, adding that he may one day change his mind, or rather lose his mind, and resort to doctors in desperation. In the meantime he has taken the trouble to write out his views on medicine to give them "un peu plus de forme," so as to fortify his natural inclinations and show that they are not the result of boastful arrogance. He would much rather be able to boast of good health.

His closing sentences are an invitation to free debate. He has set forth his own judgments but other people are welcome to express different ones, whether on the medical profession or any other subject. No two men have the same ideas: "Et ne fut jamais au monde deux opinions pareilles, non plus que deux poils ou deux grains. Leur plus universelle qualité, c'est la diversité" (p. 766). Thus diversity is the last word of Book II, and of course it has a familiar ring. Montaigne had sounded this keynote at the beginning of Book I, describing man as a creature who is "vain, divers et ondoyant," and again in the first essay of Book II, which deals with man's ever changing nature. But here in "La Ressemblance" he underscores the existence of discordant opinions which may be as valid as his own. He has not forgotten the teachings of Pyrrhonism. Skeptical suspension of judgment —whether in Montaigne or in Sextus— arises from a keen awareness of diversity, from the recognition of everpresent changes and differences in living ceatures, in the universe, and in interpretations of what seems to be knowledge or truth.

The pages for Madame de Duras constitute an epilogue at the end of Book II of the essays and carry the same message as the "Au lecteur" of March 1, 1580: here is an honest portrait, a personal memento which cannot render any service to the reading public. His opinions come from the experience of one individual and they may be widely different from the findings of others. Thus the same concept of diversity motivated his attack on dogmatic physicians and his refusal to be dogmatic himself. This doubting attitude would later be modified and absorbed into more complex modes of thought but it was surely a major preoccupation as he worked to round out his essays and prepare the text for publication. His unpretentious final chapter holds special interest as a reflection of his state of mind. It forms a satisfying conclusion to Book II because it contains so many reverberations of skeptical themes and conveys so well, along with his growing faith in nature, the author's cheerful acceptance of change and uncertainty as conditions of life.

MONTAIGNE'S READINGS FOR *DES CANNIBALES*

BERNARD WEINBERG
University of Chicago

It has frequently been stated that, for the composition of *Des Cannibales*, Montaigne relied very little upon written documents and used instead materials that he obtained from oral accounts. This is taken to be a distinguishing feature of the essay (I, xxxi) and one that corroborates the late date of composition for the whole of the essay, assigned to it through other kinds of evidence. Such was the position of Pierre Villey in his prefatory note to *Des Cannibales* (*Les Essais de Michel de Montaigne*, Paris: Alcan, 1922, I, 261):

> Bien que les relations imprimées ne fissent pas défaut à cette époque sur le pays des Cannibales (la côte actuelle du Brésil) où avait abordé en 1557 la fameuse expédition de Villegagnon, il est à remarquer que, conformément à sa déclaration, Montaigne, dans la première rédaction de son essai, semble n'avoir rien emprunté ni aux cosmographes comme Thevet, Belleforest et Munster, ni aux relations des compagnons de Villegagnon comme le même Thevet ou Jean de Léry; il paraît parler des cannibales uniquement d'après des témoignages oraux.

In his note on the same essay, Jacob Zeitlin (*The Essays of Michel de Montaigne*, New York: Knopf, 1934, I, 378) argues for a somewhat modified estimate of Montaigne's indebtedness to literary sources:

> But there is no reason for believing that the essay as a whole was not composed at the same time [1579-80].

> Both in ideas and in style it represents a sufficiently mature stage of Montaigne's art. Its freedom from dependence on the authority of books is one evidence of its late date among the essays of the first edition. It is true that Professor Chinard has thrown some doubt on Montaigne's claim to derive his material entirely from the direct oral testimony of an eyewitness. Besides the passage from Benzoni, he believes that the essayist made use of the narrative of Jean de Léry, *Histoire d'un Voyage Fait en la Terre du Brésil* (1578). But in M. Villey's opinion the resemblances are only such as would be inevitable in a description of the same things. ... The probability is that while Montaigne relied mainly on the recital of his own "domestic," he had read the account of Léry, and perhaps also André Thevet's *Singularitez de la France Antarctique* (1558), and that some details stuck in his memory and blended with his first-hand information.

The "passage from Benzoni," on which Villey based his date and to which Zeitlin here refers, is not by Benzoni at all; it is from one of the interchapters or commentaries that Urbain Chauveton added to his translation of Benzoni, entitled *Histoire nouvelle du nouveau monde* and published in Paris in 1579. There is no equivalent for it in the Benzoni original. Gilbert Chinard (*L'Exotisme américain dans la littérature française au XVIe siècle*, Paris: Hachette, 1911, pp. 197-201) first demonstrated the close parallelism between passages in Montaigne and the Chauveton translation. But it should be noted that those passages in Montaigne are concerned with authors and reports from Greek antiquity about the discovery of new lands; they do not belong to the description of the American savages and their mores. They leave intact Montaigne's affirmation that he had relied exclusively on his informants for facts about the cannibals: "je me contente de cette information, sans m'enquerir de ce que les cosmographes en disent" (ed. Villey, I, 261).

With that affirmation, Dr. A. Armaingaud took definite issue in his edition of the *Essais* (Paris: Conard, 1924, II, 241, n. 1): "Comme on l'a vu plus haut, Montaigne ne se contentait pas des témoignages de son serviteur, et il lisait très attentivement les récits des explorateurs." But it is difficult to find, "plus haut," any support for Armaingaud's conclusion. My purpose in this paper is to examine the possibility that certain "récits des explorateurs" may have contributed to the materials used by Montaigne. I shall do so by studying, in their strict chronological order, the successive parts of the essay *Des Cannibales*, in the redaction of 1580 (ed. Jean Plattard, Paris: Société Les Belles Lettres, 1946, Vol. II), and by pointing out the resemblances between certain passages in the essay and the texts of three *relations de voyage*. These are, in their apparent order of publication:

(1) André Thevet, Les Singvlaritez de la France Antarctiqve, Avtrement nommée Amerique: & de plusieurs Terres & Isles decouuertes de nostre temps. Par F. André Theuet, natif d'Angoulesme. A Paris, Chez les heritiers de Maurice de la Porte, au Clos Bruneau, à l'enseigne S. Claude. 1557. Avec Privilege Dv Roy. The *privilège* is dated "à Saint Germain en Laye, le dixhuitiesme iour du mois de Decembre, l'an de grace mil cinq cens cinquante six, & de nostre regne le dixiesme," and is signed "Fizes."

(2) N[icolas] B[arré], Copie de Qvelqves Letres Svr La Navigation du Cheuallier de Villegaignon es terres de l'Amerique oultre l'Æquinoctial, iusques soubz le tropique de Capricorne: côtenant sommairement les fortunes encourues en ce voyage, auec les meurs & façons de viure des Sauuages du pais: enuoyées par vn des gens dudict Seigneur. A Paris, Chez Martin le Ieune, à l'enseigne S. Christophle, deuant le college de Cambray, rue S. Iean de Latran. 1557. Avec Privilege. The *privilège* is dated "le vi. iour de Feburier M.DLVI. [=1557], and is signed "DuTillet." The two letters are dated "De la riuiere de Ganabara au pais du Bresil, en la Frãce Antarctique, soubs le Tropique de Capricorne, ce premier iour de Feburier mil cinq cents cinquantecinq" (signed N. B.) and "De la riuiere ... ce vingt cinqieme iour de May, mil cinq cents cinquante six" (signed N. B.), and there is a note following the first date to the effect that "ont esté ces presentes receuës le Ieudy 23. de Iuillet 1556." In spite of these early dates, February-July 1556, there is some textual evidence that Barré made use of Thevet.[1]

---

[1] E.g., the sentence in Barré, p. 18, "Nous arriuasmes le dixieme de Nouembre en la riuiere de Ganabara, pour la similitude qu'elle a au lac," makes sense only when one reads the original in Thevet, p. 48v: "ceste grande riuiere nommée Ganabara de ceux du païs, pour la similitude qu'elle à au lac." The Barré letters are given in Latin translation in Vol. II of *Americae Historiae*, ed. Theodore de Bry, Frankfurt-am-Main: Matthias Becker, 1605, pp. 285-95.

(3) Jean de Léry, *Histoire D'Vn Voyage Fait En La Terre Dv Bresil, Avtrement dite Amerique*. ... Le tout recueilli sur les lieux par Iean De Lery, natif de la Margelle, terre de sainct Sene au Duché de Bourgongne. ... Pour Antoine Chuppin. M.D.LXXVIII.

The first section of *Des Cannibales* (seven pages in the Plattard edition) is a historical and philosophical introduction to the subject, made up of the following elements: the bases for judging current opinions, with special reference to such notions as "barbare"; the discovery of new countries and changes in topography; reports in antiquity about lands beyond the Atlantic; and a consideration of the ideas of the natural, the barbarous, and the civilized. It should be noted again that the passage from Chauveton cited by Chinard corresponds to a part of this first section.

By way of preparing for the major development to come, the first section contains several references to Brazil and to Montaigne's informants. Close to the beginning, the sentence: "J'ay eu long temps avec moy un homme qui avoit demeuré dix ou douze ans en cet autre monde qui a esté decouvert en nostre siecle, en l'endroit où Vilegaignon print terre, qu'il surnomma la France Antartique." [2] A little later (p. 91), a commentary on the veracity of Montaigne's witness: "Cet homme que j'avoy, estoit homme simple et grossier, qui est une condition propre à rendre veritable tesmoignage." Finally, a brief introduction to the general position that Montaigne will take throughout the essay: "je trouve ... qu'il n'y a rien de barbare et de sauvage en cette nation" (p. 92). But here there are no possible textual sources, since the materials belong to Montaigne's experience or to his ideas.

It is when he begins to describe the mores of the Cannibals and the material conditions of their lives that resemblances to the earlier texts are suggested:

---

[2] Villey, Plattard, and others give the date of Villegagnon's first expedition as 1557; but according to the evidence of the texts studied here, Villegagnon embarked on May 16, 1555 and arrived at Ganabara on Nov. 10, 1555; this for the first expedition.

Au demeurant, ils vivent en une contrée de païs très-plaisante et bien tempérée; de façon qu'à ce que m'ont dit mes tesmoings, il est rare d'y voir un homme malade; et m'ont asseuré n'en y avoir veu aucun tremblant, chassieux, edenté, ou courbé de vieillesse. Ils sont assis le long de la mer, et fermez du costé de la terre de grandes et hautes montaignes, ayant, entredeux, cent lieuës ou environ d'estendue en large (95).

Barré: Le lieu est naturellement beau & facile à garder, à raison que l'entrée en est estroicte, close des deux costez de deux haults monts (18-19). ... L'air est temperé, tendant toutesfois plus à chaleur qu'à froideur. ... Voyla quant à la fertilité de la terre, salubrité & disposition de l'aer.[3] (22) *Léry:* ... bien sont-ils plus forts, plus robustes & replets, plus disposts, moins suiets à maladie: & mesme il n'y a presque point de boiteux, de manchots, d'aveugles de borgnes, contrefaits, ny maleficiez entre eux. Dauantage combien que plusieurs paruiennent iusques à l'aage de cent ou six vingt ans ... peu y en a qui en leur vieillesse ayent les cheueux ny blancs ny gris. Choses qui pour certain monstrent non seulement le bon air & bonne temperature de leur pays ... mais aussi ... le peu de soin & de souci qu'ils ont des choses de ce monde (108-9).

---

[3] The passage in Barré continues:
"Il reste à parler des habitans, de leurs conditions, statuts, & meurs. Ceste nation est la plus barbare, & estrange de toute honnesteté qui soit soubs le ciel, comme ie croy. Car ils viuent sans congnoissance d'aucun dieu, sans soucy, sans loy, ou aucune religion." The passage is close to Montaigne, II, 12, an addition of C: "Ce qu'on nous dict de ceux du Brésil, qu'ils ne mouroyent que de vieillesse, et qu'on attribue à la serenité et tranquillité de leur air, je l'attribue plutost à la tranquillité et serenité de leur ame, deschargée de toute passion et pensée et occupation tendue ou desplaisante, comme gents qui passoyent leur vie en une admirable simplicité et ignorance, sans lettres, sans loy, sans roy, sans relligion quelconque."

According to Thibaudet, Pléiade ed., II, 545n., the passage in Montaigne was "Presque transcrit d'Osorio, *Histoire du Portugal*, traduite par Goulard." Plattard, II, 276, note to p. 101, indicates the similarity between the accounts of Osorio and Léry and that of Montaigne. Cf. Osorio, ed. 1581, p. 62: "Ils n'ont conoissance de lettres quelconques, viuent sans religion, sans loix, ne s'aident de poids ni mesures, & ne sont suiets à Roy quelconque."

Le premier qui y mena un cheval, quoy qu'il les eust pratiquez à plusieurs autres voyages, leur fit tant d'horreur en cette assiete, qu'ils le tuerent à coups de traict, avant que le pouvoir recognoistre.

Thevet: En premier les espouuenta [le Capitaine Arual] auec ces cheuaux, qui leur estoient incongneuz, & reputez comme bestes rauissantes ... (106v-7)

For the details on the buildings in which the Americans lived, several explorers offer parallel descriptions:

Leurs bastiments sont fort longs, et capables de deux ou trois cents ames, estoffez d'escorce de grands arbres, tenans à terre par un bout et se soustenans et appuyans l'un contre l'autre par le feste, à la mode d'aucunes de noz granges, desquelles la couverture pend jusques à terre, et sert de flanq.

Thevet: Les maisons ou ils habitent sont petites logettes, qu'ils appellent en leur langue *Mortugabes* ... Ces logettes sont de deux, ou trois cens pas de long, et de largeur vingt pas, ou enuiron, plus ou moins: basties de bois, & couuertes de fueilles de palme, le tout disposé si naïfuement, qu'il est impossible de plus. Chacune logette à plusieurs belles couuertures ... (84)

Barré: Ils viuent en congregation, s'assemblants cinq ou six cents, & edifient de longues loges que les anciens appeloyent Mapalia. (26)

Léry: comme ainsi soit que les maisons des sauuages (longues qu'elles sont & de façon rondes comme vous diriez une treille de nos jardins de par deça) soyent basses et couuertes d'herbes iusques contre terre. (272-73) ... Touchant les immeubles de ce peuple consistans en maisons & ... en beaucoup plus de tresbonne terre qu'il n'en faudroit pour les nourrir: quant au premier, se trouuant tel village entr'eux où il y a de cinq à six cents personnes, encores que plusieurs habitent en vne mesme maison, tant y a que chaque famille (sans separation

	toutesfois de chose qui puisse empescher qu'on ne voye d'vn bout à l'autre de ces bastimens ordinairement longs de plus de soixante pas) ayant son rang à part: le mari a ses femmes & ses enfans separez. (304-5)
Ils ont du bois si dur qu'ils en coupent, et en font leurs espées et des grils à cuire leur viande.	*Thevet:* Il se trouue dauantage en ce païs vn autre bois iaune, duquel ils font aucuns leurs espées ... (117v)

In the same way, much attention is paid to the cotton hammocks in which the savages slept:

Leurs lits sont d'un tissu de coton, suspenduz contre le toict, comme ceux de nos navires, à chacun le sien ...	*Thevet:* ... au milieu desquelles [logettes] chacun en son quartier, sont pendus les licts à pilliers, forts & puissants attachez en quarrure, lesquels sont faits de bon coton, car ils en ont abondance ... (84-84v) *Barré*: Ils ont force cotton, dont ils font des licts qui pendent, & y fait autant bon dormir qu'en licts de plume: nous ne dormons point en d'autres licts. (26)
	Léry: (in a description of an engraving on the opposite page) & aupres des trois vn lict de couton fait comme vne rets à pescher pendu en l'air, ainsi qu'ils couchent en leur pays. (120)... des licts de coton qu'ils appellent *Inis*, faits les vns en maniere de Rets ou filets à pescher, & les autres tissus comme gros caneuats; mais estans pour la pluspart longs de quatre, cinq ou six pieds, & d'vne brasse de large, plus ou moins, tous ont deux boucles aux deux bouts faites aussi de couton, ausquelles

Ils se levent avec le soleil, et mangent soudain après s'estre levez, pour toute la journée; car ils ne font autre repas que celuy-là. Ils ne boyvent pas lors, comme Suidas dict de quelques autres peuples d'Orient, qui beuvoient hors du manger; ils boivent à plusieurs fois sur jour, et d'autant.

Leur breuvage est faict de quelque racine, et est de la couleur de nos vins clairets. Ils ne le boyvent que tiede; ce breuvage ne se conserve que deux ou trois jours; il a le goust un peu piquant, nullement fumeux, salutaire à l'estomac, et laxatif à ceux qui ne l'ont accoustumé; c'est une boisson très-agreable à qui y est duit. (95-96)

les Sauuages lient des cordes pour les attacher & pendre en l'air à quelques pieces de bois mises en trauers expressément pour cest effect en leurs maisons. (306-7)

Léry: Et ce qui est encores plus estrange & à remarquer entre nos *Toüoupinabaoults*, est, que comme ils ne mangent nullement durant leurs b u u e r i e s, aussi quand ils mangent ils ne boyuent point parmi leur repas. (144)

Thevet: leur Cahouin, qui est vn bruuage composé de mil nommé Auaty, & est gros comme pois. Il y en à de noir & de blanc, & font pour la plusgrande partie de ce qu'ils en recueillent ce bruuage, faisans bouillir ce mil auec autres racines, lequel apres auoir bouilly est de semblable couleur que le vin clairet. (46-46v) *Barré:* La terre ne produit que du Mil, que lon appelle en nostre pais bled sarrazin, duquel ilz font du vin auec vne racine qu'ils appellent Maniel ... (20) ... ils font du vin de Mil et racines, duquel ils s'enyurent ... (24) *Léry*: Les sauuages appellent ce b r u u a g e *Caou-in,* lequel a presque le goust de laict aigre: & en ont du rouge & du blanc comme nous auons du vin ... (142) ... leur coustume (du tout contraire à la nostre en matiere de vin, que nous aimons frais & clair) estant de boire ce *Caou-in* vn peu chaut & trouble, les femmes pour le tiedir font premierement vn petit feu à l'entour

	des cannes de terre où il est. (143)
Au lieu du pain, ils usent d'une certaine matiere blanche, comme du coriandre confit. J'en ay tasté: le goust en est doux et un peu fade.	*Thevet:* nous festoya d'vne farine faite de racines ... (46) [on the Hoyriri fruit:] dedans se trouue comme petites noisettes, dont le noyau est blanc & bon à manger, sinon que la quantité (comme est de toutes choses) offense le cerueau: laquelle force l'on dit estre semblable en la coriandre, si elle n'est preparé ... (62) *Barré:* d'icelle [the maniel root] ils font de la farine molle, qui est autant bonne que du pain. (20)
Toute la journée se passe à dancer. Les plus jeunes vont à la chasse des bestes à tout des arcs. Une partie des femmes s'amusent cependant à chauffer leur breuvage, qui est leur principal office.	*Thevet:* Car à vray dire, les femmes trauaillent plus sans comparaison, c'est à sçauoir à cueillir racines, f a i r e farines, bruuages, amasser les fruits, faire iardins, & autres choses, qui appartienent au mesnage. (79v-80) *Léry:* comme de fait les femmes de nos *Toüoupinambaoults* trauaillans sans comparaison plus que les hommes lesquels excepté quelques matinees (& non au chaut du iour) qu'ils coupent & essertent du bois pour faire les iardins, ne font gueres autre chose qu'aller à la guerre, à la chasse, pescher, faire leurs espees de bois, arcs, flesches, habillemens de plumes & autres choses que i'ay specifiees ailleurs, dont ils se parent le corps. (296).

After several sentences on the moral exhortations delivered by the old men of the village, Montaigne returns to the facts of material existence — before moving on to the spiritual life.

Il se void en plusieurs lieux, et entre autres chez moy, la forme de leurs lits, de leurs cordons, de leurs espées et brasselets de bois dequoy ils couvrent leurs poignets aux combats, et des grandes cannes, ouvertes par un bout, par le son desquelles ils soustiennent la cadance en leur dancer.

Léry: mesmes aucuns ont des Fifres & fleutes faites des os, des bras & des cuisses de ceux qui ont esté par eux mangez, desquelles pour s'inciter d'auantage d'en faire autant à ceux contre lesquels ils marchent, ils ne cessent de flageoler par les chemins. (227)

... Ils croyent les ames eternelles, et celles qui ont bien mérité des dieux, estre logées à l'endroit du ciel où le soleil se leve; les maudites, du costé de l'Occident. (96)

Léry: ie diray en premier lieu: ... que non seulement ils croyent l'immortalité des ames, mais aussi ils tiennent fermement qu'apres la mort des corps celles de ceux qui ont vertueusement vescu, c'est à dire selon eux qui se sont bien vengez & ont beaucoup mangez de leurs ennemis, s'en vont derriere les hautes montagnes ou elles dansent dans de beaux iardins auec celles de leurs grands peres... & au contraire que celles des effeminez & gens de neant... vont auec *Aygnan*... ou elles sont incessament tormentees. (262-63)

Montaigne's next major development concerns the activities of the priests or prophets. The essential details are also found in Thevet:

Ils ont je ne sçay quels prestres et prophetes, qui se presentent bien rarement au peuple, ayant leur demeure aux montaignes. A leur arrivée, il se faict une grande feste et assemblée solennelle de plusieurs vilages... Ce prophete parle à eux en public, les exhortant à la vertu et à leur devoir; mais toute leur science ethique ne contient que ces deux articles, de la resolution à la guerre et affection à leurs fem-

Thevet: Ces Sauuages ont encores vne autre opinion estrange & abusiue de quelques vns d'entre eux, qu'ils estiment vrays Prophetes, & les nomment en leur langue *Pagés*... Tels imposteurs pour colorer leur meschanceté, & se faire honorer entre les autres, ne demeurent ordinairement en vn lieu, ains sont vagabonds, errans ça & là par les bois & autres lieux, ne retournans point auecques les

mes. Cettuy-cy leur prognostique les choses à venir et les evenemens qu'ils doivent esperer de leurs entreprinses, les achemine ou destourne de la guerre; mais c'est par tel si que, où il faut à bien deviner, et s'il leur advient autrement qu'il ne leur a predit, il est haché en mille pieces s'ils l'attrapent, et condamné pour faux prophete. A cette cause, celuy qui s'est une fois mesconté, on ne le void plus. (96-97)

autres, que bien rarement & à certaines heures, leur faisans entendre, qu'ils ont communiqué auecques les esprits, pour les affaires du public, & qu'il faut faire ainsi & ainsi, ou qu'il aduiendra cecy ou cela: & lors ils sont receus & caressez honorablement, estants nourris & entretenuz sans faire autre chose: encore s'estiment bien-heureux ceux la qui peuuent demeurer en leur bonne grace, & leur faire quelque present. ... Dauantage il faut noter que les Sauuages ont en tel honneur & reuerence ces *Pagés,* qu'ils les adorent ou plustost idolatrent: mesmes quand ils retournent de quelque part, vous verriez le populaire aller au deuant, se prosternant, & les prier: disant, Fais que ie ne sois malade, que ie ne meure point ... Que s'il aduient quelquesfois que ces *Pagés* ne dient la verité, & que les choses arriuent autrement que le presage, ils ne font difficulté de les faire mourir, comme indignes de ce tiltre & dignité de *Pagés.* (65-67)

It was after this paragraph that Montaigne added, on the margins of the Bordeaux copy, his passage on divination.

Two subjects were of special interest both to Montaigne and to the explorers. These were the matter of wars and warriors and the related question of the treatment —and cannibalism— of prisoners. Thevet, Barré, and Léry were fascinated by these subjects.

Ils ont leurs guerres contre les nations qui sont au delà de leur montaignes, plus avant en la terre ferme, ausquelles ils vont tous nuds, n'ayant autres armes que des arcs ou des espées de bois, apointées par un bout...

Thevet: Ce peuple de l'Amerique est fort subiet à quereler contre ses voisins ... & n'ayans autre moyen d'appaiser leur querele, se battent fort & ferme. (70) ils chargent les vns les autres de coups de flesches confusement, de masses & espées de bois ...

C'est chose esmerveillable que de la fermeté de leurs combats, qui ne finissent jamais que par meurtre et effusion de sang; car, de routes et d'effroy, ils ne sçavent que c'est. (97-98)

(71) les hommes ne portans rien, que leurs arcs & flesches à la main. Leurs armes sont grosses espées de bois fort massiues & pesantes: au reste arcs, & flesches. (72) ... Aussi quand ils sont prisonniers les vns aux autres, n'estimez qu'ils demandent à echapper par quelque composition que ce soit, car ils n'en esperent autre chose que la mort, estimans cela à gloire & honneur. (78v) *Barré:* Ils font la guerre à cinq ou six nations ... (23) *Léry:* Car, comme eux mesmes confessent, n'estans poussez d'autre affection que de venger, chacun de son costé, ses parens & amis qui par le passé ont esté prins & mangez ..., ils sont tellement acharnez les vns à lencontre des autres, que quiconque tombe en la main de son ennemi, sans autre composition, il faut qu'il s'atende d'estre traitté de mesme: c'est à dire assommé & mangé. Qui plus est si tost que la guerre est vne fois declaree entre quelques vnes de ces nations, tous allegans qu'atendu que l'ennemi qui a receu l'iniure s'en ressentira à iamais, c'est trop laschement fait de le laisser eschaper quand on le tient à sa merci: leurs haines sont tellement inueterees qu'ils demeurent perpetuellement irreconciliables. (219-20) Surquoy faut noter que ces Ameriquains sont si acharnez en leurs guerres, que tant qu'ils pourront remuer bras & iambes sans reculer ni tourner le dos ils combatront incessamment. (220)

Chacun raporte pour son trophée la teste de l'ennemy qu'il

Thevet: & la teste, ils la reseruent à pendre au bout d'vne

a tué, et l'attache à l'entrée de son logis.

Après avoir long temps bien traité leurs prisonniers, et de toutes les commoditez dont ils se peuvent aviser, celuy qui en est le maistre, faict une grande assemblée de ses cognoissans; il attache une corde à l'un des bras du prisonnier, et donne au plus cher de ses amis l'autre bras à tenir de mesme; et eux deux, en presence de toute l'assemblée, l'assomment à coups d'espée. Cela faict, ils le rostissent et en mangent en commun et en envoient des lopins à ceux de leurs amis qui sont absens.

perche, sur leurs logettes, en signe de triomphe & victoire. (77v)

Thevet: Le prisonnier rendu en leur païs, vn ou deux, autant de plus que de moins, sera fort bien traité, quatre ou cinq iours, apres on luy baillera vne femme, parauenture la fille de celuy au quel sera le prisonnier, pour entierement luy administrer ses necessitez à la couchette ou autrement, ce pendant est traité des meilleures viandes que l'on pourra trouuer, s'estudians à l'engresser, comme vn chapon en muë, iusques au temps de le faire mourir. ... Ce prisonnier ayant este bien nourri & engressé, ils le feront mourir, estimans cela à grand honneur. Et pour la solennité de tel massacre, ils appelleront leurs amis p l u s loingtains, pour y assister, & en manger leur part. ... (76) *Barré:* quand ils prennent des prisonniers, ils leur donnent en mariage les plus belles filles qu'ils ayent, leur mettants au col autant de licolz qu'ils le veulent garder de lunes. Puis quand le temps est expiré ils font du vin de Mil et racines, duquel ils s'enyurent, appelants tous leurs amys. Puis celuy qui l'a prins prisonnier l'assomme auec vne massue de bois, & le diuise par pieces, & en font des carbonnades, qu'ils mengent auec si grand plaisir, qu'ils disent que c'est Ambrosie & Nectar. (23-24)

Léry: Incontinent d o n c q u e s qu'ils sont arriuez, non seulement ils sont nourris des meilleures viandes qu'on peut trouuer, mais aussi on baille des

	femmes aux hommes (& non des maris aux femmes), mesmes celuy qui aura un prisonnier ne faisant point difficulté de luy bailler sa fille ou sa seur en mariage, celle qu'il retiendra le traittera & luy administrera tout ce qui lui sera necessaire ... (237-38) Premierement apres que tous les villages d'alentour de celuy ou sera le prisonnier auront esté aduertis du iour de l'execution, hommes, femmes & enfans y estans arriuez de toutes parts ... deux ou trois des plus estimez de la troupe l'empoignans, & le lians par le milieu du corps avec des cordes de coton, ou autres faites de l'escorce d'vn arbre ... sans qu'il face aucune resistance, combien qu'on luy laisse les deux bras à deliure, il sera ainsi quelque peu de temps pourmené en trophee parmi le village. (238-39) ... celuy qui est la tout prest pour faire ce massacre, leuant sa massue de bois à deux mains, donne du rondeau qui est au bout de si grande force sur la teste du poure prisonnier, que tout ainsi les bouchers assomment les bœufs par deçà i'en ay veu du premier coup tomber tout roide mort... (242)
Ce n'est pas, comme on pense, pour s'en nourrir, ainsi que faisoient anciennement les Scythes; c'est pour representer une extreme vengeance.	*Thevet:* Et les Anthropophages qui sont peuples de Scythie, viuent de chair humaine comme ceux cy. (77v) ... la cause de leur guerre est assez mal fondée, seulement pour appetit de quelque vengeance, sans autre raison ... (73) *Léry:* plus par vengeance que pour le goust & la nourriture, ils mangent entierement tout ce qui se peut trouver ... (247)

After a long disquisition on the relative barbarity of the Cannibals and of certain Europeans, especially the Portuguese, Montaigne inquires into the causes of the wars among these savages.

Leur guerre est toute noble et genereuse, et a autant d'excuse et de beauté que cette maladie humaine en peut recevoir: elle n'a autre fondement parmy eux que la seule jalousie de la vertu. Ils ne sont pas en debat de la conqueste de nouvelles terres, car ils jouyssent encore de cette uberté naturelle qui les fournit sans travail et sans peine de toutes choses necessaires, en telle abondance qu'ils n'ont que faire d'agrandir leurs limites. (99-100)

Thevet: Si vous demandez pourquoy ces Sauuages font guerre les vns contre les autres, veu qu'ils ne sont gueres plus grands seigneurs l'vn que l'autre: aussi qu'entre eux n'y a richesses si grandes, & qu'ils ont de la terre asses & plus, qu'ils [sic] ne leur en faut pour leur necessité. Et pour cela vous suffira entendre, que la cause de leur guerre ... [etc. as above] (73)

Ils ne demandent à leurs prisonniers autre rançon que la confession et recognoissance d'estre vaincus; mais il ne s'en trouve pas un, en tout un siecle, qui n'ayme mieux la mort que de relascher, ny par contenance, ny de parole un seul poinct d'une grandeur de courage invincible; il ne s'en void aucun qui n'ayme mieux estre tué et mangé, que de requerir seulement de ne l'estre pas.

Thevet: Par cela pouuez congnoistre qu'ils ne font conte de la mort, encores moins qu'il n'est possible de penser. I'ay autrefois (pour plaisir) deuisé auec tels prisonniers, hommes beaux & puissans, leur remonstrant, s'ils ne se soucioyent autrement, d'estre ainsi massacrez, comme du iour au lendemain: à quoy me respondans en risée & mocquerie, Noz amis, disoyent ils, nous vengeront, & plusieurs autres propos, monstrans vne hardiesse & asseurance grande. (76)

After another long interruption (made even longer by the additions) devoted to thoughts on courage and victory, Montaigne "returns to our story" to describe the attitude of the prisoners in the face of death, their words and their songs:

... il s'en faut tant que ces prisonniers se rendent, pour tout ce qu'on leur fait, qu'au rebours, pendant ces deux ou trois mois qu'on les garde, ils portent une contenance gaye; ils pressent leurs maistres de se haster de les mettre en cette espreuve; ils les deffient, les injurient, leur reprochent leur lacheté et le nombre des batailles perduës contre les leurs. J'ay une chanson faicte par un prisonnier, où il y a ce traict: qu'ils viennent hardiment trétous et s'assemblent pour disner de luy; car ils mangeront quant et quant leurs peres et leurs ayeux, qui ont servy d'aliment et de nourriture à son corps. "Ces muscles, dit-il, cette chair et ces veines, ce sont les vostres, pauvres fols que vous estes; vous ne recognoissez pas que la substance des membres de vos ancestres s'y tient encore: savourez les bien, vous y trouverez le goust de vostre propre chair." Invention qui ne sent aucunement la barbarie. Ceux qui les peignent mourans, et qui representent cette action quand on les assomme, ils peignent le prisonnier crachant au visage de ceux qui le tuent et leur faisant la mouë. De vray, ils ne cessent jusques au dernier souspir de les braver et deffier de parole et de contenance. (103)	*Thevet*: [on the *défis* preceding the battles and the engraving representing them] Nous sommes vaillans (disent ils) nous auons mangé voz parens, aussi vous mangerons nous: & plusieurs menasses friuoles: comme vous represente la presente figure ... (73v) ... chantant tout le iour & la nuict telles chansons, Les Margagens nos amis sont gens de bien, forts & puissans en guerre, ils ont pris & mangé grand nombre de noz ennemis, aussi me mangeront ils quelque iour, quand il leur plaira: mais de moy, i'ay tué & mangé des parens & amis de celuy qui me tient prisonnier; auec plusieurs semblables paroles. (76) [4] *Léry*: i'ay moy-mesme, vaillant que ie suis, premierement lié & garroté vos parens: puis en s'exaltant tousiours de plus en plus, auec une contenance de mesme, se tournant de costé & d'autre, il dira à l'vn, i'ay mangé de ton pere: à l'autre i'ai assommé & *Boucané* tes frères: bref, dira-il, i'ay en general tant mangé d'hommes et de femmes, voire des enfans, de vous autres *Toüoupinambaoults* que i'ay prins en guerre que ie n'en say le nombre: & au reste ne doutez pas que les *Margaias* de la nation dont ie suis pour venger ma mort n'en mangent encores cy apres autant qu'ils en pourront attraper. (239)

---

[4] Plattard, II, 276, note to p. 103, calls attention to the similarity of the song reported by Thevet.

Several other details in the remainder of Montaigne's text complete the resemblances with the accounts that I have been examining:

Les hommes y ont plusieurs femmes, et en ont d'autant plus grand nombre qu'ils sont en meilleure reputation de vaillance; c'est une beauté remerquable en leurs mariages, que la mesme jalousie que nos femmes ont pour nous empescher de l'amitié et bien-veuillance d'autres femmes, les leurs l'ont toute pareille pour la leur acquerir. Estans plus soigneuses de l'honneur de leurs maris que de toute autre chose, elles cherchent et mettent leur solicitude à avoir le plus de compaignes qu'elles peuvent, d'autant que c'est un tesmoignage de la vertu du mary. (103-4)	*Thevet*: En ceste pluralité de femmes dont ils vsent, comme nous avons dit ... (81) *Barré*: Ils prennent autant de femmes qu'ils veulent, & ont liberté les femmes de delaisser leurs maris, pour petite occasion. (24-25) *Léry:* Mais notez que la Poligamie c'est a dire la pluralité de femmes ayant lieu en leur endroit, il est permis aux hommes d'en auoir autant qu'il leur plaist: mesmes ceux qui en ont plus grand nombre sont estimez les plus hardis & plus vaillans & en ay veu tel qui en auoit huit. Et ce qui est esmerueillable entre ceste multitude de femmes, encores qu'il y en ait tousiours une mieux aimee du mari, tant y a que pour cela les autres n'en seront point ialouses, n'i n'en murmureront, au moins n'en monstreront aucun semblant... elles viuent ensemble en vne paix la nompareille. Surquoy ie laisse à considerer à vn chacun, quand mesmes il ne seroit point defendu par la parole de Dieu de prendre plus d'vne femme, s'il seroit possible que celles de par deçà s'accordassent de ceste façon. (294)
Leur langage, au demeurant, c'est un doux langage et qui a le son aggreable, retirant aux teminaisons Grecques. [According to Armaingaud, II, 263n. his editions *a, a', b* give the following	*Barré*: Leur langage est fort copieux en dictions, mais sans nombre ... (23) *Léry:* toutesfois les lecteurs en pourront encore voir quelque chose au Colloque suyuant lequel fut fait au temps que

text: c'est le plus doux langage du monde, et qui a le son le plus aggreable à l'oreille, il retire fort aux terminaisons Grecques.] (105)

i'estois en l'Amerique, à l'aide d'vn Truchement, qui non seulement, pour y auoir demeuré sept ou huict ans entendoit parfaitement le langage des gens du pays, mais aussi parce qu'il auoit bien estudié mesme en la langue Grecque, dont (ainsi que ceux qui l'entendent ont ia peu voir ci-dessus) ceste nation des *Toüoupinamboults*, a quelques mots, il le pouuoit mieux expliquer. (340). [5]

An examination of the passages presented above suggests several conclusions. First, although each of the three travelers had lived in Brazil, both Barré and Léry supplemented their personal experience by details and texts borrowed from Thevet;[6] this is not without its usefulness in explaining Montaigne's own practice. Second, most of Montaigne's text (except for the introductory materials and for his philosophical disquisitions) is close in content and sometimes in language to the texts of one or another of the three travelers. Indeed, there is hardly a sentence —in the parts actually pertinent to the Cannibals, or the savages, or the Brazilians, or the Americans— that is not paralleled by passages in the explorers. Third, just as Barré and Léry differ from Thevet in certain details and certain emphases, presumably as each followed his own interests or called varyingly on his own experience, so Montaigne differs constantly from the texts that may have been his sources. His interests intervene: he cares less than they about cannibalism, gore, items of idle curiosity; he cares more about morals, virtue, and a way of life that might illustrate the philosophical points that he was making. His experience intervenes, in the form of his actual acquaintance and conversations with his "domestic." Perhaps his bad memory also intervenes.

I think of Montaigne as writing this essay in the same way that he wrote the other late essays of Book I. He began with a moral

---

[5] Villey cites this passage in Léry.

[6] The debt of Léry to Thevet seems to be especially great. The copies of Thevet and Barré that I used are in the Newberry Library, Chicago; the copy of Léry, at the Bibliothèque nationale.

hypothesis that he was interested in developing, a hypothesis based upon much meditation and supported by the witness of several ancient authors. When he came to the "example," to the illustrative case that would permit him to found his argument, he undoubtedly called upon his remembrance of reports made by his "domestic," he undoubtedly used the artifacts that he possessed. But he also went back to his books: the passages are too numerous, the resemblances are too close for us to deny this. Whether he went back to his books by rereading and consulting, or whether he made reference only through the memory as stimulated by those conversations, I cannot be sure. But I think that both probably took place.

BIBLIOGRAPHY OF WILLIAM LEON WILEY

George B. Daniel

"Pierre Le Loyer's Version of the *Ars Amatoria*," *Romanic Review*, XXV (1934), 118-26.
Minimum French (with Henry A. Grubbs). New York: F. S. Crofts, 1935.
"The Love Tales of Antoine de Baïf," *Studies in Philology*, XXXII (1936), 45-54.
"The French Renaissance Gallicized: An Emphasis on National Tradition," *Studies in Philology*, XXXIV (1937), 248-59.
"Jean Chapelain, the Oracle of Aristotle," *Studies in Philology*, XXXVII (1940), 51-63.
Pierre Le Loyer's Version of the Ars Amatoria, University of North Carolina Studies in the Romance Languages and Literatures, 1941.
Reading French (with J. C. Lyons). New York: Henry Holt and Co., 1942.
"Who Named Them Rhétoriqueurs?" in *Medieval Studies in Honor of J. D. M. Ford*, edited by U. T. Holmes and A. J. Denomy, C. S. B. (Cambridge: Harvard Press, 1948), 335-52.
"A Gentleman's Code of Honor in Renaissance France," *University of North Carolina Extension Bulletin*, XXIX (January, 1950), 36-47.
"A Defense of the Renaissance *Gentilhomme Champêtre*," in *Romance Studies Presented to William Morton Dey*, 1950, 185-90.
"Brantôme's Interest in Languages and Literature," *Modern Language Notes*, LXV (1950), 331-36.
"Concepts of Genteel Conversation in the French Renaissance," in *South Atlantic Studies for Sturgis E. Leavitt* (Washington: Scarecrow Press, 1953), 331-36.
"Ronsard's Ideas on the Theatre," *Studies in Philology*, L (1953), 149-57.
The Gentleman of Renaissance France. Cambridge: Harvard Press, 1954. Pp. 303.
"A Royal Child Learns to Like Plays: The Early Years of Louis XIII," *Renaissance News*, IX (1956), 135-44.
"Bruscambille's Defense of the Theater," *Modern Language Notes*, LXXIV (1959), 502-7.
The Early Public Theater in France. Cambridge: Harvard Press, 1960. Pp. 326.
"Commentary on Provincial Archives," Folger Library Conference on Society and History in the Renaissance (Washington: The Folger Library, 1960), 60.

"Commentary," Society and History in the Renaissance (Washington: Folger Shakespeare Library, 1960), 60.

"Corneille's Refinement of His Earlier Plays," *Studies in Philology*, L (1962), 171-83.

"Corneille's First Tragedy: *Médée* and the Baroque," *Esprit Créateur*, IV (1964), 135-48.

"Montaigne's Later Latin Borrowings," *Essays Presented to Honor Alexander Herman Schutz*, edited by Urban T. Holmes and Kenneth R. Scholberg (Columbus: Ohio State University Press, 1964), 246-56.

"Du Bellay and Ovid," *Romance Notes*, VIII (1966), 98-104.

"Classical Meters in French Renaissance Poetry," *Renaissance Papers*, 1966, 31-37.

The Formal French. Cambridge: Harvard Press, 1967. Pp. 317.

In addition to these separately published books and articles, William L. Wiley has written on The Comédie Française for *Collier's Encyclopedia*. He was also an active member from 1939-1959, of the committee which compiles the annual bibliography of the French Renaissance, appearing in *Studies in Philology*. He has published numerous reviews in various journals.

www.ingramcontent.com/pod-product-compliance
Lightning Source LLC
Chambersburg PA
CBHW030338240426
43661CB00052B/1671